AUSTRIAN POLITICS AND SOCIETY TODAY

Also by John Fitzmaurice

SECURITY AND POLITICS IN THE NORDIC AREA
QUEBEC AND CANADA
THE POLITICS OF BELGIUM
POLITICS IN DENMARK

AUSTRIAN POLITICS AND SOCIETY TODAY

In Defence of Austria

John Fitzmaurice

Foreword by
Bruno Kreisky

St. Martin's Press   New York

First published in the United States of America in 1990

Printed in Great Britain

ISBN 0-312-04706-1

Library of Congress Cataloging–in–Publication Data
Fitzmaurice, John.
Austrian politics and society today: in defence of Austria/ John
Fitzmaurice; foreword by Bruno Kreisky.
    p. cm.
ISBN 0-312-04706-1
1. Austria—Politics and government—1945– 2. Austria—
Civilization—20th century. I. Title.
DB99.2.F58 1990
943.605'3—dc20
                                                    90–32409
                                                         CIP

For Elizabeth

Table of Contents

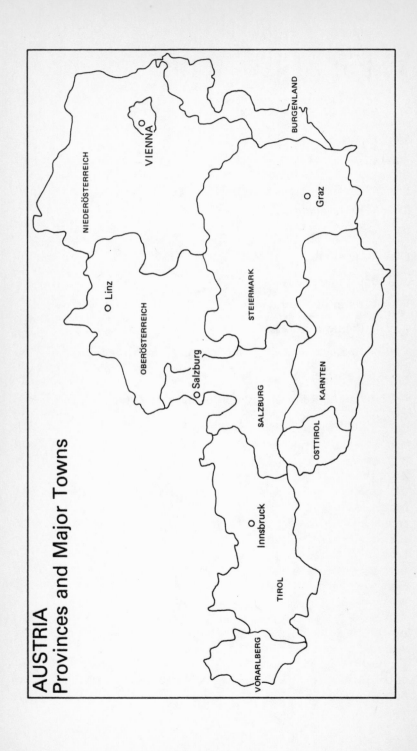

AUSTRIA
Provinces and Major Towns

VORARLBERG

TIROL

○ Innsbruck

OSTTIROL

KARNTEN

SALZBURG

○ Salzburg

STEIERMARK

○ Graz

OBERÖSTERREICH

○ Linz

NIEDERÖSTERREICH

VIENNA ○

BURGENLAND

Foreword

At a time of well-publicised attacks on Austria, it does one good to be confronted, though from a not uncritical standpoint, with this work, with its subtitle 'In Defence of Austria'. The very complex history of the Austrian nation makes these varied views most appropriate

In the year of the hundredth anniversary of the birth of Adolf Hitler, I decided to be one of the contributors to a comprehensive evaluation of Hitler in the well known critical German magazine *Der Spiegel*. There, I dealt with the use of stereotypes, as is often the case today, to unleash orgies of hatred. This was of course not my only motive, since political and historical truth must be served.

What are the most frequent reproaches levelled at Austria today? Even if a good deal of this must be reduced to its proper proportions, it still is worth looking at what remains uncontested and therefore still valid. There have been frequent collapses in Austrian history. Dreadful mistakes were certainly made in the old Austro-Hungarian Monarchy and it is worth making the attempt to analyse what, in Austrian history was so to say ineluctable and what could have been different if a radically different policy had been followed.

British historians in particular showed a very limited fairness towards the Austria of 1918. Historians like Seton-Watson or A.J.P. Taylor made no secret of their slavophile tendencies, and this led to the easy conclusion as to what should happen to the rump of Austria. Many also came to the simplistic view that all Austrians, like the old rump, had desired the Anschluss. The historical paradox that after the Second World War, the majority of Austrians did not want to hear about any 'Anschluss', is deliberately ignored now, so it is hardly surprising that some over eager supporters in Austria of the European Idea are suspected of covertly promoting an Anschluss with Germany.

What can be briefly said about the issue? Even those who are not supporters of the Austrian Nation have to admit that, apart from the years between 1938 and 1945, Austria was in fact never part of Germany. Certainly, since the collapse of Hitlerism, the vast majority of the Austrian people have supported independence. The difference between Germany and Austria is slightly reminiscent of the situation in Britain, though at first sight this may appear rather surprising. No Scot would deny the existence of Scotland merely because Scots and English people both speak English. The comparison is not of course perfect, but on the other hand, it is not as unjustified as it may seem. What I mean by it is that the Austrians are always being told that they must be Germans because they speak German. That has never been applied in the French-speaking world and certainly never in the wider Latin world. Why then should it be applied to Austria, where demonstrably, indeed as a result of greater German imperialism, the old slogan 'Ein Reich, ein Volk, ein Fuehrer' has long ceased to hold sway?

What about the Nazi aspect? Well, already in the old Austria, there was often clerico-catholic sympathy with antisemitism. This is difficult to explain in detail. Indeed, it must be very difficult to understand for the British historical tradition, where a Lord Beaconsfield, born as Disraeli, is taken for granted. It remains however a fact which can be shown through many examples such as the notorious Mayor of Vienna Karl Lueger, that it was a dominant trait of Austrian history. In the article to which I referred earlier, I show how close historically, Lueger's antisemitism was to the holocaust. This issue is still very much alive, as a controversial article written by Joel Carmichael in the April/May number of the New York review *Midstream* shows. He calls on Christian theologians to set the New Testament criticisms of the Jews back in their historical context and thereby 'transform the Jews from their status as mysterious agents of Satan, into normal non-Christians like the majority of the human race'. Religious historians are right to deal with this aspect of the problem.

As to more recent social and economic developments in Austria, I would like to insist on the fact that while I was in government, I followed a policy, called neo-Keynesian by some and which certainly went along those lines, especially to fight unemployment, but which was, I must in all modesty point out, different in both form and content. I shall illustrate this by a few comments. Certainly, the phenomenon of unemployment and the battle against it, does have historical meaning, but probably not the basic ideas themselves. I am only too well aware that the ideas that we helped promote were strongly attacked at the time of their greatest political relevance – that is the fate of all the basic ideas of political economy. However, as the Report to the US Congress by Professor Leontief, recommending closer attention to the German and Austrian experience, demonstrated, these were the only two countries in the western world to produce both high levels of employment, satisfactory growth and moderate inflation.

It seems worth mentioning that it became clear in the course of my recent work for the Independent Commission on Employment questions in Europe that precisely those policies and trends that had seemed the most unassailable over the last decade were now consigned to the past. This applies both equally to supply-siders and monetarists.

I am therefore grateful to John Fitzmaurice, the author of this book, for seeking to demonstrate these conclusions through the Austrian example. I am aware that in these few lines I have only been able to point to a very few aspects of his book. Yet, those that I have pointed to, do show that present fashion of Austrophobia, even when clothed in the greatest literary elegance is not an approach that one can admire. The author certainly therefore deserves warmest thanks and recognition for his objective presentation, especially in these times.

BRUNO KREISKY

Acknowledgements

Many people have given me enthusiastic encouragement and assistance with this project. My particular thanks go to Mrs Kadlec and Mrs Dunkelmeyer of the Federal Press Office, for their patient and resouceful response to my many, and at times difficult, requests during my several research visits to Vienna. Thanks to them, I was able to get a very broad view of Austrian affairs. My thanks also go to Dr Fehnkart of the Austrian Embassy in Brussels for both useful ideas and contacts, as well as his positive encouragement.

Very many distinguished Austrians, from a very wide range of political horizons and organisations have given up time in their very busy schedules to discuss and illuminate various areas of Austrian politics, economics and social life with me. These discussions added very considerably to my understanding of Austria and were always interesting and at times colourful. Of the many, I must single out former Chancellor Dr Kreisky, to whom I owe a great debt; the present Chancellor Dr Vranitzky; Foreign Minister and former ÖVP leader Dr Mock; FPÖ leader Jörg Haider; the then leader of the Greens in Parliament, Mrs Freda Meissner Blau. Thanks are also due to the General Secretaries of the two major parties, Dr Sallaberger (SPÖ) and Dr Kukaschka (ÖVP). Outside Vienna, I would like to thank the Steiermark authorities and here especially Dr Silcher ÖVP leader in the Landtag, for a delightful visit to Graz, which gave me greater insight into Austrian federalism.

I should also like to thank my good Viennese friend Elizabeth Figl, for many pleasant hours during my visits to Vienna and for many interesting ideas.

My thanks go to Anna Isaac for coping with my writing and turning it into an intelligible manuscript.

Finally, the views expressed, and indeed any errors and omissions, are my own.

John Fitzmaurice

List of Abbreviations

Parties

SPÖ	Sozialistische Partei Österreichs
ÖVP	Österreichische Volkspartei
FPÖ	Freiheitliche Partei Österreichs
VdU/WdU	Verband der Unabhängige/Wahlbund der Unabhängige
KPÖ	Kommunistische Partei Österreichs
VGÖ	Vereinigten Grüne Österreichs
ALÖ	Alternative Liste Österreichs
BIP	Bürger Initiative Parlament

Social Partners/Organisations

AK	Arbeiterkammer
ÖAKT	Österreichischer Arbeiter Kammertag
ÖGB	Österreichischer Gewerkschaftsbund
ÖAAB	Österreichischer Arbeiter und Angestellten Bund
ÖWB	Österreichischer Wirtschaftsbund
ÖBB	Österreichischer Bauern Bund

Other

NR	Nationalrat
GP	Gesetzgebungsperiode (Legislature I–XVII)
EC/EEC	European Communities
CA	Creditanstalt
BSA	Bund Sozialistischer Akademiker
ÖIAG	Österreichische Industrie Aktientgesellschaft
EFTA	European Free Trade Association
ERP	European Recovery Programme
MBFR	Mutual and Balanced Force Reduction Talks
CSCE	Conference on Security and Cooperation in Europe

Preface, Spring 1990

It is the well known nightmare of every author on contemporary political issues that important events should occur during the grey period between completion of the manuscript and committing it to the printing press. This has happened with a vengeance in relation to Austria's place in Central Europe. The implications for Austria of the 1989 year of revolutions in central and eastern Europe are considerable and require at least a preliminary comment. At the same time, the Austrian domestic political scene is far from static, with 1990 an election year. These issues fully justify a short 'preface 1990' dealing with both the external and internal trends affecting Austria as at the time of writing in the spring of 1990. Those trends seem dramatic and potentially far reaching, but that may belie the Austrian penchant for stability. Nothing at present observable in these trends suggests the invalidation of the basic hypothesis of this book, that Austrian stability is durable and viable due to its adaptative qualities and is at present in the process of considerable change and adaptation, without abandoning the basic positive characteristics of the 'Austrian Model'. On the contrary, present trends seem to confirm the analysis.

The general election is due in the autumn of 1990 at the latest. It is now rather unlikely that the election will be held earlier. There was some internal debate in the SPÖ at the end of 1989 about an early election in the spring of 1990, but this was rejected by the Chancellor, who did not wish to appear politically opportunistic, undermining his image as being above party politics. At present, the opinion polls suggest that the likely outcome will be much as below:

SPÖ   40%
ÖVP   35%
FPÖ   15%
Greens   8%

This suggests that the two large coalition parties will together lose some 5%, a large loss in Austrian terms, but a more limited triumph for the FPÖ than expected. The Greens, despite their at times destructive internal debates, now seem to be part of the political landscape. This suggests that the SPÖ remains within striking distance of its objective of at least a blocking majority with the Greens, preventing any possibility of an ÖVP and FPÖ coalition. Probably only an even more dramatic loss for the ÖVP would lead it to seek to form a Small Coalition with the FPÖ. The present leadership of the ÖVP remains weak: the change to Riegler has not improved the image of the party. The groups in the ÖVP that support Riegler, such as Josef Krainer and Minister Schlussel, have a longer-term strategy. They have written off this election and this time support a new Grand Coalition, even under SPÖ leadership. They are preparing for the next election but one, under Schlussel. The SPÖ is clearly still dominated by Chancellor Vranitzky. Despite the compromises of the coalition, he remains a popular, dominant leader, whose approval rating runs well beyond that of his party. The trends, therefore, would suggest the continuation of a strong Grand Coalition under Vranitzky.

This suggests that, despite the muddying of the waters over the last few years with the Waldheim affair and persistent scandals and economic difficulties in the state sector of the economy, the electoral message is 'steady as it goes'. This desire for stability may be reinforced by the dramatic events in eastern Europe. It should, however, not obscure the fact that a more serious and intensive debate about the Austrian past and about the balance between stability, consensus and change has got underway, though it has made little apparent impact on the political mainstream as yet.

The most dramatic developments are, however, on the international front. The changes in eastern Europe can be expected to have a major impact on Austria and on Austrian thinking about her future development.

Austrian neutrality may require considerable rethinking. In the new situation in central Europe, it may lose its clear original focus as neutrality between east and west, as these antipodes no longer exist in any meaningful sense. The question then arises, should neutrality be redefined as a more general concept, independent of the now non-existent Cold War division of Europe, making it closer to the 'old' neutrality of nations like Sweden and Switzerland? Austrian neutrality as a specific low-tension component of the European system may decline in importance, as the Cold War and its attendant structures and mind-sets are wound down. That does not, of course, mean that neutrality has not served other latent functions, such as contributing to the building of Austria's specific national identity in the Second Republic and differentiating her from the two German states. Were neutrality to become so reduced in importance, redefined or else, lose its salience, so that it no longer contributed significantly to such a differentiation, then Austria would certainly be forced to redefine her national identity.

She had already, by way of pre-emption so to speak, begun this process with her application to join the EC in July 1989. Two applications, which may or may not be accepted on Austria's terms, and indeed may or may not be relevant in the prevailing international climate in the mid-1990s, will not be substantively addressed by the EC before 1993 at the earliest. This is known and accepted with equanimity in Vienna today. The application is now seen more clearly for what it always was, as part of an internal debate about Austria's western identity and alignment and her commitment to economic and social modernisation. It was and is a symbol and a signal at home and abroad, which may even – possibly – lead to EC membership, for which there are certainly both disadvantages as well as advantages. Environmental, regional development, macro-economic, agricultural, traffic in the Alps and sectoral-corporatist disadvantages are emerging with more clarity and the initially negligible opposition to EC membership is clearly increasing, as people ask whether on balance, with a likely net contribution of $1 billion to the EC budget to set against perhaps only 1%–2% in lost GDP growth, there is a real need for membership – especially one deferred to some unknown future time. The issue is clearly now, by consensus, more or less on the back burner.

Official policy clings more strongly to the various traditional rationales for membership and to Austria's western alignment, but does so perhaps a touch too pointedly to be entirely convincing. Speaking recently to an international conference at Havard University, Chancellor Vranitzky said: 'Austria never was and never will be something between the two Europes. In its political system, in its traditions, in its economy, as well as its international stance, it has always been firmly and solidly part of western Europe.'

In the same speech he argued that Austria was not a 'bridge' but was firmly on the western bank, and rejected a revival of the 'Mitteleuropa' concept and above all rejected the view that the German question affected Austria, stating, 'Whatever form the German question is going to take Austria is not, nor ever will be part of it.'

He was at pains to rehearse the strong arguments which justified the EC application, which he strongly defended but called for 'an open and flexible one (EC) comprising ultimately more than its present member countries', ready to grant Austria certain exemptions for situations where its neutrality would become relevant.

The Chancellor, like broader Austrian opinion, noted a responsibility (for supporting the eastern European revolutions) derived from interest, history and the special Austrian experience in central Europe, but Austrian policymakers appear – at present – determined to avoid having their west politik blown off-course by events in eastern Europe.

However, the broader political, economic, intellectual and cultural debate in Austria is less sure that old certainties based on the traditional post-1955-style neutrality and a resolutely western orientation for Austria, with some limited economic assistance for eastern Europe, is in any sense an adequate response to the new post-revolutionary situation. 'Mitteleuropa' is perhaps a myth, but it is a powerful and perhaps useful myth today. There is a new excitement abroad in Vienna and Austria as the old Bohemian, Hungarian and Slovenian hinterlands are opened up again culturally, politically and economically.

Furthermore, Austria can not remain indifferent to the success of democracy and market liberalisation in central Europe, as this will condition Austria's own success. At best, it could eliminate the constraints of neutrality and open up new economic opportunities, especially for eastern Austria which has experienced lower growth rates than the western provinces. This would increase Austria's political and economic options in a fast-changing world.

On the other hand, a more pessimistic scenario in which economic failure led to the failure of democracy, and hence Balkanisation and Third Worldisation of the central European and the Balkan area as well as the former Soviet Union, with ethnic conflicts, authoritarian or military régimes and perhaps sub-nuclear conflicts, accompanied by Russian intervention not on ideological grounds but on traditional national security grounds, could impact very seriously on Austria. She, therefore, has a vital stake in the success of the new democracies in central and eastern Europe – so runs the argument. Indeed, her interest may be greater than that of the NATO or EC states. Interest, experience, tradition and expertise may all flow in the same direction. A small, independent, neutral but activist Austria, with a strong and adaptable economy, with many market-taming social components; a democratic and consensual, but evolving political system; a western and central European economy and culture – these may be exactly what is required at the moment. Perhaps, echoing Musil, we can say that it is hard to define the 'Austrian idea' but it is definitely worth celebrating it.

1. Introduction

Austria has been in the news frequently over the last three years. Indeed, rarely has there been so much interest in the country. Most of this new interest is negative and critical. Earlier, in the 1950s and later again in the 1970s, there was a tendency to discuss the 'Austrian Model' or the 'Austrian Way', as if it was a model of perfection. It is therefore difficult to achieve a balanced and objective view of modern Austria, which neither overlooks its faults nor its very real achievements. That is the aim of this book.

Today, Austria is to many people simply the Waldheim Affair, the problems in her state industries and an interminable series of political scandals. These are no more than superficial symptoms of a wider malaise which requires a deeper analysis than that accorded by the news media, which have highlighted only the more sensational aspects of Austria's problems. It has been too rapidly concluded that the Austrian Model has been a failure and could only be a failure. It has also been too rapidly concluded that Austrian society and government is incapable of adapting to changing circumstances.

It will be the central thesis of this book that the Austrian model does indeed have problems, but that these problems are widely recognised in Austria and that the necessary adaptation is taking place. Thus, the model will prove more adaptable and hence successful than its critics are prepared to concede.

The problems of Austria today are in a very real sense the downside of success, for every successful model extracts its price. In the case of Austria, there has been a rush to judge that the price was exorbitant. Such a judgement should, however, be balanced against the cost, and indeed the very real possibility of failure, which faced Austria in the early years of the Second Republic after 1945.

The pillars of Austria's post-war success have been three-fold. In the first place, Austria has built her self into a nation, with a strong and effective sense of identity and a policy of active permanent neutrality. This identity and indeed acceptance of nationhood was lacking in the First Republic between the wars. The Kleinösterreich nation, imposed by the Allies in the Treaty of St Germain (1920), then reimposed after 1945, finally took and Austria became a nation in fact as well as in name. Thus, whilst in 1956, 46% of those polled

1

did not consider Austria to be a nation, that had fallen to a mere 11% by 1980. By this date, 86% considered Austria was a nation and 91% opposed an Anschluss with Germany.

Austria has developed a policy of active neutrality, which has proved to be a positive national asset. At first, permanent neutrality was a necessary part of the delicate East/West compromise which enabled the State Treaty to be signed (1955), by which Austria regained her full independence and the Forces of the four Allied occupying powers left her soil. This status has not hindered Austria from building a close relationship with Germany and the countries of the European Community, as the current debate on Austrian full membership of the Community shows. Her neutral status, coupled with the historical ties of the old Monarchy, has given her a special position as a bridge to that area of central Europe so evocatively called 'Mitteleuropa' in German, to which all of the old Empire belonged. Her neutral status has also enabled her to develop ties with the Third World and especially with the Arab nations and with OPEC, whose seat is in Vienna. Indeed, Vienna – as the seat of OPEC, of several UN agencies, its position as an East/West bridge and as the venue for several important CSCE follow-up meetings and disarmament talks such as the MBFR talks – is recovering its lost status as as an international and cosmopolitan city, albeit in a new guise.

The troubled political scene, and above all the total lack of even a minimal degree of consensus in the period between the two wars, was a serious impediment to any nascent national cohesion, ending in civil war in 1934 between the Catholic right and the SPÖ and the imposition of the authoritarian Austro-fascist dictatorship of Doll-fuss, paving the way for the Anschluss in 1938. The bitter lessons of this period were learned in the post-war period. Austrian political leaders recognised that only unity and a degree of political consensus and social peace could save the country, which all came to accept had come to stay, in the face of the Allied occupation and above all the presence of Soviet forces in Eastern Austria and Vienna. Out of the habits of consensus, which were so successful in the ten years of occupation, grew the politics of consensualism (between the Christ-ian Democrats and the Socialists, and between the two sides of industry), which was institutionalised in the Grand Coalition, which lasted from 1945-66 and was renewed in 1987.

Pragmatic acceptance of the fact of nationhood, with active neutrality and political and social consensualism, were the pillars of the Austrian Model, which has proved to have considerable success in the post-war period. These pillars are, of course, closely inter-linked and can hardly be dissociated from each other. Each has played its own vital part in the whole.

Yet there have been real costs, which the Waldheim affair and the current difficulties in the Austrian public sector illustrate well. Nation-building requires a degree of broad consensus in support of that objective. It was the absence of consensus in favour of the 'der Staat, der keiner wollte' in the interwar period that made its eventual collapse inevitable and ensured that there was so little will to oppose the Anschluss, which came as relief or logical conclusion even to those who had reasons to oppose it.

The pan-Germanic lager (camp) obviously strongly opposed the building of an Austrian State after 1918. The Socialists also opposed what would be a clerically dominated State (except in red Vienna). They looked to what was initially a socialist Germany. Only the Christain Social Party (Catholic) was remotely favourable to the new State in the early years, yet the Allied Powers insisted on creating the new State from the rump of the old Monarchy which they had dismembered. They did this less from positive reasons than by a process of elimination. The Allied Great Powers, much influenced by the various émigré pan-Slavic movements, considered the Empire to be a reactionary anachronism, standing in the way of national self-determination, which was the progressive principle of the future, or so it seemed from the standpoint of 1918. As the war progressed, the elimination of the Empire became a war aim in itself which was independent of the specific demands of the Allied neighbours of the Empire – such as Italy, Serbia and Romania – and of the national minorities within the borders of the Empire, though this was not the case in 1914.

The logical Anschluss of German Austria with Germany was rejected by the Great Powers since it would strengthen Germany. The successor States pressed territorial claims against the old Empire – going beyond non-German areas – and hence the Treaties of St. Germain and Trianon dismembered the Empire and left a rump German–Austrian State, which was specifically forbidden to join Germany.

Perhaps not surprisingly, this State enjoyed little popular support and was seen as not being viable in the long term. It was inevitably associated with defeat and was seen as an imposition of the Allies. No political group saw an interest in close association with the new State, which association was likely to discredit them. Indeed, several groups on both left and right, such as Communist, pan-Germanists and later Nazis, and even residual Habsburg Monarchists, saw their main interest lay in undermining and smashing the new State. Only the Christian Social Party reluctantly settled into the new State and indeed governed it in an increasingly authoritarian manner after the civil war in 1934. Few mourned the passage of the First Republic at the time of the Anschluss in 1938. Of course, at the time no-one realised what terrible years lay ahead in the Third Reich.

As in 1918, the Second World War victors, for conflicting reasons and again in the absence of acceptable alternatives, resuscitated the Austrian Republic within its pre-1938 frontiers and subjected it to a ten-year occupation, which was only ended with the signature of the State Treaty in 1955. In effect, the Allies re-established Austria by fiat. Austria was required to make a success where she had failed in the inter-war period.

The pan-Germanic lager and indeed the former Nazis, though defeated and discredited in 1945, did not disappear and could have constituted a serious source of alienation and opposition, capable of preventing the development of a distinct Austrian national unity and consciousness. Though most of them were disenfranchised at the 1945 election and the Allied council only authorised three parties, the problem would not go away. Hence, both major parties (ÖVP and SPÖ) were conscious of the need to integrate these elements into a positive national consensus.

Thus, in 1949, a fourth party, first called the Independents (VdU), was permitted. It organised the old pan-Germanic lager and the re-enfranchised national socialists. However, a broader policy of national reconciliation was needed and was actively promoted by the two major parties, who vied for votes from the old National lager. Naturally, though perhaps necessary as part of an exercise in nation building, this policy precluded any examination of the Nazi period or responsibility for the Anschluss, let alone a serious de-Nazification programme. In fact, this area was in principle, until 1955, an area reserved to the Allied Occupation authorities, which gave Austrian governments an excellent alibi for inaction, although the Allied jurisdiction was never exclusive. Hence, in retrospect, the occurrence of a Waldheim affair was always a possibility and earlier less noticed affairs can be found. It was indeed a risk, a calculated risk to be accepted and if necessary to be confronted as the inevitable price of what was otherwise an extremely effective approach to the problem of national cohesion in post war Austria.

Alongside the policy of integration, a second source of strength was the Grand Coalition, first formed in 1945 with the ÖVP + SPÖ + KPÖ and later exclusively with the ÖVP and SPÖ. The coalition continued until 1966 and the two parties have never represented less than 84% of the electorate at any election. The originality of the coalition was that it was formed so easily in 1945 and lasted for over twenty years, until 1966, when it was reluctantly broken off to be revived in 1987. In the intervening years, it was frequently canvassed as a possibility and always retained well over 50% support in opinion polls as an option. Indeed, one could say that it became a kind of 'ideal' against which any current government was measured.

Clearly, alongside its very positive consensus building character, it also had negative aspects. The very formation of such a coalition eliminated any parliamentary opposition, as the only other parties in the Nationalrat were at first the KPÖ, then the KPÖ and FPÖ and later the FPÖ alone. At the time, these were parties of protest, confined to permanent opposition. Effective decision-making did not take place in Parliament or in public debate, but rather within the Cabinet and the Coalition Committee, established by the two parties. Difficult issues on which there was no apparent consensus were simply shelved. Similar problems have arisen in the revived Grand Coalition after 1987. Despite the coalition's relative success in several key areas of its programme such as tax reform, the law on competition, the state industries, agricultural subsidies, all of which have required a considerable degree of political courage and the government's high positive poll ratings, there is a distinct feeling of malaise. There have been a very large number of corruption scandals and there is a feeling that the coalition has limited democratic debate and accountability. The coalition parties have suffered severe losses in all Landtag (provincial) elections since 1987, to the benefit of both opposition parties, but especially the populist FPÖ under Jörg Haider. He has been able to capitalise on the anti-government, anti-consensus mood, which dominates despite the government's not inconsiderable successes and the excellent state of the economy.

Economic and social stability was achieved to a remarkable degree through the operation of a form of parallel coalition, the Economic and Social Partnership. Thus, the key actors in the Austrian economy – unions, employers and agriculture – were co-opted with government into an elaborate and effective consensus-building forum, which became a kind of parallel government. This structure survived the first Grand Coalition and continues to function today. Here too, there are those on both sides who consider that consensus has meant paralysis or excessive concessions.

The two levels of coalition – political and economic – involved trade-offs in appointments and in policies. The State had to meet simultaneously the concerns of both parties and their clientèle: measures against unemployment, a strong State sector, assistance to small industry and agriculture. Inevitably, considerable subsidies, State intervention and controls were required. Appointments also had to obey the law of 'proportz' or balance, with the resulting duplications and inefficiency.

The system certainly maximised integration, ensured a strong economy and rapid growth and minimised political and social conflict. The price was high subsidies, a large public sector debt, some inefficiency and fudged solutions, or problems shelved in order to avoid conflict within the coalition in Austrian society. Consensus meant slower decision-making, expensive compromises and a tendency to allow the longer term problems to drift, especially if their solution would cause conflict with powerful interest groups. At the same time, inevitably, the democratic transparency of decision-making was limited. The Grand Coalition and its associated Social Partnership shifted the locus of decision-making away from the electorate and Parliament and towards party and interest group bureaucracies and the public sector industries. Even after the break up of the first Grand Coalition, the associated habits of consensus seeking continued in many areas and it was thus easy to revive the coalition in 1987. Indeed, it was almost a relief to do so.

Until recently at any rate, however endemically criticised, their system was seen by most Austrians as the most successful and the most appropriate to Austrian conditions. Despite an ÖVP absolute majority in Parliament in 1966 and SPÖ absolute majorities in 1971, 1975 and 1979, there was always considerable nostalgia for the Grand Coalition both in the electorate and among political leaders. Functional consensus remained intact and a habit of mind throughout the period of single party government and the Small Coalition (SPÖ/FPÖ). The political parties have often seemed reluctant to exercise power alone and it is very revealing that following the break up of the Small Coalition in 1986, both large parties ran for cover and took the formation of a new Grand Coalition virtually for granted during the 1986 election.

Our theme will be the delicate weighing of costs and benefits in the Austrian Model, as it has often been called, based on the triple pillars of effective nationhood and neutrality, political consensus and Social Partnership. We shall look at the building of the Austrian State and the painstaking erection of each of the three pillars. We shall attempt a penetrating, at times critical evaluation of Austrian society and political life and of her image and self-image, at this critical juncture in her short life as a nation.

It may well be that Austria is entering a new and questioning period when much that was previously taken for granted will be critically examined. Such a critical transition can be both salutary and beneficial, leading to a new synthesis. The old model can be adapted to the demands of the very different circumstances of today. More open and critical domestic political debate could be permitted than was desirable in the delicate period of post-war reconstruction and occupation. In that sense, the model thus seems to have considerable adaptability and durability.

At all events, we shall seek to avoid either taking a too complacent view of post-war Austria's not inconsiderable achievement or accepting the recent tendency to regard the model as a failure because of the price which has been paid for its success. It should not be forgotten that Austria's realistic options were few. She has in fact played the poor cards that history dealt her with considerable skill and determination, creating a modern nation, a strong economy and a generous welfare state, which can form the basis for a more open and critical society in the future.

2. From Empire to Nation

Even more than in 1918, Austria in 1945 seemed to have reached the bottom of the abyss and to face a very uncertain future in a Europe which was in the process of radical change. She had few cards in her hand.

Fundamentally, her status was unclear: she was cast by the Allies as part victim and part co-aggressor with Nazi Germany. She was again cut off, and this time more decisively, from both Germany and her traditional Central European hinterland. She was occupied and under Allied supervision. Vienna and Eastern Austria were under Soviet occupation and the Renner government, installed by the USSR, was at first not recognised by the three Western Allies. Despite the promises of the Moscow Declaration, the future seemed bleak and would obviously depend as much on the latitude accorded to her by the Allies as on the will of her people.

To understand either of these elements which would determine the future of Austria, it is necessary to go back well beyond 1945. The makings of modern Austria's situation are to be found in the nineteenth century and even before. Indeed, what did the term 'Austria' signify in 1945? It certainly was not a clear, self-confident and unequivocal declaration of nationhood. For many, it was like an old garment which, being all that one had, one had to make the best use of. In such a situation, there was an inevitable tendency towards nostalgia and a preference for looking back to the better past, rather than towards the uncertain future. The past had, though, seen several fatal turning points, on which the 'if only ...' schools of history hinged. These fell in the years 1849, 1866 and 1867 and 1918. All represent vital turning points in modern Austrian history.

In 1849, revolution was defeated and the chance of creating a liberal German State was lost. In 1866, Prussia defeated Austria and excluded her from German affairs. A conservative and narrow German State came into being under Prussian leadership. All chances of a democratic Germany evolving was lost. Austria lost her possessions in Italy, was turned towards the Balkans and eventually became tied to the German alliance against pan-Slavic Russia. In 1867, a weakened Empire was forced to compromise with Hungary, creating the dual Monarchy, in which Hungary possessed full internal autonomy. With this compromise, any serious hopes of structural reform of the Empire was lost. Finally, the defeat of 1918 led to the break-up of the Empire, under the combined pressure of its component peoples. The Treaty of Trianon then denied the rump Austrian territory the right to join Germany, as it would have wished. This was the second exclusion. Austria was forced into existence as a State and that existence was then confirmed in 1943. So the die was essentially cast by 1867, but what was Austria in that year?

Austria was a vast, sprawling, multinational Empire astride the Danube, stretching from the Alps to the approaches to the Black Sea. Her destiny had been sealed: she was a middle European or even Balkan Empire and not a German State, as her earlier history down to the demise of the Holy Roman Empire in 1806 might have led her to expect. The State was above all a dynasty – the Habsburgs. The first Habsburg Archduke of the Lower and Upper Austrian Lands was elected Holy Roman Emperor in 1273 and ensured the Germanic character of its inner core by defeating Ottokar II of Bohemia at the gates of Vienna.

It was only after the accession of Maximilian in 1477 that the Habsburg Empire came to take on the familiar form that we recognise. His marriage to Anne of Bohemia and the dynastic arrangements with the Jagellon Kings of Poland led in 1526-27 to the unification, under his successor Ferdinand, of the German Austrian areas, Bohemia, Hungary and the Triune Kingdom of Croatia. In 1521, the Pact of Brussels had split the western, Spanish and the eastern parts of the Empire between two quite separate branches of the family. The separation of the eastern and western branches of the Empire was definitive.

On the abdication of Charles V in 1566, Ferdinand also became Holy Roman Emperor. He set in motion important administrative reforms that gradually began the process of integration of the various disparate lands of the Empire, which process eventually established links going well beyond the dynastic. The Turkish threat, the battle against Protestantism and the economic subsidiarity of the various lands all contributed to this process. Now the Imperial Crown was, despite its formally elective character, a hereditary Habsburg apanage.

Following the decisive battle of the White Mountain against Protestant Bohemia in 1621 and the Peace of Westphalia, which ended the Thirty Years War in 1648, Catholic domination of southern Germany was assured.

The destruction of Kara Mustapha's army at the walls of Vienna in 1683 was the last great surge of the Ottoman Empire. This defeat began the Ottoman Empire's lengthy decline and expulsion from Europe, which was to take a further two centuries and bring Austria and pan-Slavic Russia into conflict in the vacuum left behind by the Turks.

It was during the War of the Spanish Succession that Austria, in alliance with England, began her rise to the status of a Great Power. The process was to be continued in the wars of Maria Theresa's reign (1740-80). During her reign and the short and, in many ways, unfortunate reign of Joseph II, which immediately preceded the Revolutionary Wars, the Empire was given a sense of nascent patriotism and an administrative structure to replace the patchwork of feudalism. However, this was far from espousing the even more modern forces of democratic nationalism which underlay the movements of the revolutionary period down to 1815. Thus, by the opening of the modern period, the Empire had attained certain basic characteristics. It was a central European, multinational Empire, but it was deeply involved in German affairs.

The Turkish threat was giving way to the Turkish problem, which was later to lead the Empire into conflict with Russia. The Empire was a mosaic, held together by the dynasty, the army and the administration, rather than by political or cultural bonds. It was thus inevitably autocratic rather than democratic. It gravitated naturally towards a conservative, if not reactionary position in the concert of Great Powers in 1815 and thereafter. All these basic features were to prove to be a central weakness in the last century of the Empire.

Thus, Austria was built on ambiguity. She was the multinational Empire of the Habsburgs. She was also a German State, being a member of the German Confederation. She was a major Balkan power, with millions of Slavic subjects. She was a major European power and leading player in the Holy Alliance of Conservative States, established to maintain the Congress Settlement and the European balance of power associated with it under the Metternich system. These different rôles held within them the seeds of contradiction.

In the early post-revolutionary war period, the Monarchy as a whole had a population of 35.4 million, of which only 6.4 million were German. In 1840, there were 14.8 million Slavics, 5.3 million Hungarians, 4.5 million Italians and 1.3 million Romanians. The Slavics, which included both Catholics and Orthodox, were dispersed to the north in Bohemia and Slovakia and to the south. Inside the German Confederation, Austria was the leading power, with a population of 9.5 million (5.0 million Germans), followed by Prussia (7.9 million), Bavaria (3.5 million) and Wurtemberg (1.4 million). In all, there were thirty-five States and four city-State members of the Confederation. Austria was to become the southern pole and Prussia the northern pole of the Confederation.

As we have seen, the situation of the Empire had essentially been created by the Congress of Vienna, one of the great remakes of the Continent, together with the events of 1648, 1918, 1945 and those in, one might say, 1989. The aim of Congress itself and the concept of a Congress system, was to restore the *status quo ante bellum* as far as possible, as far as such a course was in the interests of the victorious powers. Just as important was the creation of mechanisms for the preservation of this conservative settlement.

Napoleon was defeated, yet the turbulent years which preceded that defeat held the seeds of danger for the Empire which, in 1815, seemed at the apogee of its power. When the century opened, Napoleon was at the high point of his power. He established the middle German Rheinbund under his tutelage, destroying in the process the last vestiges of the authority of the Holy Roman Empire. The renewed anti-French coalition of Austria, Russia and England was defeated – at least on land – at Ulm and then at Austerlitz. At the subsequent peace of Bratislava, Austria lost two million subjects. Prussia, a late entrant into the alliance, was in turn defeated at Jena in 1806 and lost all her territories west of the Elbe. Russia was defeated at Friedland and concluded peace and even a temporary alliance with Napoleon. The Holy Roman Empire was wound up.

Austria now faced a difficult strategic choice. Archduke Karl had urged her to seek a central European and Balkan destiny; urgent appeals from the Serb rebel leader, Kara George, had called on her to champion the Christian Serbs against the Turks rather than seek a German destiny. At the same time, both France and Russia were seeking to create a Serbian State as a counterweight to Austria. Austria failed to seize the chance of putting herself at the head of a Balkan movement. The chance was then lost forever and, as we shall see, the German option also failed.

A second war led to rapid defeat in 1809 and placed the integrity of the Empire in jeopardy. A severe peace was imposed, losing Austria her last Italian possessions, including the ports of Trieste and Fiume, part of Galicia and the Tirol. Napoleon married the Princess Marie-

Louise, thus making Austria a reluctant ally until 1812; she even contributed 30,000 troops to the Russian campaign. Following Napoleon's Russian defeat, Austria, Prussia and Russia formed a new coalition, sealing his fate at the battle of Leipzig in 1813. Prussia's contribution to Napoleon's defeat was at least as significant as that of Austria, who could not recover her dominance of the new German Confederation.

Austria, host to the peace Congress, seemed to be at the high point of her influence and her idea of a reactionary alliance to police the continent did indeed emerge from the Congress. Yet she had made her fatal choice of the German option without obtaining a winning hand in the forthcoming battle for Germany, which was to polarise into a war with Prussia in 1866. For that, she had abandoned the rôle of leading power in the Balkans and retained Italy, which in her long term strategic interest could only prove a liability. These problems were reinforced by the ideological heritage of the French Revolution: democracy and nationalism. These ideas were potent and could not be erased from human memory, though they could be driven underground for a time. Both concepts would inevitably re-emerge and together or singly were very dangerous for Austria in Hungary, the Balkans or Italy.

In the period down to 1830, the reactionary course charted at the Vienna Congress had held the line. This was the period of Biedermaier conservatism and relative quietism in foreign affairs. The Congress system itself soon came under strains, and while the Holy Alliance was able to intervene in Italy and Spain the Congress of Verona in 1822 could no longer count on British support in these conservative police actions. However, it could not prevent Greek or Belgian independence, nor stop the Orléanist Revolution of 1830 in France. However, uprisings in Italy and Poland in the same year and the Polish uprising of 1846 were quelled without too much difficulty.

In Germany, the conservative structures put in place following the Congress of Vienna also held. The battle for control of Germany was as yet only latent. The German Confederation was reorganised in 1815 and consisted of fewer States than the old Empire – just thirty-nine – of which Austria, Prussia, Bavaria and Saxony were the most powerful. The German Bund was a confederation, with very weak central powers and institutions. The Bundestag was in effect an intergovernmental conference, in which the member States were virtually equal. There was no popular elective body and the Bund had almost no executive machinery. Indeed, the Bund in Frankfurt had a mere twenty-seven permanent officials. It established basic defence arrangements and was able to act against what it considered liberal subversion, but its powers in the trade field remained a dead letter, not least because of Austrian opposition.

Trade links developed piecemeal through the South German Zollverein and the Zollverein of 1834, in which Austria did not join. Following the assassination of the dramatist Kotzebue by a fanatical liberal-nationalist, the forces of reaction, led by Austria with the active support of Prussia, pushed through a catalogue of repressive decrees at the Karlsbad conference in 1819, covering censorship, control of the universities and a rudimentary confederal police apparatus. These measures were confirmed in 1824 and, after a new but extremely limited wave of liberal demonstrations in the early 1830s and following the French revolution of 1830, some 60 new repressive laws were enacted at the Vienna Conference of 1834–35. Until the 1840s, there was a relative peace in the Bund, despite permanent Austrian fears of liberalism, especially in the southern States which had more advanced constitutions. Indeed, Austria had imposed restrictive constitutional clauses on the Bund, aimed at preventing the establishment of liberal régimes in the Confederation. Austria was more concerned with containing liberalism than with any other political goals in Germany.

In the period between the outbreak of revolution in that year of revolutions, 1848, and her final exclusion from Germany, the Austrian Empire faced battles on many contradictory fronts and was unable to develope a coherent strategy or to establish priorities between threats in order to operate within her real capacity. She faced the almost simultaneous threats of internal upheaval, revolts in Italy and Hungary, key choices in relation to her German policy and difficult foreign policy decisions. In reality, she did not make sufficiently ruthless choices between problems and sought to deal with every threat at once. Cutting losses was not a concept that Austrian statesmen of that time were able to apply, though such an approach would have been considerably more effective.

The year of revolutions began in February in Milan and spread to southern Italy, Munich, Paris and Hungary. Kossuth set Hungary aflame with his speech to the Hungarian Parliament on 3 March and the movement then spread to Vienna, with a Citizens' Petition, a student demonstration and a mass demonstration outside the Estates

and in the First World War. Prussia carefully remained outside the Crimean War. Hence when the showdown came in Germany, Austria could not rely on Russian support, as might otherwise have been logically expected in Russia's interests. The Crimean War left Austria with gains in the Danubian region, at least insofar as Russia was excluded, but with more potential enemies (France, Russia, Italy) and no allies for the coming struggle for Germany.

In a certain sense, the battle for Germany had been going on since the dissolution of the Holy Roman Empire by Napoleon in 1806. Austria and Prussia had brought forward competitive plans for the reorganisation of conservative Germany and for the winning of the 'Third Germany' to their side. The democratic movement, that led to the hopeful election of the first German Parliament that met in Frankfurt in 1848–49 to write a constitution for a democratic German Reich, was a failure as the revolutionary moment had passed by 1849 and the Parliament was too divided; it never succeeded in creating an executive power of any substance and with any authority, but it sealed the fate of Austria and, in the end, strengthened Prussia. The constitutional debates and the final text adopted on 28 March 1849 offered Austria a stark choice and, indeed, had already led to the withdrawal of the Austrian Deputies from the Assembly as early as 5 April after the decisive vote on the text.

As early as October 1848, the Assembly had adopted the famous articles 2 and 3 which provided that any member of the Bund with territories outside the Bund would have to place its German and non-German territories under separate governments though not necessarily under a separate Head of State. The Head of State of the German territories would have to reside in them and be German. This was an expression of the rising nationalist principles. Austria would have to split into two or more personal unions or else remain outside the new Reich and maintain only inter-State relations with the new Reich. Forty-one of the 115 Austrian Deputies voted against these articles and the remainder supported them, favouring a personal union. However, the conservatives, led by Schwartzenberg, were now recovering ground. He sought to table a counter-proposal for a Grossdeutsche Union, including the whole of Austria – the seventy-million Reich.

The new Reichsministerpräsident Gagner was also looking for a compromise on the lines of an 'inner' and 'outer' Reich, which would have preserved both the unity of Austria and its close links with the new German Reich and a special status for the German part of the

Empire. The parliamentary situation in Frankfurt was fascinating but confused and changeable. The four broad groupings (left, centre-left, centre-right and right), were later joined by a united-left which, with the right, formed the Grossdeutsch Coalition grouping. They opposed the broad centre that favoured the Kleindeutsch solution with the Prussian King as a hereditary German Emperor.

There were in all some ten parties, named after the inns where they met: 'Deutscher Hof', 'Casino', 'Steinernes Haus', etc! It was not possible to find a majority for those compromise solutions. Thus on 27 March 1849, the final text of the Constitution, including the controversial articles 2 and 3, was voted upon. 267 voted in favour and 263 against. The following day, Friedrich IV was elected Emperor by 290 votes with 248 abstentions. Many German States, including Austria, recognised the Constitution, but Friedrich IV refused to accept the Crown from a democratic assembly rather than, as later in 1871, from his peers the other German princes. So the Constitution was still-born and soon important States such as Bavaria rejected the Constitution and the Assembly, and with it the campaign to obtain recognition of the Constitution. The sceptical attitude of those such as the Czech Palacký, who still accepted the Monarchy but had refused to participate in the German national–liberal construction, saw their attitude fully justified by this turn of events. The revolution had run its course.

Austria sought to seize the initiative that she had lost and rescue something from the confusion. With the so-called Punctuation of Olomouc in 1850, she won the first round. In a conflict over the Bund – the old Bund was still in existence and had been reactivated at Austria's behest – and a Prussian intervention in Hessen-Kassel, Prussia was forced by an ultimatum to withdraw her troops from Hessen. The Schleswig– Holstein affair which had first erupted in the nationalist wave of 1848, was resolved with the Convention of London in 1852. Denmark retained the Duchies, which remained in the Bund, but was forbidden to bind them into the Kingdom.

Bismarck, who come to power in 1862, used this issue as a lever to bind northern Germany to Prussia and to revenge the Olomouc humiliation. This finally provoked a row which excluded an isolated Austria from Germany and enabled the unification of Germany under Prussian hegemony in 1871. Austria called a 'Fürstentag', an assembly of all the German princes, in Frankfurt for August 1863 to consider a revision of the Bund Constitution to create a five State Directorate and a two chamber Parliament for a Union of States. The

Prussian King declined to attend and even when the King of Saxony, as the envoy of the Fürstentag, invited him to do so, he still refused under Bismarck's pressure. The Austrian initiative failed and counter-proposals flew up and down Germany, but Bismarck remained firm. Austria's position was weakened by the need to preserve the unity of the Empire, as in 1849.

Bismarck now seized on the convenient problem of the succession line to the Danish Crown and to the Duchies, which became relevant with the death of the Danish King in 1863. At the same time, Danish efforts, such as the Constitution of 1855, to bind the Duchies closer to Denmark represented provocations to German nationalist opinion. Following the failure of the Vienna reform initiatives, Austria saw an alliance with Prussia – ignoring the Bund – as the way forward, and so joined Prussia in war with Denmark. The war was rapidly over and both Duchies were annexed to Austria and Prussia who, at first, ran a joint administration. Bismarck secretly offered assistance to regain Lombardy against Prussia's part in the Duchies. This initiative failed as the two Monarchs rejected the plan. In any event, it would have led to war with France. The alliance was, however, the cause of serious mistrust of the 'Third Germany'.

Bismarck oscillated cleverly between conflict over administration of the Duchies and proposals for joint action against the other German states. However, conflict grew and gained the upper hand. Bismarck wanted a showdown and probably had already opted for war by late 1865. Austria supported the Augustenborg claims to the Duchies – an anti-Prussian move as Bismarck aimed at annexation – and she renewed her drive for the support of Middle Germany. Bismarck set the scene. He convinced his Emperor of the need to take preventative measures against Austrian provocation and on 8 April 1866, signed an alliance with Italy. This assisted him in obtaining French neutrality, which Austria also 'bought' with Venetia. Britain and Russia were easily persuaded to remain neutral. He also sought rapprochement with the Middle German States such as Bavaria, which prevented Austria from developing a strategy with them. The pretext was conflict over administration of the Duchies. Prussian troops entered Holstein. Austria called for the mobilisation of Bund troops against Prussia. Prussia declared that she had left the Bund, an illegal move.

War had now become inevitable, as the only way of determining hegemony in Germany. Austria and her allies were ill-prepared and were no match for the modernised Prussian army under von Moltke. Austria's allies were geographically divided, with Hannover and

Oldenburg in the north cut off from Hessen, Pfalz, Baden, Wurtem-berg, Saxony and Bavaria in the south. There was no military coordination and Austria received little support. The Prussian plan involved a northern offensive against Hannover and Hessen and a three pronged attack on Bohemia. The war lasted a mere six weeks. Austria stood and fought at Königgrätz on 4 July 1866 and her army was defeated. The road to Vienna was open. In Italy, Austria was victorious, winning the land battle of Custoza and the sea battle of Lissa. Yet as Austria had already agreed to cede Venetia to France (to be passed to Italy) in return for her neutrality, these victories had no relevance. To avoid the threat of French intervention on behalf of Austria in order to save the balance of power in Germany, Bismarck realised that he needed to reach a rapid and magnanimous peace with Austria. With great difficulty, he persuaded his Emperor to make no territorial demands on Austria. At the Peace of Prague, Austria recognised the dissolution of the German Confederation and hence her exclusion, after almost 600 years, from Germany, and the reorganisation of North Germany under Prussian leadership. Her own territorial integrity and that of her ally Saxony was respected.

It was a shattering defeat for Austria, with multiple consequences. She was excluded from Germany and Italy (Peace of Vienna), but Italy remained dissatisfied as her Prussian ally had not assisted her in gaining the South Tirol or territory on the Dalmatian Coast. In the field of foreign policy, paradoxically it soon became clear, especially after the defeat of France in 1870, that Austria had only one possible, reliable, long-term ally. Hence the fateful system of alliances was built up. The cornerstone of alliance with Germany was the dominance of the German and Hungarian national groupings in the Empire as a bulwark against Slavic advances to the West. This meant that despite the introduction of constitutional government in the Austrian 'Reichshälfte' in 1867, there was limited room for maneouvre in the matter of serious reform of the Empire. Indeed, under the 1867 Ausgleich, Hungary became virtually independent and could not be compelled to make concessions to her very large Slavic and Romanian minorities. The powder barrel of 1914-18 was thus buried and primed.

The next 50 years was taken up with a slow, but inevitable decline, having some of the elements of a Greek tragedy. Was there any chance of reform that would have saved at least some form of democratic multinational organisation in the regions covered by the Empire? Was a gradual democratic transformation possible? It has to be said that by this time, given the contradictions between the interests of the different peoples of the Empire, the intransigence of Franz-Joseph and the obligations of the German/Hungarian alliance, the answer must probably be no. Austria had failed to seize the possibility of a Balkan or Central European destiny; now her destiny, it was about to be forced upon her. The next period, down to the First World War, is the history of the creation of the Alliance system, the development of Slavic nationalism and the struggle, inevitably vain, to square the circle in internal reform.

Bismarck, having defeated Austria and France and unified Germany, sought to bring Austria into his system of alliances. Bismarck organised the Three Emperor League (Germany, Austria, Russia) in 1873. Would this agreement lead to Russian–Austrian co-operation in the Balkans? It was soon tested with the Serbian supported revolt against the Turkish régime in Bosnia-Hercegovina. Russia gave its support to associated risings in the eastern Balkans. Under the Reichstadt Agreement (1875), Austria pledged neutrality in the coming Turkish War and Russia accepted Austrian occupation of Bosnia and Hercegovina.

The 1877–78 war led to a Russian victory and her control over the Dardanelles as well as the creation of a Grand Bulgaria under Russian tutelage. Austria and Britain protested and in the Congress of Berlin held under German auspices in 1878, Russia was forced to abandon Grand Bulgaria, now reduced in size, and the Austrian occupation of Bosnia and Hercegovina was accepted by the powers. The benefits were small: Russia remained revisionist, Serbia was dissatisfied, (though she became fully independent) and Bosnia and Hercegovina remained formally Turkish; the Slavic population of the Empire had increased alarmingly. Above all, the settlement increased Austria's dangerous dependence on Germany.

An alliance was signed in 1879 that would commit Austria to a two-front war against Russia and France at the side of Germany. Austrian policy was now subordinated to Germany and since that alliance reposed on the German-Magyar axis inside the Empire, the German external guarantee of the Empire was bought against its prospect of internal reform and hence paradoxically destroyed it. In 1882 this alliance was extended, to include Italy, as the Triple Alliance. This was intended by Bismarck to strengthen the Alliance against France and reconcile Austria and Italy. This new ally was of very dubious value as her behaviour in 1915 was to show.

In 1883, the Alliance was extended to Romania, who also deserted during the First World War. The Three Emperors League, less binding than the interlocking alliances, was renewed several times. It aimed at reducing conflict between Austria and Russia, but as Bismarck made clear in a speech to the Reichstag in 1888 where he stated that 'the Balkan problem was not worth the sacrifice of the straight limbs of even one single Prussian grenadier', here Austria was on her own and could count on no German support. Here, Germany made a serious miscalculation destined to cost her and Europe dearly. Germany and Austria were inexorably bound together, because their system of alliances was responded to by the creation of the Franco-Russian Alliance in 1894 and the later Anglo-French and Anglo-Russian Alliances thus creating the entente block to stand against the central powers, who were later joined by Turkey. Furthermore, the German post-Bismarck leadership neglected his 'reinsurance' policy, enshrined in the 1887 Treaty with Russia, under which Bismarck pledged neutrality in an Austrian offensive war with Russia and more significantly accorded Russia a free hand in Bulgaria.

A series of crises in the Balkans (Bulgaria 1885 and 1896, the Serbian dynastic change of 1903, Bosnia 1908, the Balkan Wars) tested and, when coupled with other crises in which Austria or Germany and Austria (Morocco) were isolated and forced to back down, wore down the goodwill necessary to preserve peace. Each crisis made it more likely that the next would prove fatal, as the Powers and especially Austria lost their incentive to compromise, and accepted even greater risks to avoid defeat. At the same time, Austrian domestic considerations made compromise even more difficult. Thus, for example, the Foreign Minister was forced to resign in 1908 as his policy of accommodation with Russia and Serbia was unacceptable to Hungary.

The most significant internal development resulting from the defeat of Austria was the Ausgleich with Hungary in 1867 and the introduction of constitutional government in Austria at the same time, replacing the various authoritarian or absolutist forms of government introduced since the defeat of the revolution in 1849.

The compromise represented a political structure *sui generis*. It was neither a Federation nor a Treaty between completely sovereign States. It was a personal and real Union (Realunion) between two equal States with a common Emperor and some common functions and institutions involving foreign affairs, defence and the necessary common financing, the respective share being subject to review every ten years. Customs, currency and railways were separately administered according to common principles. The Empire remained an economic area. Each government was responsible to its own Parliament and the three joint Ministers of Defence, Foreign Affairs and Finance to Delegations from each Parliament. The joint Ministers with two Prime Ministers formed the joint Ministerial Council. In addition, the Hungarians viewed the whole arrangement as being contingent on the maintenance of the 1867 Constitutional Laws in Austria, which established a unitary State.

The Imperial Manifesto of Emperor Karl in 1918 that called for a federative structure in the Austrian 'Reichshälfte' was taken by Budapest as the pretext, legally sufficient, to end the Union. Thus, the way to the reform of the Empire towards any form of democratic federation was triply blocked: by Germany, in Hungary, and in Austria by the need to preserve the 1867 laws in order to maintain the Union. No solution could be found for the minorities in either part of the Monarchy, let alone those (Croats, Serbians, German, Romanians, Ruthenians) that lived in both parts.

These constitutional laws could not be passed in Austria except with the united support of the German members of Parliament since the Czechs and Poles rejected the compromise, as well they might. That meant compromise with the Liberals. A series of relatively liberal constitutional laws were thus passed creating a bi-cameral Reichsrat with much wider legislative powers, and established the principle of Ministerial Responsibility to Parliament. Yet under the infamous article 14 which accorded the right to issue emergency decrees to the Cabinet and the Emperor, democracy was relative.

At the same time, a hidden consequence was to force the Emperor to govern almost exclusively with the support of the German deputies, who were hostile to any reform of the structure of the Empire and were able to block the so-called Fundamental Laws (1871) which would have represented a move towards an 'Ausgleich' with the Czechs, many of whom, like the great Czech and pan-Slavic Nationalist Francis Palacký, believed even now in a solution within the Empire. Within Hungary, a limited 'Ausgleich' was enacted with Croatia in 1868. This was essentially the constitutional structure of the Dual Monarchy and its geographical extension until its collapse in 1918.

Austrian political life in the period down to the first World War was characterised by several important trends, some of which were potentially disturbing. The movements associated with Georg von Schönerer and Karl Lueger, Mayor of Vienna, brought a populist antisemitism into the political arena and were later regarded as models by Adolf Hitler. These, and other less radical liberals and numerous clubs and societies, represented a pan-Germanic strand. The period also saw the rise of the Social Christians, supportive of the Monarchy and the Ausgleich, and the formation of the Social Democratic Party at the Hainfeld Congress in 1888, under Victor Adler. The period saw a sharpening of conflict over language issues, especially in mixed areas, and a radicalisation of Czech opinions, especially in the Young Czech and National Socialist Parties and with the emergence of Thomas Masaryk as the leader of Czech Nationalism. In 1905, Austrian and Hungarian Croats and Serbian political leaders came together in Fiume and Zador, in defiance of their governments, and proclaimed their unity. No one had as yet obtained undisputed leadership of the moves towards a southern Slavic entity within or outside the Empire, but the movement had received an important impetus.

These events are inextricably linked up with the Bosnian crisis in 1908 and the Balkan Wars in 1912 and 1913 which were preludes to the First World War. In 1908, Turkey became a Constitutional Monarchy and hence might theoretically seek reversion of full sovereign rights in Bosnia–Hercegovina. This was taken by Austria as a pretext for a piece of dangerous adventurism. A secret deal, later repudiated, was supposedly made with Russia to permit an outright Austrian annexation of the territories. This provoked a major crisis in which the entente powers and Serbia faced an Austria backed by Germany. Austria gave some nominal satisfaction to Turkey, but forced Serbia to demobilise. Russia backed down. She would, however, not do so again. Serbian hostility has been assured and a large, hostile Slavic population added to the Empire. The second Moroccan crisis, the Italian war against Turkey (1911), and the two Balkan wars, worsened the international situation. The disintegration of Turkey now seemed assured and with it the problem of the union of the Slavs inside and outside the Monarchy.

In the first War, a coalition of Greece, Montenegro, Serbia and Bulgaria pushed Turkey out of Europe. In the second War, the other victors, plus Romania, joined forces against Bulgaria and shared Macedonia and southern Dobroudja. Austria had blocked Serbian access to the sea by an ultimatum and by creating Albania as a satellite State. This behaviour redoubled Serbian hostility and set the stage for Sarajevo.

It was the assassination of Franz-Ferdinand, the heir to the throne in Sarajevo, on 28 June 1914 that lit the fuse to the long-buried powder keg of the Balkans. The explosion was to carry away, for better or worse, the multi-national Empire. Almost any event could have lit this fuse. A Balkan war, involving Austria and Serbia at least and probably also Russia, had become increasingly inevitable. The Austrian ultimatum to Serbia was designed to provoke a war to a point where even a compromise response by Serbia was ignored. The Austrian leadership got the war that it sought, to try to reverse the reverses that it had suffered in the region. A pre-emptive strike was seen as vital.

It, no doubt, did not expect that by the end of July all Europe would be at war, the deadly cogs of a quasi-automatic system of alliances, whose foundations had been laid in the last century and in the early years of the new century, having functioned with precision. The broadening of the conflict to include all Europe and eventually from 1916 Italy, Romania and the United States was the death knell of the Empire. Her fate was linked with Germany. Her bitterest enemies were all in the Allied Camp and the Slavic cause was able to exercise considerable political leverage in the United States. It was precisely this global and political character of the war that was so fatal to the Empire. Initially, the Allied Powers had no intention of dismembering the Empire, nor undertaking a comprehensive remake of the map of Europe. Indeed, as late as 1917–18 when secret peace feelers were put out from the Austrian side, this was not so.

Indeed, Austria lost the war more politically than militarily. Her ally Germany was defeated and the central powers were exhausted economically from four years of war. Yet the Army, the backbone of the Empire, despite its multi-national character, remained intact. Before the Russian Revolution, the fortunes of war in Galicia had varied, but at no time had the Russian armies achieved a decisive penetration into Austrian territory. Naturally, after the Revolution, this threat disappeared. In the south, Serbia and Montenegro were occupied by 1915. It was only in 1918 that the Allies, moving north from Salonika broke into southern Serbia and overwhelmed the Bulgarian positions. On the Italian front, after some initial modest Italian gains in Istria and north of the Lake Garda, the Austrians pushed them back south to the Po and almost reached Venice.

By failing to react to any of the Western (particularly American) attempts to reach a compromise peace, the Central Powers had played a dangerous 'all or nothing' game entirely of their own making.

In 1914, the chancelleries of Europe had seen the Empire as a necessity. That had largely been true even in early 1917. Of course, the more radical Slavic movement and in particular the Czechs under Thomas Masaryk, aimed at the dismemberment of the Empire as the only way that they could by then obtain a Czech State. Yet the collapse of Russia as a power factor could have even reduced their weight in the peace Councils. A compromise peace would no doubt have preserved the Empire and some multinational organisation of the region.

Would this have been worse than what actually resulted from the intransigence of the Central Powers and their failure to accurately read the new moral force of President Wilson's ideas of democracy and self-determination? (However, the young Emperor Karl had made one inept effort to escape from his strait jacket, only to be shown the limits of his power by his German allies in brutal fashion. This was the Sixtus affair – secret negotiations through Sixtus). Failure to show any of the famous adaptability of the Habsburgs at this key point, doomed the Empire to an outcome close to the unconditional surrender of 1945, (which had not been asked of it).

From October 1918, total confusion reigned. On 28 October, the Czech Republic, already recognized by the Allies, was proclaimed. On 29 October, the Slovak National Council decided to join the Czech Republic. Earlier, the Slovenes, Croats and Serbians issued the Corfu Declaration (20 July) in favour of a Southern Slav Kingdom. Meeting in Zagreb, the Croation National Council within the Empire, voted on 29 October for membership of that Kingdom. On 21 October the German Reichsrat members voted for the creation of a Deutsch-Österreich Nation, which would take in all German-speaking areas including the Sudetenland. At last the Austrians accepted Wilson's fourteen points as the basis of negotiations but sought a limitative interpretation of point ten which specified 'autonomous development' for the people of the Empire. By now, this was no longer acceptable to the Allied Powers, who had already recognized the Czechs, and was becoming increasingly irrelevant in view of the internal developments. On 27 October, a request for a separate peace was made and on 4 November a truce was signed for the Italian front. On 12 November, after the end of the European War, the Emperor abdicated.

The First Republic was born in almost total chaos, a condition which was, with the exception of a short period of relative stability in the late 1920s, to remain its lot. The borders of the new State were unclear, its constitution was confused and disputed, and the economic situation was desperate. The period before the Peace Treaties of

St Germain and Trianon in 1919 and 1920 was chaotic. Initially, the majority of the members of the 'Provisional National Assembly' for German Austria, set up in response to the Emperor's proclamation of 16 October 1918 urging the creation of assemblies in all the Crown Lands, had seen the 'Klein-Österreich' State as non-viable and voted for union with the democratic German Reich. This was not immediately possible. As a result, an Austrian provisional government under Karl Renner (SPÖ) was formed with a Social-Democrat-dominated Volkswehr to maintain order.

Elections to a Constituant Assembly were held on 19 February 1919 and seventy-two SPÖ, sixty-nine Social Christians, twenty-three Nationalist, three Peasants and three others were elected. The Social Democrats retained the chancellorship, but were forced to compromise as to the federal nature of the constitution, and the failure of the Committee of Nationalisation of Industry to provide results soon showed.

The new State was set about with problems. It was very weak. Three Communist putsches were attempted in the first year. The ex-Emperor was only forced to leave the country in March 1919. There was violent conflict between Slovenes and the Freischärler defenders of Kärnten. South Tirol was occupied by Italy and there were Soviet Republics on her borders in Bavaria and Hungary, which supported the Red Guards in Austria. Political violence in both urban and rural areas was frequent. Unemployment, demobilised soldiers, serious food shortage and the lack of fuel were serious problems which fuelled unrest. Austria's industrial areas had been in Bohemia, her main agriculture in Moravia and Hungary, her markets to the East and her outlet to the sea in Istria and Dalmatia. All these were lost. The peace negotiations also hung over the new Republic like The Sword of Damocles. The Republic was hanging-on by its fingernails.

Certainly, Allied peace terms were severe. Commitments had been made to Italy (in the secret Treaty of London 1915) and to the Czechs and Southern Slavs. Both Austria and Hungary suffered severe territorial losses and considerable restrictions. In order to avoid 'unpacking' delicate inter-allied (Italian versus Yugoslav claims) compromises, the two Peace Treaties of St Germain and Trianon were in effect diktats on which no concessions were offered. As Clémenceau is supposed to have politely put it, 'Austria is what's left'. Austria lost the Sudetenland area, the whole Croatian, Dalmatian and Istria areas, the South Tirol, including Bozen (Bolzano), part of Kärnten. Reparations and military restrictions were imposed. However, after considerable diplomatic manoeuvering involving both Czechoslovakia and Italy, the German-speaking west Hungarian areas (minus Pressburg and Ödenburg) were ceded to Austria under the Treaty of Trianon. This settlement had seen the two main parties involving foreign powers in their quarrels: the SPÖ made an arrangement in Prague to gain support on the west Hungarian areas (Burgenland) and the Christian Party looked to Italy and Hungary. The Heimwehr, a rightist private army, obtained support from Hungary. This was a very dangerous precedent that was to be repeated in the 1930s and destroy Austria.

After the Peace Treaties, the State began to function. A federal constitution was adopted. The coalition under Renner fell and the SPÖ was to remain in opposition for the remainder of the First Republic. The economic situation began to improve and successive cabinets with independent or Christian Social chancellors such as Dr Seipel held office throughout this period. The Socialists had suffered severe losses at the 1923 elections falling back to sixty-eight seats with eighty-two for the Christian Social Party and 15 for the Deutschnationale and Farmers Party (joint list). The Christian Socialists, now led by Dr Seipel, a strong centralist in his party and opposed to the representatives of the Länder who argued for more decentralisation, held their position in 1927, with eighty-five seats (with the Deutschnationale), seventy-one SPÖ and nine Farmers party members. Indeed, Dr Seipel's bloc obtained an absolute majority. The 1920s saw a considerable improvement in the economic situation and the currency was saved. At the same time, the alliance of the Christian Socialists with the Deutschnationale against the Social Democrats who, rhetoric apart, remained pragmatic during this period, and the division between 'red' Vienna with its progressive municipal housing (60,000 apartments built 1923–33) and the 'black' countryside, was a dangerous polarisation in a democracy with shallow roots.

The Social Democrat Linz programme on which they went to the polls in 1927 was actually a defensive programme, but was seen as anti-democratic and a 'Marxist' programme by the bourgeois parties. The SPÖ did not win power, but with 42.3% of the vote and its auxiliary organisations, including its private force the Republikanisch Schutzbund, remained a force to be reckoned with if the economy fell apart, as indeed it did in 1929. Yet, it proved to be a paper tiger. The period between 1927 and the final collapse of political democracy in Austria in 1934 was characterised by increasing and escalating violence between the antagonistic political private armies of the Socialists, the National Heimwehr and the National Socialists.

The democratic system became weaker and less and less capable of governing effectively in the face of successive bank failures, including that of the Creditanstalt in 1932, and unemployment which rose above 400,000. The country was in almost permanent negotiations with its external creditors and it became increasingly difficult to cobble together parliamentary majorities behind rescue packages. After the 1930 elections, the government – essentially authoritarian Christian Social – with shifting allies, was eventually reduced to a majority of one when the Nationalists witheld support. In the Landtage and local authorities, the Nazis represented a new threat, with 15% of the vote in Vienna in 1932. New elections were not the preferred option for the right, which was increasingly attracted by the concept of an Austrian authoritarian corporate State on the Italian model, propagated by the social philosopher Dr Spann. The opposition to parliamentary democracy was growing in the Heimwehr in the new Christian Social Party generation such as Dollfuss, Fey and Schuschnigg and Starhemberg. Those men were prepared to act against democracy. The first step was the use of old wartime emergency powers to rule without parliament by decree.

Then in March 1933 came the tragic-comical end of Austrian parliamentarism. Under the rules of the Nationalrat, the President-in-the-Chair could not vote. For tactical reasons, the SPÖ persuaded Karl Renner to resign as President to 'win' his vote. This won the vote, but destroyed Parliament, the Socialists' only weapon, since each of the other Presidents also resigned! Parliament could not now be called into session. Chancellor Dollfuss now had a perfect pretext to liquidate the 'old régime'. It had in effect liquidated and ridiculed itself. Yet, in the Austrian fashion, compromises were sought and nearly achieved. However, a new factor was the external one: Hitler had been in power in Germany since 30 January 1933. The Austrian Nazis were now a bigger threat than the Socialists. Only the Italian alliance, and hence a corporate State, could provide the Austro-Fascist régime with some backing against Hitler and did so until 1938. As a result, Dollfuss rejected the compromise route with the Socialists and refused to compromise with the NSDAP, who he rejected on religious grounds.

On 12 February 1934, the Socialist Schutzbund, almost unplanned and uncoordinated, did fight back against attempts to seize their weapons. There were three days of fighting in Vienna, Linz, Graz, Leoben and Hallein near Salzburg. The Socialists lost 137 dead and 399 wounded and the government 105 dead and 319 wounded. The Socialists were crushed, the party banned and its leaders forced into exile. On 17 March, Dollfuss signed a Treaty of Alliance with Italy and Hungary. On 25 July 1934, the other threat materialised and was defeated. The Austrian Nazis organized a putsch. They captured the chancellory and murdered Chancellor Dollfuss. Otherwise the putsch was rapidly put down in Vienna and other places, notably in Kärnten, Steiermark and Salzburg. The aim had been to install a Nazi-front government headed by Dr Rintelen, a former Minister but not an overt National Socialist. The army was not favourable, as the putschists had supposed. The new Chancellor was Dr Schuschnigg who assumed easy and rapid control of the authoritarian State and its political organisation the Vaterländisches Front. He was to govern for almost four years until the Anschluss in March 1938.

These victories were short-lived and pyrrhic. The German occupation of the Rhineland in 1936, the manifest weakness of Italy in the Abyssinian War and her rapid subordination to Germany, showed Austria that she was alone. Italy was a broken reed. In 1936 Dr Schuschnigg concluded an agreement with Germany that freed putschists, authorised National Socialist political activity and led to the appointment of several Nationalists close to the Nazis to the Austrian government. Despite this compromise and the appointment of the 'moderate' Fritz von Papen as Ambassador to Vienna, the pressure did not weaken. The visit of Foreign Minister von Neurath in February 1937 made it clear to Schuschnigg that he had miscalculated: the demands would escalate. A German intervention in Austria was accepted by Mussolini in late 1937; he had no choice. Austria had no other allies and Schuschnigg refused to seek a compromise with the Austrian left, to mobilise the people. Finally he was called to meet Hitler. He accepted his demands for German 'observers' in the Austrian forces. His only step was to announce an ill-thought-out referendum. This finally provoked an ultimatum to appoint Dr Seyss-Inquart (later executed for his brutal reign as Gauleiter in Holland) as Chancellor or face armed intervention.

Again Schuschnigg accepted. The new cabinet then decreed the Anschluss, later approved by 99.7% of the voters, and German troops marched in on 12 March 1938.

Yes, Hitler was acclaimed on the Heldenplatz. Yes, many brutal Nazis were Austrians; yes, 99.7% did vote for the Anschluss in a technically fair vote; yes, leading figures like Karl Renner or Cardinal Innitzer did support the Anschluss with reservations. However, it was difficult for almost half the population to regret the passing of the Austro-Fascist régime after the events of 1934 and earlier. There was too quick a reversal of opinion. As early as 1939, the attitude was changing. The Viennese Special Court alone tried 17,000 cases involving political crimes between 1938-45. There was an active Austrian underground. There was active Austrian solidarity, even among Nazis or from Nazis to non-Nazis. The new Austria was full of contradictions but it was born of common suffering and as victims of Hitler, however naive the initial expectations may have been in 1938.

In 1945, the situation was not easy. The country was as clearly defeated, economically devastated and isolated as in 1918. Worse, many urban areas, such as Vienna, were severely damaged and then threatened with the dismantling of industrial plant for reparations. The country was also occupied by the four Powers. Certainly there was the basis of a new democratic national spirit, but there were also 700,000 Nazis....Above all, there was uncertainty about the future. Yet, there was a dawning belief that, whatever might have been historically preferable, the only nation that the Austrian people would have was the 'Klein-Oesterreich', the rump State. It was up to them to make the best of it.

As we shall see in Chapter 3 (Austria in the World), the future of Austria after the Second World War was determined by the Allies, who were to a large extent indifferent to Austria, or else looked at the question from the standpoint of their own interests in the region. These interests were contradictory or cancelled each other out.

Despite scepticism based on the unfortunate failure of Austria to develop into a viable nation in the inter-war period, the simplest solution, and indeed the one arrived at by a process of elimination, was to re-establish Austria as an independent nation within her pre-1938 borders and declare her to have been the 'first victim' of Nazi aggression whilst applying a carrot and stick approach by warning Austria that her final treatment would depend on her own contribution to the anti-Nazi cause. That was the balanced approach of the Moscow Declaration of 1 November 1943, which was to remain the policy keystone of the Allied Powers towards Austria. It was decided to subject Austria to a four Power occupation régime, similar to that in Germany, and to the tutelage of an Allied Council. Yet, from the start, allied policy was much milder in Austria than in Germany. By the end of April, a provisional government was installed and by the autumn, it was recognised by the four Allies for the whole country. By November 1945, the first elections since 1930 were held and a democratic government, the Grand Coalition (until 1947 ÖVP + SPÖ +KPÖ) was installed under Chancellor Leopold Figl (ÖVP).

The party system took its basic contours, modified in 1949 by the establishment of the small precurser of the FPÖ, into a two and a half party system. The coalition was born from a new sense of reality and a genuine broad based desire to make the Austrian nation work this time. To do so, no one could claim total power and exclude the other camp. Compromise, comprehension and recognition of the merits of others, qualities forged in the common experience of the Nazi camps, were needed.

It was a new and promising start. The coalition was held together by two central objectives, both of which were achieved: economic reconstruction and the State Treaty (1955). Both parties recognised the external and internal constraints. Both recognised the need for a mixed economy. Both recognised that in dealing with the other, patience and compromise were needed. Differences were mostly over method and tactics rather than fundamentals. There was no alternative to the Grand Coalition or to the essential elements of its policy. The political battle was about their respective influence within the Coalition. An ÖVP absolute majority strengthened its hand. Had the SPÖ won more seats, as it did votes in 1953 and in 1959, it could have claimed the Chancellorship. For the most part the parties carved out spheres of influence, such as agriculture for the ÖVP and social policy for the SPÖ, and limited the battleground to certain key areas such as influence in the State industries. Thus, throughout the 1950s, electoral changes became a barometer of the respective parties' control over the industrial sector. This self-restraint, this mutual accommodation that by the late 1960s became paralysis, was an accepted and acceptable price for successful reconstruction and nation-building.

The process by which Austria recovered her independence as a neutral State, but was forbidden to undertake an Anschluss with Germany whose military capacities were also limited by the State

Treaty, and the progress of the Austrian economic miracle are examined in detail in later chapters.

Austria was forced to become a real nation – and succeeded. As she succeeded, her self-confidence grew and her people increasingly came to identify with the new State and her success. When the Grand Coalition came to an almost natural end in 1966, having achieved its initial goals, having run out of steam and with one party (the ÖVP) again having an absolute majority, the SPÖ chose opposition. The skies did not fall in. Austria was a stable, successful western democracy. Her system could and did take the move to two-party competition and alternation in power in its stride.

The 1970–85 period was an intense period of democratisation and modernisation in all areas of Austrian life. In retrospect, the ÖVP majority government (1966–70) was transitional towards this period of rapid reform and innovation. This Kreisky era – the period of Dr Bruno Kreisky's chancellorship – saw significant and lasting innovations both in style and substance of politics and policies.

Political parties changed. Political leaders became more 'presidential'. Dr Kreisky actively 'worked' the media, with press conferences and briefings, in a way that had not been done before. Parties became more open to new ideas and new influences. They sought to expand the boundaries of their 'magnetic field' beyond their traditional lager. Extension and reaching out to those who in a famous Kreisky dictum, 'were prepared to go part of the way' rather than consolidation, were the name of the game, as a new looser post-materialist and mobile class structure developed in Austria. Alongside this new style came new policies for a new era. Many of these structural reforms in education, the legal system in training, the social policy field, were key elements in the Austrian economic model (see Chapter 5).

A new foreign policy based on contractual trade relations with the European Community, a 'good neighbour' policy to the East, an active and at times controversial foreign policy in the Middle East, the Third World and the non-aligned movement, has put Austria on the map and has given her a profile as a nation with something to say in world affairs that goes beyond her small size, which profile was also an important contribution to the building of a national consciousness.

By 1983, the reform wave had seen its course and come to a provisional end, having achieved considerable success towards its twin goals of modernisation and democratisation. New tasks and difficult choices involving retrenchment and a clearer concentration on a small number of priorities were on the horizon. In this context, the 1983–86 'Small Coalition' can be seen as a transitional stage on the road back to the Grand Coalition in its new form.

With the loss of the SPÖ absolute majority Dr Kreisky resigned as chancellor though he guided the creation of the small SPÖ–FPÖ coalition under Vice Chancellor Sinowatz from the Burgenland. Both his initial 'dauphins', Hannes Androsch and Leopold Graz had been swept away in political scandals that increasingly came to characterise this almost 'fin de régime' period.

The coalition was weak, with a new chancellor and the inexperienced FPÖ taking its first steps in government. For the most part, the government was defensive and continued the old policies in attenuated forms. The government was hit by continuing scandals, rising unemployment, the massive crisis in the State industries in 1985 and the enervating battles of the Waldheim affair in 1986. With the election of Dr Waldheim, the SPÖ lost the presidency for the first time, which seemed to signal a political 'Wende'. The popularity of the FPÖ collapsed and Vice Chancellor Norbert Steger was ousted as leader in a dramatic rightist–populist putsch at the 1986 Parteitag led by Jörg Haider.

The new model SPÖ Chancellor Franz Vranitzky, former banker and Finance Minister, who had taken command following the resignation of Dr Sinowatz after the election of Waldheim in June, sought a surprise election to save the SPÖ's relative majority and to form a Grand Coalition under his leadership. He broke the coalition which both Jörg Haider, and from the sidelines Dr Sinowatz and Dr Kreisky, would have been prepared to continue. The strategy worked. Despite some losses, the new pragmatic SPÖ retained a lead of three seats and the chancellorship and finance ministry in the new Grand Coalition which was formed in January 1987, at least for the duration of the XVIII Legislative (in principle 1986–90). The coalition seems to be working. It is popular (70% positive rating) and has achieved some results: tax reform, agricultural policy reform, reforms of the State industries, and its budget reforms are on target. Perhaps after a lean period of falling self-confidence, the Austrian Model has recovered some of its élan. In all events, Austria is clearly a nation with a past and a future, an identity and a consciousness.

3. Austria in the World

For Austria, foreign policy has been a matter of national identity. Until Austrians collectively decided what they were, there could be no meaningful foreign policy. In the inter-war period, no consensus emerged as to the national identity and that seriously undermined any chance of resisting Nazi subversion or the Anschluss itself. Austria had no collective sense of itself and hence no will to defend its interests against outside threats. It was therefore impossible to develop either a national consensus or effective alliances that would have given Austria a degree of security.

As we shall see, these grave errors were not repeated after the Second World War. The decision to recreate the Austrian State was certainly taken without consultation by the Allied Powers and enshrined in the Moscow Declaration, from which all else effectively flowed. However, this decision was rapidly and effectively endorsed as a working basis, and then as an irrevocable and definitive situation, by almost all political forces in Austria, even the Socialists, who had been the most reticent in the inter-war period. It was, indeed, highly symbolic that the first chancellor of the new Austria was Karl Renner (SPÖ) and that his government immediately issued a declaration of Austrian independence.

It took longer for the mass of the population to assume full nationhood, but the people soon came to accept the pragmatic wisdom of their leaders and, beyond that, came to believe in the Austrian nation and its rôle in world affairs – the Austrian way in foreign policy.

Naturally, the development of a national consciousness and a clear national identity did not take place from one day to the next. It was a gradual process, made up of several phases, in which a number of events played a leading part. The first event was the 1848 revolution, which had laid the political and constitutional basis for specifically Austrian institutions within the Empire. The exclusion from Germany followed by the 'Ausgleich' with Hungary was the next major step. The collapse of the Empire in 1918, the creation of the corporate state in 1934 and the Anschluss (1938) were all decisive elements, whose true impact only became cumulatively evident with the Moscow Declaration, the four-Power occupation in 1945-55 and the State Treaty construing Austrian sovereignty and neutrality. A decisive and, indeed, irrevocable process had taken place which had achieved popular acceptance and then support.

A survey conducted in 1980 showed that 67% of those questioned believed that Austria was a nation and 19% that it was in the process of becoming one. Thus, in all, 86% considered themselves Austrians and accepted that identity. Only (although it is a large enough figure) 11% rejected Austrian nationhood. In 1965, 15% rejected nationhood and in 1956, almost equal numbers considered Austria to be a nation (49%) as did not (46%). This shows how dramatic the change has been down to the present.

Table 1   When did Austria become a nation?

	Before 1918	At the break-up of the Empire	1934 –1938	Anschluss	1945 –1955	1955	Later	Not at all	DK
All	14	9	1	2	14	26	5	4	25
Men	16	10	1	2	16	25	6	6	18
Women	12	8	1	1	13	27	5	3	30
Age									
<30	9	9	0	2	14	36		5	20
30–50	13	7	1	2	15	28		6	24
>50	20	11	1	2	13	17		5	27

In 1970, support for a new Anschluss was only 7%, whereas 91% rejected it. Analysis of a more detailed survey made in 1972 shows that even among FPÖ voters, only 11% rejected an Austrian identity. Pan-Germanism was at its strongest in Salzburg, Oberösterreich and Kärnten (8%).The case of Vorarlberg is probably different (11%). The greatest support for pan-Germanism (less than 10%) came in the higher social groups and among those with better education. It is interesting to analyse respondents' perception of when Austria became a nation (see Table 1).

Interestingly, a significant proportion of respondents saw the origins of Austrian nationhood being before or at the break-up of the Empire (23%) and this figure rose to 31% for those over 50 years of age (in 1972). However, 40% saw the occupation period and the State

Treaty as the most important milestones. This proportion rose to 50% among the under-30 age group. Interestingly, neither the 30–50 age group (born between 1922 and 1942) or the over 50s (born before 1922) were significantly less 'Austrian' than the under 30 age group (born after 1942). Indeed, in the words of the Austrian Professor Felix Kreissler, the creation of an Austrian national identity is 'a learning process with many obstacles on its way', but that process is now virtually complete.

Austrian public opinion accepts the fact of Austrian nationhood, sees it as irreversible and rejects the Anschluss but, more positively, also supports a conception of Austrian foreign policy based on active neutrality. Thus in 1982, a survey showed that 56% approved of the 'active' SPÖ foreign policy and only 3% disapproved. Ninety per cent supported neutrality, 80% went further to say that they felt more secure in a neutral state, and 76% held that neutrality contributed to Austria's then good image abroad and increased her capacity to play a positive rôle in world affairs. Thus both the general foundations of Austrian foreign policy and the development of this 'Austrian way' have found a broad basis in popular support.

How has this happy but radical transformation of the state of affairs been brought about? To understand that, we shall look at the recent evolution of Austria's self-image, the process of nation building which has always been an inner and an external process, and her relations with both her immediate neighbours and the Great Powers who have influenced her destiny.

For Austria, foreign policy has been at the centre of political concern and, indeed, literally a matter of national life and death. As in the domestic field, lessons have been learned from the unhappy inter-war period, when the lack of a national consensus on the nation's foreign policy and on its very existence was to prove a fatal flaw. Our aim in this chapter will be to look at the making of Austrian foreign policy, at the main aspects of this policy, and at the changes she must face in the coming period.

As we shall see, there was a very broad consensus on foreign policy during the Second Republic, which consensus has been vitally important in ensuring the success of Austrian policy. In the first phase, when there was a Grand Coalition, the aim of policy was to achieve the State Treaty and the withdrawal of the occupying forces. The second phase, which opened in October 1955, was based on a policy of permanent neutrality as enshrined in the settlement that had led to the signature of the State Treaty. This is the foundation stone of Austrian foreign policy. On other issues, such as relations with the European Community or the Middle East, there can be divergences, but there has been broad unity on the fundamentals.

Unlike the unhappy history of the First Republic – the State no one wanted – there was, from the start, a broad consensus behind the foundation of the new Austria, on the premises established by the Moscow Declaration.

The aim of Austrian policy was to recover full sovereignty as soon as possible, to end the four-Power occupation. Almost no one contested the existence and the economic and political viability of the Austrian State. That was the central premise of the Moscow Declaration, accepted by the three, then four, Allied Powers. In any event no other alternative was realistic. The British had lost the argument over the creation of a new Danubian or Middle European grouping as both a means of dismembering Germany and as a counterweight to Soviet power.

As the Cold War became more marked, there was little interest in Austria for links with the States of the old Empire which were falling victim to a tight Stalinist dictatorship, which almost all Austrians fervently hoped to avoid. Germany had also lost its attraction. The crimes of the Third Reich made Germany an international pariah. The German State and its Economy was in ruins.

The Austrian pan-Germanic lager thus had few arguments and was fatally compromised by its association with National Socialism. A new realism, not evident in the inter-war period, took hold. The key question was not to seek a chimera of ideal solutions, but to make the best of the situation as it was. Realism dictated that Austrian sovereignty could only be regained with the consent of the Allied Powers and in particular with agreement of the Soviet Union.

Austria was forced to come to terms with being the object rather than the subject of history. This was no more than the recognition of facts which had become ever more evident. Austria had ceased to be an independent great power after her exclusion from Germany in 1866 and her subsequent alliance with the German Empire in 1879. Her fate was umbilically linked to that of Germany. All her efforts from 1916 onwards to obtain a separate peace were doomed to failure.

The Allies were, in turn, pressed towards adopting the dismemberment of the Monarchy as a war aim, which had not been the case until very late in the war. In the inter-war period, foreign policy was dictated by the conditions created by the collapse of the Empire. The

Anschluss with Germany, desired by the majority of the Deutsch-Oesterreich Parliament in 1918, was forbidden under the Peace Treaties. The only alternatives were to develop normal economic relations with the successor states, seek the protection of fascist Italy against Nazi-Germany between 1933–37 or await the change in the situation heralded by the seizure of power by the Nazis in Germany in 1933, which came to fruition in 1938. All the approaches, contradictory as they were, had supporters and were tried. As events were to prove, no independent foreign policy for Austria was possible and none could have succeeded.

The foreign policy of the Second Republic was based on the lessons of the past, reflections of the exile groupings and above all on a realistic appraisal of the situation as it was in 1945. The Moscow Declaration and the intentions of the Allies was the central starting point. The Allies naturally did not attach major importance to the future of Austria and came to the problem very late in the war. In any event, the policy of the various Allied Powers depended less on specific Austrian conditions than on broader geo-political interests and considerations. The Allied governments knew little about conditions inside Austria and placed no faith in the various exile groups which had no common line and little contact with the Allied governments. Austrian policy was therefore made in a void.

The obvious and early starting point was to repudiate the Anschluss as being an act of National Socialist aggression. Even this was not the immediate reaction. Only Mexico entered an early protest in the still existent League of Nations, followed by Spain, Chile, China and the USSR. Britain's Prime Minister, Winston Churchill, declared that the Anschluss was void in a speech at the Mansion House in November 1940, and listed Austria as a victim of Nazi aggression. In 1942, Foreign Ministers Eden and Hull also issued a (joint) declaration that the Anschluss was void. In the meantime, the British Foreign Office had began the process of defining a policy for Austria. From then on, Britain was to be the most actively involved in pushing for inter-Allied agreement on Austria.

The first internal study identified four main options. The first was a pure restoration of the *status quo ante:* Austria would become an independent State, as in the inter-war period. The second option was to consider the Anschluss as definitive. The third option involved the creation of a Danubian confederation and the fourth proposed several states hewed out of Austria, Bavaria and other neighbours. Under this plan, Austria would be dismembered. All these options raised serious objections either from the point of view of their realism or because they did not accord with the aims of UK policy. The basic aim of UK policy, or at any rate its maximalist goal at this time, was to exclude the USSR from the region and create an effective counter-weight to both Germany and the Soviet Union. From that point of view, and given concerns about the viability of Austria alone, the least worst option was the creation of a Danubian confederation. However, the attitude of allied successor states, such as Yugoslavia and Czechoslovakia, was likely to be negative and the position of the Soviet Union was by no means clear at this stage in the war. As it turned out, Anglo-American forces penetrated into Austria, Czechoslovakia and almost into Yugoslavia in the spring of 1945 and, had Churchill's advice been followed, might well have reached Prague, Zagreb and Vienna before the Red Army, and might have even extended into western Hungary. That they did not was more a matter of the lack of political will than military difficulties.

Yet in 1942 it seemed urgent to reach some kind of minimum agreement with the Soviet Union, about the organisation of the post-war world and as a safety net, whatever the outcome on the ground. It was also imperative to commit the USA to a significant involvement, which she was by no means ready to accept at this point. In any event, the aspirations of the Austrians, in Austria or in exile, played no part in those calculations, or those of the other Allied Powers. Indeed, the aim of apparent concessions towards Austrian particularism and the 'first victim' thesis – as exemplified by Churchill, the Eden–Hull statement or various utterances of Stalin, which drew distinctions between Germans and Austrians – was to drive a wedge between Austria and the Reich – but nothing else. There is evidence that the 'first victim' thesis had a purely tactical significance in its origin.

Such was the position in 1942. British soundings with the Soviet Government had shown opposition to virtually any design other than a pure and simple restoration of the Austrian Republic as it had been before the Anschluss in 1938. The British government was still looking for various confederal 'reconstructions' of the region, but now saw the absolute necessity of involving the United States of America, as Britain alone would inevitably be too weak to assure the necessary long-term commitments in the area.

For Britain – the main driving force in seeking an inter-Allied agreement on Austria – the first preference would have lain in a confederal solution. The next preference lay in the exclusion of the

USSR from Austria and a joint occupation (provided the United States was involved and that other solutions were not formally excluded). The Soviet Union also favoured an American presence in Austria but in no other point agreed with the British position. America was not interested and came to define her policy late and under pressure from her Allies. For her, even the Moscow Declaration by no means implied American participation in an allied occupation of Austria. As late as the beginning of 1943, the view of President Roosevelt was that Austria would naturally be in the Soviet sphere of influence after the war.

Britain, eager to avoid that outcome by tying the matter down before the situation on the ground created an irreversible fait accompli, pushed for a decision and provoked what was to become the Moscow Declaration. A first British draft was distributed on 22 July 1943. The soundings in Washington and Moscow had brought the realisation that there was only a very small margin for manoeuvre and that the only common denominator in the positions of the three Allies was agreement on the restoration of Austria as a State. For Britain, that was a first step, which should not prejudice other later changes in status. For the USSR, it was her whole policy. The British draft included the tell-tale phrase: 'Austria shall be re-established as free and independent, in connection with her neighbours to guarantee her economic future....'. This was the greatest opening towards a later reconstruction of the region that could be proposed in the light of the positions of the other Allies.

Reactions to the draft were numerous. The Americans wanted a reference to the Atlantic Charter built into the passage on Austria being a victim of Nazi aggression, and wanted to make the text less of a classic 19th century diplomatic statement. Commonwealth States argued that the Austrian State would not be viable and proposed division or partition. There was no reaction from Moscow, however, before the first meeting of the Allied foreign ministers which began in Moscow on 18 October 1943.

The British draft was merely retouched and subjected to minor amendments to meet the views of other governments. The reference to links with 'her neighbours' was made more vague and the passage on the responsibility which Austria must bear for her future treatment – a carrot and stick method – was strengthened. This text, issued on 1 November 1943, became the basic Allied document on Austria and contained within it all the elements of ambiguity about

Austrian history and the appropriate judgement upon it that even today are at the centre of debate, not least in the Waldheim affair.

Thus, Austria is seen in the Declaration as 'the first victim' of German aggression and the Anschluss is seen as null and void; yet it states at the same time that Austria must bear a degree of responsibility for her own situation. She is to be restored, but her exact treatment will depend on her attitude. There is no specific reference to an Allied occupation in the Declaration. Austria is thus neither to be considered a liberated ally nor merely a defeated axis State.

The scene then shifted to the European Advisory Committee (EAC) which began its work in London in January 1944, and to the various military and civil planning groups which dealt with Austria, often without a clear political mandate. Indeed, whilst the Americans persisted in their ambiguous attitude to their own rôle, Britain maintined that it had entered into no commitment and excluded no development by signing the Moscow Declaration. At the Teheran and Quebec Conferences, Winston Churchill returned to the theme of an association, if not a confederation, of Danubian States, implicit in the initial British draft of the Declaration and in his view still not excluded. The vigorous opposition of allied successor states in the region, principally Yugoslavia, Poland and Czechoslovakia, supported by the USSR, and the developments on the ground, forced Britain to abandon the confederation concept and fall back on solutions which would minimise or block Soviet influence in Austria. This revolved essentially around balancing Soviet influence with an American involvement and later supporting French involvement. As before, the British sought to force the pace both by presenting several proposals to the EAC, (for example, 'The military occupation of Germany', one part of which dealt with Austria) and by persistent pressure on her two Allies to react.

In parallel, the military planners, in London and Washington and in SHAEF and the Mediterranean theatre, began planning for a military occupation and administration of Austria. The Americans had not as yet taken any decision on their own participation or its level. British planners sought to reduce Soviet participation to a minimum. In the British view, different arrangements would be appropriate than for Germany. However, on 18 February 1944, the Soviet counter-proposal was made to the EAC, involving a three power-occupation and administration. Britain sought to grant sole responsibility to the United States who still had no clear policy.

Indeed, a matter of broad principle – the longer-term presence of U.S. troops in Europe outside Germany – was at stake. It was only resolved in favour of an American involvement after considerable difficulty and a contradictory debate between the military, the State Department and the President in May 1944. At this point, serious planning for the zonal-division and the organization of the Allied administration could begin. Britain was forced to accept the Soviet proposal, for a three-way zonal-division, as a compromise. The zone issue had arisen as a solution to divergent views on the rôle of a unified Allied administration for Austria.

By late 1944, France was admitted to full membership of the EAC and participation in the occupation of Germany and Austria. French policy had traversed several phases. Initially, as she sought to regain a rôle in Europe and hoped to rebuild the pre-war links with Central Europe, she sought to stand between the Anglo-American Allies and the USSR. The treaty of 1944 was the culmination of General De Gaulle's efforts to achieve great power status. In reality, the USSR did not adopt a more favourable attitude to France, and in the last phase of the war France returned to a 'Western' reading of the European situation, and opposed any excessive Soviet influence, rejecting any future Anschluss and insisting on her right to reparations. French analysis of the Austrian problem in the period prior to the Moscow Declaration had given consideration to ambitious but wholly unrealistic restructuration and federation plans for the region, which were abandoned with her acceptance of the Moscow Declaration on 16 November 1943 and with the realisation that such a plan would find opposition from both the USA and the USSR.

From late 1944 onwards, the EAC and other more technical planning bodies began to see Austria as a specific issue and no longer deal with it as part of a geo-political debate about the future shape of Europe. The Powers argued about zones, frontiers with Italy and Yugoslavia, control of Austria's industry and oil production and the system of control over local Austrian authorities. France and the USA continued to see the issue in terms of small symbolic forces and a political rôle only.

This then was the background to the occupation of Austria in 1945. As it was, Vienna and Eastern Austrian Austria was occupied by the Red Army and the Western Allies were only able to take up their zones in Vienna in September 1945, following the 4 July 1945 Four-Power Control Agreement and the zonal agreement of 9 July 1945.

All the powers had approached the problem from their own specific and different perspective. For the British, Russians and French at least, Austria was an insignificant element in much broader geo-political concerns in which, however, she had a place. For the British, the key aim was to create a counterweight to the USSR in this vital region. The concept of a Danubian federation was a maximalist aim that had to be abandoned in favour of an occupation which would minimalise Russian influence and guarantee American involvement.

The USA had no pre-conceived views on Austria and reacted pragmatically under pressure from her Allies and events on the ground. She was initially prepared to see Austria in the Russian sphere, but slowly came to the view that Western influence should be preserved as far as possible; she aimed at as limited a commitment as possible.

France, late in the field, initially concurred in the aim of the reconstruction of Central Europe, but was unable to give any practical expression to these goals, not least because her Allies had already abandoned them and because the policy of 'special relations' with the USSR produced no concrete results. France joined the American pragmatic and minimalist line, but supported the USSR on reparations and the treatment of German property in Austria.

Russian policy was perhaps the most consistent and logical. Before the Nazi–Soviet Pact of August 1939, the USSR had strongly protested against the Anschluss and called for collective action in the League of Nations. During the war, despite some temporary hesitations, she consistently opposed British moves to create any form of confederation or association. However, her policy was essentially pragmatic and cautious. Austria was, as for the British, part of a whole. She was not of key strategic importance to the USSR. She served as a 'forward position', a laboratory for experimentation, a shop window in relations with the western Allies. As no essential interests were at stake, compromise was always possible. Hence the choice of Renner as Chancellor, hence the support of the Allies over the Kärnten border, hence the acceptance of the holding of genuine elections in 1945 and a government without KPÖ Ministers after 1947 and indeed, the State Treaty in 1955.

The new Austrian Republic had two border problems that required solutions by the Allies, though the *status quo* was implicit in the Moscow Declaration. The Italian border, as it had been fixed in 1920, was once again an issue. Italy was defeated too. However, British and later western policy was to seek rapprochement with the new Italy, which above all was not to be weakened in face of the strong internal Communist threat. Hence, no border rectification in favour of Austria, which might itself go Communist, was to be expected. Yugoslavia also had territorial demands in Kärnten, claims which were backed by the presence of elements of the Third Yugoslavian Liberation Army. However, after high level contacts, these were evacuated by the Soviet command and the agreed British occupation took effect; the Yugoslav claims received no backing from the Soviet Union.

How did the large Austria diaspora – some 150,000 in all – affect allied policy towards their homeland? The short answer is: very little. Indeed, though there was, in typical Austrian fashion, intense and often strongly divergent émigré political activity, it impinged but little on the governments of the three Allied Powers, as they sought to define their policy towards Austria. The main centres of émigré political activity were in Stockholm, Paris (until 1940), Washington, Moscow and above all, London. From 1934, the Socialists and KPÖ established themselves in Czechoslavakia, setting up a KPÖ organisation and the ALÖS (SPÖ under Otto Bauer). These groups moved to Paris in 1938, as did the moderate and conservative opposition groups, which then in 1940 mostly moved to London. The KPÖ elements went to Moscow. Some SPÖ groups had already gone to Stockholm. There were active Socialist, Conservative and Habsburg groups in the United States.

Communists saw the struggle as both a national and an ideological battle, but were almost totally uninfluential with Soviet policy-makers with whom they had little contact. Their pressure for a National Committee was not accepted and Soviet use of KPÖ activists during the war was very limited. In 1943, Austrian observers were appointed to the German national Committee, though this was prior to the Moscow Declaration and the émigré statement 'Die Wiedergeburt Österreichs' was very moderate in tone and in line with the general Soviet 'broad front' policy of that period, proposing only the election of a constituent assembly.

In the United States of America, Otto von Habsburg sought to obtain the creation of an Austrian Legion, which at first was not discouraged by the President. However, the project was eventually blocked by the Secretary of War, Stimson, and was in any event not regarded with favour by the State Department. The Austrian National Committee (Christian Social), under the former Minister Rott, and other more aristocratic groups under Czernin and the

Socialists, organised in the Austrian Labour Committee under Adler and Deutsch, continued pre-war political hostilities and were unable to establish any meaningful co-operation or even contact with like-minded compatriots in Europe. American policy-makers did nothing to encourage émigré political activity and took no account of it.

The Stockholm socialist grouping, Österreichische Sozialisten in Schweden around Bruno Kreisky, were the first to break with previous SPÖ doctrine elsewhere in favour of the Anschluss. The Stockholm group came out in favour of Austrian independence in July 1943, having obtained some insight into Allied thinking, and therefore were supportive of the Moscow Declaration when it was issued. The real battle for the organisation of Austrian opinion abroad took place in London. The most serious source of division, apart from pre-war bitterness, remained the SPÖ position on the national question. The SPÖ had only very recently removed reference to the Anschluss from its party programme and still believed in some form of 'Gesamtdeutsch' movement towards Socialism and thus rejected the re-establishment of Austria and all forms of Austrian patriotism saying they were redolent of the Dollfuss régime. Those who disagreed, such as the former Member of Parliament Maria Kostler, were expelled. She formed the Austrian Socialists in Great Britain as a dissident grouping from the main Austrian Labour Movement. A Council of Austrians in Great Britain was formed, regrouping a large number of political tendencies (1938), but not the SPÖ, which remained aloof. This body was a very loose organisations. In addition to the Socialists and Communists, the Legitimists around Sir G. Franckenstein, the Liberals (Austrian Democratic Union) around S. Meinl and the Christain Social group around K. Kerzfeld, were formed.

In June 1941, after the German attack on the Soviet Union, the Council of Austrians issued a call for unity, and a new umbrella body was formed by the KPÖ and 13 non-Socialist organisations, the Free Austria Movement (FAM). The Socialists rejected co-operation with the KPÖ led FAM. However, in order to keep the door open, FAM adopted a very cautious policy position. At first, it did no more than to espouse an 'attentiste' position, favouring self determination, which then shaded into support for independence, and by 1943 it backed the Moscow Declaration. With some non-Socialist groups such as the Liberals and Christian Socialists, (but not the Communists), the SPÖ established an alternative body called the 'Vertretung', or Assembly, which was negative towards the Moscow Declaration and was, indeed, shocked by the Swedish based SPÖ, which had, as we have seen, aligned itself with the Moscow Declaration.

The Allies recognised none of these groups and, indeed, in all three capitals tended to discourage the émigré groups, which they regarded as having no base in Austria, as unrepresentative and as unreliable in terms of Allied policy as set out in the Moscow Declaration. In both London and Moscow, there was an awareness of the internal division in the Austrian diaspora, which could lead to the Allies recognising different groups. Above all, the aim of the Moscow Declaration was to weaken Germany by stimulating resistance in the country. The Declaration was aimed at internal opinion and here the émigré groups could offer almost no assistance and hence received no support.

The Allies were interested in the resistance inside the country and indeed it was the anti-Nazi forces in Austria itself, rather than the various groupings abroad, that came to play a major part in the vital immediate weeks and months after the arrival of the Allies in Austria. Indeed, paradoxically at this point, the absence of an exile government or even of external groups to which the internal resistance owed a degree of allegiance, was almost an advantage. There were no restrictions and the resulting confusion offered opportunities that were seized. As Austria had no exile government and the émigrés remained fractious and divided to the last, inside Austria a new and unexpected spirit was dawning which enabled the rapid and harmonious establishment of the Renner three-party Cabinet in April 1945. Its recognition by all the four Allies as the national government of Austria by September was a fact never subsequently seriously questioned.

Ten thousand Austrians served in the Allied Armed Forces and 2,000 Spanish Civil War Veterans served in the French FFI. There were also five battalions of Austrians with the Yugoslavian Liberation Army operating in Southern Kärnten. However, and more significantly for the future, was the resistance which came forward to take power from the Nazi administration in the last days of the war. This became the nucleus of a new political structure and was, for the most part also the nucleus of the subsequent 'Grand Coalition'. There was an immediate realisation that the old pre-war political mores had to end and that a new political consensus had to be forged. Miraculously, it happened.

Naturally, there was considerable confusion in Austria at the end of the war. However, the behaviour of the Nazis in Austria had sewn the seeds of a new Austrian national consciousness. Those who were contacted to join the 20 July conspirators against Hitler, such as Hurdes, Seitz or Schärf, later ÖVP or SPÖ leaders, took the line that, however much they sympathised with the aims of the conspiracy, Austria's destiny no longer lay with Germany. Even among leading Austrian Nazis there was a degree of 'Austrian nostalgia', and Hitler had always opposed proposals to unify the two Austrian Gaue into a single 'Gau Ostmark' which would have encouraged Austrian particularism and created a central 'Austrian' administration.

In the resistance as such, there was considerable confusion about aims and methods. The resistance world had many forms and organisations which, for obvious reasons, were often not in communication with each other. There were the growing Austrian battalions in Kärnten with the Yugoslavian partisans. There was also a military resistance, albeit small in Austria, which had no links with the political parties or the other resistance bodies.

The most important resistance organisation was the O5 (so called because O and E – the fifth letter in the alphabet – spelt the first letters of Oesterreich) which, had it not been decapitated by arrests, would have played an even more significant rôle in the battle for Vienna. On 18 December 1944, the O5 established a political umbrella body, the Provisorische Oesterreichische Nationkomité (POEN), which was recognised by the western Allies, but not by the Soviet Union, although it held talks with Moscow. The POEN included representatives of the ÖVP, SPÖ,KPÖ and Liberals, but these individuals had no mandate from their parties and the nascent political parties and the Soviet authorities in Vienna ignored the POEN, which had a 'bourgeois' majority.

At both the federal and, for the most part, also at the Land level, a pattern was established where the parties agreed, with surprising ease, on a tripartite provisional executive which was recognised by the locally dominant Allied power. At that stage there was as yet no inter-Allied agreement on zones. Indeed, some Länder, such as the Steiermark, were occupied by two different allied armies at the end of the war. Usually, the older party leaders had become inactive and did not play an important part in the process, nor did the resistance groupings or the POEN.

In some areas such as Salzburg and the Tirol (Karl Gruber and Fritz Molden), there was a degree of overlap. In most areas the new executive was formed with new men who had learned, through the hard school of the concentration camps, that they were closer to other Austrians of different political views than they had believed possible. This new generation, of both Christian Socialists and Socialists, was attuned to the new realities as they arose from the Moscow Declaration and the occupation of the country: cooperation on a broad basis was essential.

In some areas such as Salzburg, the Tirol, Steiermark and Kärnten, especially where there was no fighting and the Allies arrived late, local arrangements for the transfer of power from the Nazi authorities to a Provisional Land Executive were made peacefully before or as the Allies arrived, and these arrangements were, with some exceptions and temporary difficulties in Salzburg, subsequently respected by the Allies.

The first Allied troops to enter Austria were the Soviet forces, moving on Vienna from Hungary through the Burgenland, on 29 March 1945. These units of the Third Ukrainian Front reached Wiener Neustadt on 1 April. After a week's heavy fighting, Vienna was taken and by 15 April, Soviet troops called a halt, turning northwards. Soviet positions in Austria served to cover their flanks in Hungary and Czechoslovakia during and after the war. Soviet forces did not seek to penetrate any further west than they expected to obtain as a zone in the talks in the EAC in London, despite the fact that no American, French or British forces entered Austria until late April.

Thus, in those decisive early days, Vienna – the key to Austria – was in Soviet hands and their's was the political initiative. Contrary to the Western Allies, whose aim was to constitute an Austrian administration only slowly and locally from the roots upwards and, in any event, reducing Communist influence to a strict minimum, the Soviet policy was to create tripartite administrations immediately at all levels, from the 'Bezirk' through the city to the Land and national level. Indeed, the National Provisional Government was formed as a first not last stage. Leading Communists such as Johan Köplenig and Ernst Fischer were returned to Austria to take part in the formation of the National and Lower Austrian Governments.

Ironically, the decision about the provisional government had been taken by Stalin himself and therefore could not be contested by the

KPÖ, although they would have preferred almost anyone – General Körner (SPÖ) for example – to Karl Renner, whom Stalin had chosen. Probably the KPÖ were right, seen from their viewpoint. Renner was not easy to manipulate and his prestige was considerable. He was no doubt less intellectually diminished by age and more energetic than Stalin had imagined. In any event, this choice, perhaps rather lightly made, was determinant for the future of Austria. Perhaps Karl Renner was the only Austrian politician, other than Adolf Hitler, that Stalin knew of!

As early as 16 April, the Soviet Commander had agreed to the appointment of General Körner as Mayor of Vienna. By 23 April, Renner had reached an agreement on a Cabinet with an inner political Cabinet of a few members (himself, one SPÖ, ÖVP, KPÖ) and in all three SPÖ, three ÖVP, two KPÖ and two non-party. The key men in the Cabinet were Renner, Schärf (SPÖ), Kunschak (ÖVP) and Köplenig (KPÖ). The government was approved by the Soviet authorities and officially took office on 27 April. At the same time, it issued a proclation of Austrian independence signed by the party leaders.

The Soviet authorities informed – as did Renner – the remaining Allies. Britain protested at the formation of the 'Staatsregierung' and the western Allies did not recognise the Renner government. Consequently, its writ did not run outside the areas occupied by the Russians. The other Allies had strong reservations of principle and also saw great danger in the presence of a Communist (Franz Honner) in the key post of Interior Minister. Renner abandoned the idea of recalling the rump of the last Austrian Nationalrat, because there had been no KPÖ deputies, even though there were no Soviet objections.

The 1920 Constitution, as amended in 1929, was declared to be in force and Allied efforts, especially Russian, to open a discussion about a new constitution, were blocked and the 1920 text remained. This text remains the basic law of Austria. Thus, the type of constitutional development which led to the establishment of people's democracies in Eastern Europe was avoided and the Renner government found a basis of continuity and legitimacy.

Agreements between the Allies were reached in the EAC on the structure and powers of the Control Commission (4 July) and on Zones (9 July), following a visit to Vienna by Western Allied delegations. The Allied Commission was able to take up its work in September and held its first formal sitting on 11 September. The

Allies faced the question of the Renner government. The Russians demanded full recognition and hence an extension of its remit to cover the whole country, while the British demanded as a pre-condition a radical reconstruction involving at least the removal of the Communist Interior Minister.

During the summer, there had been discussions about extending the government to include representatives of the Western Länder, reducing the KPÖ relative weight and increasing ÖVP representation. These questions had been discussed in the ÖVP and SPÖ in the Western Zones and their demands were similar to those made by the British. Renner was prepared to hold discussions with the Länder and extend the government.

The American compromise proposal, that Renner should be given a chance to reshuffle his Cabinet following talks with the Länder, was accepted on 14 September. Thus, following conferences of both the ÖVP and SPÖ in the Western Zones in Salzburg, the first of three Länder Conferences was held in Vienna from 24 – 26 September. Two key decisions emerged: the cabinet reshuffle, and an agreement on a date for elections which were proposed to be held on 25 November 1945. The two issues were not unrelated. The elections would strengthen the Western Länder and weaken the KPÖ, even if it did well, which few expected it to do as the Russian Party. Furthermore, the Western Länder could not accept that the organisation of the elections should remain in the hands of the KPÖ Interior Minister. At the conference, a compromise was reached under which one additional State Secretary and three additional ÖVP Under-State Secretaries, (including Gruber in the Foreign Ministry), were added and electoral affairs were placed in the hands of a Ministerial Committee, although Honner remained as Interior Minister. Finally, the Western Allies accepted this rather minimalist change and the Renner government received *de facto* recognition on 20 October 1945 and the way was opened for elections on the agreed date.

The Western Allies probably saw the compromise as acceptable when linked with the decision to hold elections. It is remarkable, in the light of events elsewhere in Eastern Europe, that a genuinely free election was able to take place in the whole of Austria, including the Soviet Zone. Here the Russians did give some assistance to the KPÖ, but it was very limited and had little effect. Certainly the KPÖ vote was higher in Vienna than elsewhere, but that would have happened in any case.

The elections were free, fair and peaceful. Three parties were admitted: ÖVP, SPÖ and KPÖ. National Socialists were not allowed to vote in this first election. The Landtage were also elected on the same day. The result was perhaps somewhat surprisingly an ÖVP absolute majority and an almost insignificant result for the Communists:

Table 2   Elections Results 25 November 1945

Party	% of the vote (Turnout 94.3%)	Number of Seats
ÖVP	49.80	85
SPÖ	44.60	76
KPÖ	5.42	4
Other	0.18	—

The ÖVP also controlled seven of nine Länder, leaving the SPÖ only Vienna and the Kärnten. The KPÖ obtained significant results only in Vienna (8.0%), Kärnten (8.1%) and Steiermark (5.4%). In Soviet occupied Burgenland, they obtained only 3.3%. These results were important as they gave the new Austrian government a legitimacy and credibility with the Western Allies and showed that there was no likelihood of Austria going Communist. The influence of the KPÖ could be reduced at last. However, it was considered positive in relation to the Soviets to retain the tripartite formula and include one KPÖ Minister in the new government which was led by Leopold Figl, one of the 'new' ÖVP men.

It should not be imagined that the elections resolved every problem with the Allies; on the contrary. After the British, it now was the Soviets who, in the new situation after the election where their Austrian protégés – the KPÖ and to a lesser extent Renner's SPÖ – had not done well, expressed a lack of confidence, accused the Austrians of foot-dragging over de-Nazification and insisted on retaining and even strengthening Allied control.

Recognition of the Cabinet was delayed and some ÖVP Ministers were rejected and had to be changed. The Allied Commission also demanded to examine the government's programme, given to the new Nationalrat on 21 December 1945. The Allies only accorded *de jure* recognition of the Figl government on 7 January.

This period is characterised by increasing self-confidence and frustration on the part of the Renner and then the Figl cabinets. On a series of questions, the government with Renner as President after January 1946, did not fear open opposition to the Allied Commission and individual Allied governments. They did so on the solid basis of a national consensus. The key issues were the increasing, rather than decreasing, interference in Austrian legislation and administration by Allied experts, the on-going issue of the definition of German assets in Austria, the restrictions on inter-zonal movement, the occasional arbitrary arrests, the progress (or in Soviet eyes, the lack of progress) of de-Nazification, and the treatment of some 330,000 Reichs-, Volks-and Sudeten-Germans in Austria, as well as several hundred-thousand other DPs (or Displaced Persons).

The most serious conflict was over the Südtirol question. Already at the discussions preceding the first Länder Conference, the issue of the return of Südtirol to Austria was raised and over the following months an impressive series of petitions, mass meetings and less spectacular forms of political pressure on the Allies, was set in motion. The Allies, and above all the British, preferred the Italian card. Italy was strategically more important and elections were still awaited. The PCI was also a mighty threat compared with the KPÖ. Austria's demands were summarily rejected with only a vague promise of possible minor frontier rectifications in a future peace treaty.

There was, however, one area of real progress: the agreement on the Second Control Agreement, signed on 28 June 1946, which significantly extended the autonomy of the Austrian government. The British took the initiative of opening discussions, as the first Control Agreement required, once elections had been held and a government recognised by all the installed Allies. The Western Allies were now prepared to progressively reduce control over the Austrian government. The French and Russian governments were less inclined to do so initially. A compromise was found in terms of defining certain areas of direct allied intervention, such as demilitarisation, de-Nazification, war-criminal questions, and the treatment of German assets. Otherwise, Austrian laws could be enforced unless the Allied Commission unanimously objected within thirty-one days.

Constitutional laws still required prior unanimous consent of the Commission. International border controls were eased and, as the Russians wanted, the way was opened to bilateral agreements between Austria and individual allied governments.

The new agreement, whilst retaining a degree of control and a considerable reserve of powers of direct intervention, represented a great advance for Austria – although the Americans had not been able to use the talks on the Agreement as a means of moving on to an Austrian Treaty: there was no Soviet willingness on this issue. So this agreement was to remain in force until the end of the occupation in 1955.

At this point, the issue of German assets, which had smouldered away below the surface and which was, in part, to remain a major issue throughout the lengthy negotiations leading to the State Treaty in 1955, surfaced as the key issue destined to overshadow others. Indeed, its resuscitation was to prove central, together with the neutrality issue, to unblocking the negotiations for the State Treaty and indeed creating the basis of the large public sector in Austria.

It was agreed at the Potsdam Conference that, despite Soviet and indeed to a lesser extent French objections, Austria should be treated differently from Germany in that she would not be required to pay reparations as such, but that German property and assets in Austria were at the disposal of the Allies, on the basis that each allied power controlled the German assets in its own zone.

There had been long and fruitless negotiations about the definition of German assets and some on the western side felt that the USSR 'had its price' in the sense that if it was given a free hand on the assets question, it would be prepared to relax the control measures. Here, the coincidence of the June agreement on a new control system, and significant events in relation to the German assets question, were indeed evidence in favour of that view. There was no disputing, in principle, the Soviet claim to the German assets. However, the Western allies feared that the Soviet enterprises (USIA) already created, Soviet control of Austrian oil refining and the Danube Shipping Company, would give the USSR an excessive leverage over the Austrian economy even after the conclusion of a State Treaty.

To break the deadlock both in the Allied Council and in diplomatic negotiations, the Soviets acted, issuing the Directive Number 17 on 27 June 1946, which laid out the takeover of some 280 enterprises with 50,000 workers, as well as the DDSG and 157,000 hectares of farm-land. The Austrian riposte was a law nationalising 73 enterprises on 26 July. This Austrian law was possibly against the Control Agreement, but no unanimous veto was possible and the Russians declared a readiness to negotiate whilst, as the Control Agreement allowed, declaring the law inoperative in their zone. The Western Allies conditionally abandoned their rights to German assets in their zones.

These measures and the problems of getting American aid to the Soviet zone exacerbated the differences between the two zones and convinced the Americans of the need to take measures to accelerate the economic recovery of Austria. The food situation and the general economic situation was very difficult. The Americans abandoned their right to occupation costs and, most importantly, Congress voted 85 million dollars for Austria in May 1947. On 5 June 1947, Secretary of State Marshall proclaimed the Marshall Plan (ERP), which led to an aid agreement with Austria as early as 28 June. The situation had deteriorated to the point where a special secret session of the Nationalrat was held in October 1946 to review the state of the nation. However, the economic measures taken by the United States offered a new hope.

There was no serious progress on the State Treaty in 1946, 1947 or 1948, despite the fact that the Second Control Agreement was supposedly concluded for six months only and a treaty was supposed to be concluded rapidly. This was the result of a fast deteriorating international situation, from which Austria remained, internally at least, partially protected. Indeed, during the whole period from mid-1947 to 1949, which covered the total Sovietisation of Central and Eastern Europe, including the Czechoslovak coup at the end of May 1948, the division of Germany into two states in 1949 and the formation of NATO, the four-Power machinery continued to operate in Austria on a perfectly functional, if at times difficult, basis as if Austria was an isolated island of tranquility in a storm.

Yet, the events in neighbouring states inevitably had an impact in Austria, as did the broader strategies of the Great Powers, for Austria was never more than a relatively small element in a wider picture. Thus, the division of Germany, and above all the events in Prague in the Spring of 1948, were watched with considerable trepidation in Vienna. Was the division of Austria imminent? Was the installation of a pro-Soviet régime in eastern Austria planned by the Soviet Union? It seems that, with the benefit of hindsight, these fears were unfounded and certainly exaggerated, but what is important is what political leaders and public opinion thought then, which determined how they reacted and acted. Certainly, the threat was seen as real enough at that time.

Those events, which influenced the climate of opinion in Austria, did much to cement the cracks which were showing up in the coalition and which led to at least one threat from the SPÖ to withdraw from the coalition. The existence of the coalition, the strength and firmness of the SPÖ, the weakness of the KPÖ, the existence of a functional government for the whole state, the presence of non-Soviet forces in western Austria and even in Vienna, meant that the conditions for a Czechoslovak-style coup or a German-style division of the country simply did not exist. Yet, the economic divergences between the western and eastern area, especially in currency reform matters could have been dangerous. Hence the Western Allies and the Austrian government were careful to ensure that aid did reach the Soviet zone, even if some procedural concessions had to be made to achieve this.

The currency reform of 1947 was carried out nationwide, after negotiations with the Soviet authorities, despite KPÖ opposition. The exit from the government of the KPÖ over this issue caused few ripples on the Soviet side. Soviet policy certainly shifted but did not seem to be linked to the Communist cause in Austria as such. Indeed, with the consolidation of pro-Soviet régimes in both Hungary and Czechoslovakia by mid-1948, there was no Soviet strategic goal in Austria.

American and Austrian policy also evolved in response to those events. The Truman Doctrine (March 1947), the Marshall Plan, the establishment of the Federal Republic and the foundation of NATO in 1949 were part of the new policy of containment of Communist expansionist tendencies, or perceived tendencies.

In Austria, the result was a clearer American involvement in Austrian concerns than before, but a broader analysis of the problem. In 1947 and 1948, the USA moved strongly away from the idea of a Treaty at any price or, as it was said, changed, from the view (much held in Austria) that any treaty was preferable to no treaty, to the view that no treaty was preferable to a bad treaty. A bad treaty was seen as one under which an excessive permanent economic, political or military influence would be accorded to the Soviet Union after the treaty. Indeed, even the ÖVP Foreign Minister Gruber, not popular in Moscow, called on the Americans to adopt a more flexible line. Another Allied and indeed Austrian concern, relating to those events, was the danger of a vacuum in Austria after the withdrawal of foreign forces ninety days after the coming into force of a State Treaty. Here, perhaps, there could be political unrest and no acceptable Austrian force to meet it. Britain had long argued for an Austrian frontier force to stand guard in Kärnten against the Yugoslav threat. The Gendarmarie was strengthened and the idea of authorising an Austrian army on the basis of an agreed article of the draft State Treaty was considered.

Certainly, the backwash of the Berlin blockade (which led to some incidents at the Enns demarcation line and around the Vienna airfields used by the Western Allies, KPÖ and even Soviet campaigns against the Austrian Cabinet), the build up of the Communist Werkschutz, and above all the 1948 food demonstrations and general strike in September 1950, gave serious grounds for concern and created an atmosphere of uncertainty. The reaction of the Western Allies was a firmness and a readiness to wait; they had concluded that they were in no hurry to conclude a State Treaty in the present climate. The USSR had no reason to stay in Austria and now merely wanted to achieve the best possible terms. But these she would not obtain in an atmosphere of confrontation.

The main areas of contention had also come clearly into focus. The first was the security of Austria after a State Treaty or, in plain language, her denial to either power-block as a base of operations. The second was the question of German assets. By the end of 1947, the French had put the so-called Cherrière plan on the table. This involved a 100 million dollar buy-out of Soviet claims. Privately, the Western Allies were prepared to 'up the ante' to 150 million dollars and the USSR was asking for 200 million dollars. A deal was possible. There, matters rested despite the long and complicated rounds of discussion, until the death of Stalin in 1953.

Austria had become a 'position', a bargaining counter in the greater game. In that context, the Western allies reduced or abandoned claims to occupation costs, supported the Austrian economy and (sometimes alone – sometimes à quatre), considerably reduced the restrictions of the occupation régime which were, at least on the western side, less and less directed at the Austrians and more a matter of geo-politics, as the renewed talks in 1949 showed.

Despite progress on details, there was no political will. As President Renner had predicted and as the USA foresaw, the cost of a treaty would be massive for the weak Austrian economy and an agreement in 1949 or 1950 would find Austria with no time to create a credible defence force.

Austria had become a sort of no-man's land, a forward position for both sides: protecting Hungary and Czechoslovakia for the Soviet side, and linking Germany and Italy for the West. No one wanted to leave Austria, nor give any political signal until the broader issues had been decided. The outbreak of the Korean War in June 1950 only reinforced those considerations, to an equal degree on both sides.

Austria, however, had her own interests to advance, and as we shall see, did so whenever possible. Thus, the Americans forced the pace on the development of the Austrian Gendarmerie. They sought to militarise it and to integrate Austria into American military planning. Above all they opposed the idea of neutrality, while the Austrian leaders kept sight of the broader objective and maintained a balanced policy.

The 1951–53 period was a waiting period. On 5 March 1953 Stalin died. A new coalition, under Julius Raab, was formed in Austria, after the elections. Not long afterwards, the former Chancellor, Leopold Figl, replaced Karl Gruber as Foreign Minister. There is no doubt that these internal changes placed Austria in a better position to react favourably to the accelerating pace of change and to follow up the new and positive gestures coming from Moscow. All at once, Soviet decisions and proposals led to a significant easing in the occupation régime, an amnesty, and proposals for new negotiations.

Austria reacted positively and proposed returning to the 'long version' of the State Treaty. In 1952, in order to obtain a propaganda advantage – or, in the eyes of the Austrian government, as the basis of serious negotiations – a 'Short Treaty' dealing only with the immediate withdrawal of foreign forces was tabled by the West. Predictably, the proposal was refused by the Soviet side. Overcoming an initial concern at Austria's openness to the Soviet overtures, the West made its contribution by declaring its readiness to abandon the Short Treaty. Austria was now a full participant in the game with her own middle-way policy, soon to find its expression in neutrality as the concept best able to unblock the talks. For the first time, Austria was also formally at the negotiating table when the January 1954 Foreign Ministers' talks opened in Berlin.

For reasons that to this day remain unclear, the USSR did not follow through on its élan. On the contrary, Mr. Molotov's statement to the conference was a serious step back. He went back to the 1949

Treaty proposals, added a neutrality clause, which would have put the evacuation of the occupying forces off until a German peace treaty was signed, and regurgitated an older and now irrelevant junktim with the Trieste question. The conference came to an abrupt end in February 1954 and produced no positive results; on the contrary, hopes were dashed. Possibly, the Soviet Government wanted to issue a warning relating to Germany. Equally, there were severe factional battles going on inside the Soviet leadership. Perhaps the line was not yet clear.

Soon – indeed, by August 1954 – and despite the clear lack of any progress on Germany, the Russians began to abandon their positions. In February 1955, Molotov indicated that the withdrawal of forces would not need to depend on a German treaty. Austria was invited to bilateral talks. She accepted as soon as all the Allies consented to discussions about neutrality.

The Austrian delegation, led by Chancellor Raab (ÖVP) and the Vice Chancellor Schärf (SPÖ), went to Moscow in April 1955 and reached an outline agreement, reflected in the Moscow Memorandum of 15 April 1955. This called for the withdrawal of forces in ninety days – at the latest by 31 December 1955 – on the basis of Austrian neutrality on the Swiss model and a payment of 150 million dollars for claims to German assets, ten years of oil exports and 2 million dollars for claims made by the DDSG. The detailed negotiations on the Treaty text then became simple. They were concluded on 12 May 1955 and signed on 15 May 1955. After ratification, all foreign forces had left by 26 October 1955 and the Nationalrat passed the Neutrality Act unanimously.

Soviet policy had radically altered. Faced by a NATO strengthened by German membership, she needed to create her own military pact and to re-group. The new détente could be symbolic, above all for the smaller political neutrals or semi-neutrals. A neutral Austria created more strategic problems for NATO than for the USSR. As always, Austria was a political laboratory for Soviet policy.

Austrian foreign policy since the signature of the State Treaty in 1955 has had little room for maneouvre. Its basic outlines were in any case established by the State Treaty and the Moscow Memorandum that preceded it, around which there has been a firm national consensus over the last thirty years. This included almost the whole 'National' lager and the two large coalition parties that concluded the State Treaty. The FPÖ voted for the neutrality clause in the Nationalrat, as did the KPÖ deputies. However, Austrian 'permanent neutrality' has never had the positive connotations of Swiss neutrality, even though, as we have seen, Swiss neutrality was cited as a model by both Austrian and Soviet negotiators.

Whilst Austria makes much play with the voluntary nature of her neutrality, the reality is – and the Moscow Memorandum attests to this – that neutrality was part of a package under which the occupation of Austria was ended and as such was far from 'voluntary'! It is virtually an international obligation and places Austrian foreign policy under a degree of surveillance. At the same time, the freedom of manoeuvre which Austria can enjoy will depend on the international situation, placing her in a situation only marginally more favourable than Finland, with whom Austrians certainly do not invite comparison. In reality, both have a statute deriving from the settlement after the Second World War and both have considerably expanded their freedom of action. Rather than speaking of the Finlandisation of Austria, it would be more appropriate to speak of the Austrianisation of Finland!

Foreign policy is usually the most consensual area of policy, even in states where otherwise consensualism is not sought. Inevitably, therefore in Austria, where the search for élite and mass consensus is a way of life, consensus about foreign policy is very strong and the tendency to leave its conduct to specialists has dominated. As we have seen, there is now very strong public support for both the fundamental principles of Austrian foreign policy, as laid down in the period of the Grand Coalition (1945-66), maintained since and now reiterated by the new Grand Coalition. Aside from attempts, later abandoned, by the ÖVP to attack the 'activist' Kreisky worldwide 'tous azimuths' policy (in itself largely watered down after 1983 with formation of the 'small' SPÖ-FPÖ coalition), there has been a considerable political calm on this front and little activity or conflict in Parliament, the parties or the media over foreign policy.

Not surprisingly, therefore, Parliament has been little involved. Under the Constitution, the Federal President concludes State Treaties (article 50) and conducts foreign policy (article 65(1)), but he may delegate these function to Ministers and has, under a Decree of 1920 largely done so. In any event, he may only act on the advice of his Ministers. Thus, the rôle of the President is largely symbolic or protocolar, in fact of some importance in view of the Waldheim factor. Foreign policy is thus largely conceived and carried out by the Chancellor, the Foreign Minister and a limited number of other ministers whose competencies are involved.

Parliament, in particular the Nationalrat, has the general function of controlling government, which naturally extends to foreign policy. Here the normal instruments of control such as committee hearings, written questions, interpellations and resolutions can be applied. However, in reality there is little Parliamentary interest in foreign affairs: the occasional set piece 'tour d'horizon' debate is held. In the XII G.P. (1970–71), only two out of sixty resolutions related to foreign policy. In 1972, for example, forty-eight of fifty-one State Treaties (requiring the Nationalrat's approval) received the support of all parties. In the XVI G.P. (1983–6) 105 of 108 State Treaties were unanimously approved. Only one 'interpellation' (on weapons exports) was remotely on foreign policy and only 131 out of 2,365 written questions were on foreign policy matters.

The Nationalrat has a Foreign Affairs Committee which prepares plenary debates on State Treaties and keeps a watching brief on foreign policy matters, often on the basis of a report from the government. In 1973, an inner-committee, composed of the Chairman of the Committee and one named member per party, was established to monitor policy on a bi-monthly basis in between full Committee sessions and on an informal basis. In 1976, a Foreign Affairs Council was established on the Nordic Model, to permit broader and more general debate on foreign affairs (Law 96/1976 of 23 June 1976) as well as permanent flows of information to the opposition parties. These measures have slightly increased debate, but the conclusion is clear that foreign policy is not a major area of political controversy.

The central plank in Austrian foreign policy has been a policy of permanent but active neutrality, aimed at ensuring good relations with the major Powers that signed the State Treaty, and developing and improving relations with her immediate neighbours in order to create an atmosphere of low tension and cooperation in the region. In short, Austria has sought to continue the special situation that she had during the occupation period, under which she was relatively isolated from the tensions of the cold war. Thus Austria had sought to be a centre of East–West meetings – a catalyst, a go-between, a bridge, able to speak to both sides – and even in the heightened tension of the early 1980s, this remained true. Austria has much to lose from a retreat from détente and worked to develop and preserve it.

These are positions and approaches that all the main parties subscribe to, in broad outline, but naturally there have been minor differences between them. Domestic debate about foreign policy has since the State Treaty – and indeed before – has only concerned itself with these nuances, whereas in the First Republic disagreements about foreign policy were central to political debate. Since 1945, it has been a debate on the margins. Accents and rhetoric have been different and parties have allowed themselves some latitude in non-European issues such as the Vietnam war, South Africa, Central America, the Middle East.

From the period of the Grand Coalition, a tradition of strong bi-partisanship and mutual consultation survived through the ÖVP (1966–70) one-party government and into the early years of the SPÖ government. Indeed, senior ÖVP figures remained in the upper reaches of the Foreign Ministry and informally represented the party on foreign policy issues. Even at the height of the Kreisky era, these bi-partisan tendencies remained strong on European policy, but it was the style of Bruno Kreisky, as much as the substance, that caused opposition from the ÖVP, although there were indeed issues of substance involved.

Bundeskanzler Kreisky sought to play a much more active and challenging rôle in world affairs. A neutral and non-aligned Austria should be able to act as a bridge, as a catalyst. He promoted Vienna as the Third UN Centre, alongside New York and Geneva – Vienna as an East-West meeting place and conference centre (for the MBFR talks for example) – and as the headquarters of OPEC. He saw Austria as playing a mediating rôle in various conflicts, such as the Middle East, hence his remarkable decision, as a Jew to receive Yasser Arafat.

The more active and more ideological foreign policy of the SPÖ government during the later 1970s and 1980s led to a degree of domestic political controversy at the margins. The ÖVP and the FPÖ had other priorities in foreign policy. These were essentially the development of a good-neighbour policy, and relations with the European Community. The FPÖ has long argued for a rapprochement with the European Community, and full membership (as part of its Pan-Germanic vision), is considered desirable and possible. The SPÖ and ÖVP have been more reserved about full EC membership, though neither have ever excluded it from consideration.

Austria has taken as full a part in the various European organisations as her neutrality has allowed and her economic interests have dictated. Early attempts at negotiations on a form of trade agreement with the European Economic Community (EEC) floundered on the conditions that Austria sought, which included the right to opt out at any time and to offer at least as advantageous conditions to other trading partners, which meant Eastern Europe.

Members of the Community recognised Austria's special problems, but were not prepared to offer a special status that would water down the Community politically or economically. Thus Austria was able to join the United Nations and the Council of Europe in 1956, but did not achieve an agreement with the Community because of concern in Austria, the Community and the Soviet Union about compatibility with her neutral status.

Like other neutrals, including Finland, she joined EFTA when that body was founded initially under British leadership as a counterweight to the EEC, without supranational or political pretensions. However, like the other 'non-candidate' states, Austria faced the problem of relations with the enlarged EEC if and when the UK, Denmark, Ireland and (as it was then expected) Norway joined the Community. Austria thus asked for negotiations, again setting out its position in terms of the three reservations: freedom of option in trade policy; a right to withdraw; the right to take unilateral action in the case of military conflict. These positions were seen as unacceptable within the Council of Ministers and the talks which had begun in 1963 failed following objections from within the Council and the USSR. The talks reopened in 1966, only to fail (until 1969) again on an Italian veto linked to the problem of the south Tirol.

Following success in the main talks with the four candidate states, the remaining EFTA countries were invited for talks on a trade agreement in 1970. The agreement was signed on 22 July 1972 and gave Austria full free-trade in industrial goods, the easing of agricultural restrictions, and the right to opt out or suspend the agreement in the event of a military conflict. Neutrality was respected.

Austria has subsequently been active in promoting a coordinating and bridging rôle in EFTA. In 1977, the EFTA summit agreed on an Austrian initiative, to propose new and broader forms of cooperation to the EC. At the same time, in 1980, the EFTA states agreed to intensify and coordinate their mutual relations and approach to the EC. In 1984, the joint EC–EFTA Ministerial Conference in Luxembourg agreed on an intensification of relationships. The need for this has been greatly reinforced by the decisions taken by the EC at the European Council in Milan in 1985 to move to a single internal market by 1992. All EFTA States fear isolation and exclusion from this market and see the pressing need to be more closely involved in the process of European market integration.

This naturally applies strongly to Austria and this need, together with statements of the Commission to the effect that there was no 'à la carte' membership of the internal market, and strengthened by a reluctance to consider new membership applications before 1992 (especially if that would weaken the 'acquis communautaire'), has reopened the debate in Austria about the question of full membership of the EC.

The SPÖ–ÖVP Grand Coalition formed in 1987 set the improvement of relations with the EC as the absolute priority for Austrian foreign policy, especially in the light of the coming internal market in 1992. The section of the Coalition Agreement on economic policy states:

> Participation in the development of the process of European integration is central to Austria. With the enlargement of the EC to Greece, Spain and Portugal and the plans to achieve a full internal market by 1992, the importance of the Community has increased even more.

The agreement goes on to state that all forms of participation will be examined and it was clearly indicated in parliamentary debates on the programme that a membership application was not excluded. Here, the ÖVP Vice Chancellor and Foreign Minister Alois Mock favoured an early application: he considered that neutrality was not a problem. Indeed, Soviet comment was notable by its absence. Opinion was divided, even in the ÖVP. The SPÖ was concerned about neutrality and the general effect on regional stability and saw the ÖVP's enthusiasm for the EC as also linked to ÖVP plans for a more market oriented economy. This raised some fears. The ÖVP farming lobby also expressed concern.

In December 1987, the Cabinet agreed on a plan for participation in the internal market, which did not exclude membership as an option. The ÖVP did come out for that option, but not the government as such, though Economics Minister Graf said that an application should be expected in late 1989. The SPÖ remained more sceptical and the first Soviet reactions (via Mr Gerassimov) have also been sceptical, despite discrete soundings. Yet the Soviet reaction was more sceptical than negative. Once COMECON opened relations with the EC, the situation altered and will, as always, be viewed by Moscow in the broader context of East-West relations. In any event, closer relations, a degree of participation in the internal market and pure Community programmes such as EUREKA will build bridges which could lead to full membership in due course.

For the moment, the ÖVP is seeking to force the pace and to present itself as the European Party. For them, neutrality is not an obstacle and there is a tendency to ignore potential Soviet objections. The SPÖ remains less ready to espouse this European enthusiasm. Chancellor Vranitzky sought to hold to the agreed deadlines and not accelerate them. For him, neutrality is more important than membership. This issue will depend on the development of the Community towards a political and military union. Other SPÖ spokesmen note that there could be dangers for Austrian labour law and environmental protection standards. The Greens who also see these dangers and who are openly opposed to membership and intend to campaign against it, and have raised demands for a referendum that the larger parties will certainly reject.

Various factors led to a delay in reaching a decision to make an application, which after approval by the Nationalrat, was delivered to the Community on July 17, 1989. Soviet reactions were cautious and at times contradictory, but at no time seemed to present a major difficulty. Events in Eastern and Central Europe moved very fast, as both Hungary and Poland moved towards a form of multi-party democracy, with probable implications for their relations with Western Europe and the EC. In the EC itself, opinion hardened both against any new members in general before the full consolidation of the 1992 programme, and, in some circles at least, against neutral states (such as Austria in particular). These delays led to second and third thoughts about membership, especially in the SPÖ, whose left wing, represented by parliamentary Party Chairman Heinz Fischer, emphasized the social and environmental aspects, as well as the better known issue of neutrality.

Finally, in April 1989, the SPÖ adopted a definitive position paper, which cleared the way for a decision in the Cabinet. This paper makes neutrality and its formal acceptance by the EC an absolute prerequisite of membership. For the SPÖ, membership would be the best and most logical form of association with the 1992 programme, especially as other forms of association remain vague, but it would not be a matter of life and death for the Austrian economy. If the EC does not wish to accept her as a neutral, she should remain outside. Meanwhile, in the ÖVP, many of the corporatist interests closest to the party also began to have second thoughts and the election of former Agriculture Minister Reigler as leader in place of Alois Mock in May 1989 meant that the ÖVP position would be perceptibly more pragmatic on the issue. Public opinion has as yet to focus seriously on the issue. The Greens and the KPÖ are opposing membership and demanding a referendum. There is some evidence of a backlash on the issue, affecting the ÖVP in rural areas and in areas affected by the transit question. At all events, it will be a long marathon run, with no serious negotiations starting before 1992, despite the radical changes in central Europe in late 1989 that have blurred the East/West conflict and hence Austrian neutrality.

The other key concern in Austrian foreign policy is, as it has always been, her relations with her neighbours to the east, who were for the most part previously part of the Empire. For many years, she has pursued a good neighbour policy and sought to expand trade. However, increasingly since the early 1980s, a new conceptual approach to this region has been discussed, embodying the notion of a new 'Mitteleuropa', a central European cultural and political space, in which both practical cooperation and solidarity, based on a common historical experience and (in a subtle sense), a common approach, would be possible.

This concept would give Austrian foreign policy a broader conceptual basis and lift the country out of a certain provincialism. She would rediscover a historic role as a bridge between the blocks in a period of radical change in central Europe, which she could do much to assist.

This approach has little official support or recognition because of its lack of specific substance and because of the dangers of an adverse reaction in neighbouring countries, such as Yugoslavia and Czechoslovakia. Yet, as the processes of change in central Europe gather force, above all in Slovenia, Croatia, Hungary and Poland and as the debate about the future of 'Mitteleuropa' develops, there are subtle signs of reaction – not negative – in these countries. The idea of a kulturraum without barriers (shades of 1992) from Vienna to Lemberg (now Lvov) in the USSR, through Czernowitz and Hermannstadt in Romania, to Prague, Budapest, Agram (Zagreb) is an appealing concept. Yet, it was precisely the failure to take into account the barriers of ethnic, cultural and political divergences that doomed the old Empire. Today, the barriers seemed greater and the fears that such a concept arouse were very real in a world divided at Yalta. And yet.... And yet, today, the east/west barriers are weaker than at any time since 1945. Radical change is everywhere evident. Perhaps it is an idea whose time has come. What is the reality behind these ideas?

Austrian foreign policy has sought to develop a good neighbour policy towards those countries to the East: Hungary, Yugoslavia and Czechoslovakia. This has been difficult in that all three of those states were formerly part of the Empire, were suspicious of Austrian intentions and were involved in frontier disputes with Austria. At the same time, despite these specific problems there has been a strong sense of belonging to a common cultural area, influenced by the Empire. This is the Mitteleuropa idea, which was originally considered suspect and reactionary both in Austria and in the Middle European States, but which has made a strong come-back in the 1980s.

To a great extent, 'Mitteleuropa' was and remains a diffuse and vague concept, going little beyond more or less reciprocated cultural references, a sense of common historical roots, a sense of belonging. Vienna is not western Europe and Budapest is not eastern Europe; nor is Prague. As a cultural concept promoted or supported by Austria rather than Germany, the idea has become less threatening and considerably more acceptable, not least as an attempt, however symbolic for the moment, to surmount the division of Europe into two rigid blocks.

A flourishing literary, historical and cultural debate based on symposia and publications has arisen in the 1980s around this idea. There is a new sense of discovery of belonging to a wider central European community both in Austria and the other states concerned. Yet, this concept is not without its problems. Firstly, it must be kept in balance with Austria's 'Westpolitik', her rapprochement with the European Community. It must also develop greater substance beyond a cultural smoke-screen. Without trading and political links of a more substantial character, the idea cannot progress beyond cultural nostalgia and the cultural expression of taboo political hopes. Yet, Austria is not Germany – an important consideration. Austria's neutral status makes the development of ties based on these essentially cultural concepts less problematical for the participants, within limits. Naturally, the structure of the region as laid down in 1918 and 1945 cannot be directly challenged and must, on the contrary, be respected. Yet the development of such ties inevitably weakens it or ignores this structure. But now..? That is a contradiction and an ambiguity. It is no accident that relations have developed best with Hungary and less well, not to say little, with Czechoslovakia and with Yugoslavia.

Since the break-up of the Empire in 1920, this concept of 'Mitteleuropa' has returned periodically, like an unquiet ghost. Naturally, in the inter-war period, it found little echo in the successor states, yet it was from the Czech side that several proposals were made, as the fear of reviving German and Russian power again became a factor in political calculations.

Dr Benes proposed a Danubian confederation under Czech leadership in 1921 and again in 1924, he proposed a cultural European community. Proposals even came from Belgrade and Prague to include Austria in the 'Little Entente'. This did not prove possible and was strongly opposed by the Austrian Socialists and Nationalists. Only the Christian Social Party had some understanding for the idea. Was this a missed opportunity? How different history might have been!

Once Austria had achieved full sovereignty in 1955, she began to develop relations with her Eastern neighbours in a step-by-step process of normalisation. During the last years of the Grand Coalition, there were already attempts to develop relations with her Eastern European neighbours, beginning in 1964 with Hungary and establishing agreements with Yugoslavia, Bulgaria and Romania in the 1970s. Joint Austria–Hungary, Austria–Czechoslovakia Trade Commissions have been established. Trade with the COMECON States is important, amounting to 10.6% of all Austrian trade; that is, more than Switzerland or Italy. Austria has a positive trade balance with COMECON but a negative one with the EC. Some 70,000 jobs in Austria depend on Eastern European trade. So in sum, this trade is of considerable significance and has been able to operate to some degree in a counter-cyclical way. However, it has proved difficult to achieve a rapid growth of trade or a relaxation of restrictions with some states such as Czechoslovakia.

Trade and political relations are the key issues of substance which could gradually develop a form of modern regionalism not responding to the logic of the two block division of Europe, and which could eventually lead to a degree of rapprochement between the two halves of Europe. That is certainly a seriously held long term hope in Austria and here the concept of 'Mitteleuropa' gives a useful philosophical contour to what would otherwise be *ad hoc* cooperation with neighbours.

This thinking is underpinned by a reservoir of opinion which tends to regard the break-up of the Empire as a historical tragedy ascribable to a key failure of vision and imagination in Austria in the period between 1866–1914. This view is surprisingly widespread and occurs where one might not expect it to be found. Thus, Bruno Kreisky states in his memoirs:

'The fall of the old Empire was a step back in three respects: economically because the idea of a Central European Economic Community could have been an excellent model for Western Europe ... It was also a political step backwards since the successor states fell, through excessive nationalism, into undemocratic reaction that prepared the way for Communism. Furthermore a supra-national cultural community, with many faces but a basic unity was destroyed'. (p 47)

He goes on:

'The Monarchy was a great unused opportunity....The fall of the Empire did not inevitably mean the end of the multinational State. It was not inevitable. A supra-national Republic could have developed out of the Monarchy . . .' (p 48)

These views are more common than one might expect, both in Austria and, at least as an expression of an inner hope, even in the successor states. But the main difficulty is to translate them into any kind of political reality at the present time. Perhaps the most fruitful route is that which avoids the larger political questions at this delicate stage by ignoring them, seeking instead to create regional and technical links on a step-by-step basis, without challenging or threatening the present European order. Here, indeed, some action has been taken and some substance given to these ideas, if only in a very fragmented way. The ÖVP Vienna political leader Edward Busek produced a plan entitled 'Projekt Mitteleuropa' which was an important contribution to the debate, launched in 1986.

In Northern Italy, Civita Mitteleuropa, based in the North East, has become a significant, popular movement on the cultural level. Josef Krainer, the Landeshauptsman of Oberosterreich, launched the 'Arbeitsgemeinschäft der Lander und Regionen der Ostalpengebiete' in 1978. This body was based on a joint declaration of cooperative principles covering both broad philosophical questions of cooperation and specific areas of concrete cooperation. Six commissions have been set up: Planning and Environment, Transport, Culture, Economic Cooperation, Agricultural and Forestry, and Health. The members are the Austrian provinces of Kärnten, Steiermark, Oberosterreich, the Italian regions of Friul-Ventino, Südtirol (Trentino) and the Yugoslavian republics of Croatia and Slowenia. This was followed in 1984 by the initiative from Lower Austria for the creation of a body for the 'Middle Danube'. The Lower Austrian capital project is also linked with ideas for the creation of a Danubian Festival and University of Sankt Pölten. No doubt the constitutional revision, enabling the Austrian Länder to conclude international agreements within their own areas of competence, will give fresh impetus to these movements. It is noteworthy that the initiatives come from Austria for the most part. The problem is to find a response, and more active partners in the East in Hungary and Czechoslovakia in particular. Now, in the new political climate, it can be expected that real life can be breathed into the concept as democracy establishes itself all over the old Monarchy.

There is thus a distinct Austrian way in international relations. Austrian neutrality is, given her geographical situation and economic requirements, an asset rather than a hindrance. Neutrality has enriched rather than limited her capacity for independent action on the European and world scene, whether it be in the more 'mondialiste' manner of the Kreisky era when Austria sought to play a bridging and mediating rôle in the major world conflicts, or whether it be in the more limited frame of reference of Europe, in which the present government places the main weight of Austrian foreign policy. The leitmotiv of present policy is to balance an active Westpolitik with an Ostpolitik of good neighbour relations. The vision of Austria playing a rôle as a leader and a bridge to the West in that presently incoherent region of 'Mitteleuropa' is distant, but it is what lifts Austrian policy, at least potentially, above self-satisfied provincialism.

Can one ignore the Waldheim factor? Kurt Waldheim was elected in June 1986 after a long and bitter election campaign, in which, ironically, outside interference was even stronger than during the four-Power occupation. It may well be that, however well-intentioned and even well-founded it may have been, this outside intervention was in fact counter-productive and in fact assisted Mr Waldheim by enabling him to appeal to Austrian national pride and independence. Yet, the foreign interest served to internationalise the issue and focus unwelcome and unfavourable foreign attention more generally on Austria and her situation. Mr Waldheim has received visits from only two Heads of State: King Hussein of Jordan (1988) and the Pope (1988). He has undertaken only few State visits, and only to Arab States. He is in effect *persona non-grata* throughout the Western world. The states of Eastern Europe have been less open in attacking him, but have not invited him to make state visits. His term of office lasts until 1992 and could be renewed until 1998, a long period of diplomatic quarantine.

Beyond the immediate personal problems which, given the limited real powers of the President in foreign affairs, is of small direct practical significance, there is the more subtle and dangerous problem of Austria's image abroad, especially in the United States and Western Europe. This fact is admitted even by ÖVP leaders. The effect is hard to quantify, but is certainly a serious handicap for Austrian diplomacy and shows a different and more disquieting face of Austria than that of the statesman Bruno Kreisky or the youthful moderniser, Franz Vranitzky. At best, it is an undesirable negative, as Austria's image has changed from that of an effective and modern society building on long traditions, to a much more doubtful one of blandness, indifference to the past and a certain provincial arrogance. As we have seen, this negative image is certainly greatly over-stated and is probably, on balance, false. The positive achievements of Austria, both internally and externally, are real and deserve to be predominant in evaluating her image and position in the world, but the Waldheim factor, too, is real and will leave its mark. It too is part of the ambiguity of the Austrian heritage.

4. The Political Process

The 'political pillar' is central to the whole edifice that is the Austrian Model. It is the cement, the binding that holds the whole structure together. The Austrian political method, which has certain distinct consensual features, pervades every aspect of Austrian life and almost every aspect of corporate and collective activity.

In countries such as France, a clear and interesting distinction is made between the narrow domain of the political sphere and the broader 'société civile' or civil society, from which, for example, a number of non-political ministers have been drawn in the Rocard cabinet appointed by President Mitterand after his triumphant re-election in May 1988.

Such a distinction would also be understood in Britain or the United States, but has hitherto had little meaning in Austria. Indeed, developments in Austria has, at least until the mid-1980s, been in the opposite direction, that is towards the politisation of every sphere of activity, almost to the point of caricature. Not just political groupings in the trade unions and professional bodies, but even Socialist and Christian chess clubs.

Austria is the most obvious example of a society in which the 'verzuiling' or pillarisation principle, as defined by the Dutch political scientist Lijphardt, retains its most effective relevance. Austria is, relatedly, a consensual society, in which political battles are fought inside the basic parameters of society and consensual ground-rules that ensure a balance between organised and representative interests, but obviously thereby exclude other interests.

The ground-rules are well understood and were respected by most actors in the political process at least until the early 1980s. There was a strong tendency to seek compromise and avoid sharp political conflict even if it meant that political and economic power was always shared. The consensus mentality and the types of political machinery and processes that it engenders became all too pervasive in Austria, and retained broad support. Now this approach has, interestingly, come under attack as undemocratic and elitist, and is seen as the cause of a certain immobility and provincialism in Austria society. Yet, in all this new concern about the dangers of consensus, it should be remembered that Austria's post-war success has, in large measure, been built on this system.

In this chapter, we shall seek to examine the origins, functioning and survival potential of the Austrian political method, in the light of the various critical movements that have emerged in Austria in the early 1980s. The success of the Austrian political model in the Second Republic is all the more remarkable when compared with the political difficulties that developed in the 1930s and destroyed the fabric of Austrian society, leaving her defenceless against the internal and external pressures of Nazis and the siren call of the Anschluss.

As we have already seen in examining the political history of modern Austria, the political leaders who emerged from the concentration camp experience, from the underground, or from enforced retirement to assume power under the Allied occupation and under the conditions of the Moscow Declaration (namely the permanent restoration of an independent and democratic Austria), cautiously moved towards national reconciliation in order to make the Second Republic work.

As far as possible, it was jointly decided to make an entirely fresh start and draw a veil over what had happened both in 1934 and in the later 1930s. Quite deliberately, no attempt was made to determine 'responsibility' for these events or apportion blame. No serious attempt was made to extend the political interdict imposed on Nazis to the groups that had supported the post 1934 'Ständestaat', the Austrian system of Dollfuss and Schuschnigg. Even the KPÖ (Communist) accepted this form of historic compromise, though it may well be that they did so only because the Soviet occupation authorities required them to adopt such a moderate attitude. The foundations were laid in April 1945 in the formation of Karl Renner's very first Provisional Government and subsequently in the formation of the first Cabinet after the Nationalrat elections in November 1945, under Leopold Figl (ÖVP). These basic principles came to be so fundamental to Austrian politics that we should pause and analyse them in greater detail.

Dr Renner, almost without deeper debate, as if by instinct, homed in on the formula that was to prove so enduring, the Grand Coalition. This was composed of the new United Socialist Party (SPÖ) and a party rapidly stitched together from various Catholic and Conservative groups (that had not been compromised with the Nazis), which became the ÖVP. Indeed, the party was not fully formed in 1945, but the principle of it was so well established and understood that its putative leaders were able to enter the Coalition and then complete the building-up of the party. The party landscape was simplified to a basic two-party system by a number of factors.

The old third pan-German lager had, by force of events, disappeared and was not to reappear until the relaxation of the political 'interdict' on the Nazis in 1949, by which time the basic pattern of the party system and the Grand Coalition had become set in concrete, and the third lager was reduced to almost total impotence. At the same time, a significant proportion of the former voters of the third lager found their way into the SPÖ (if an anticlerical or liberal ideology was more salient), or into the ÖVP (if they were Catholic Conservatives). The ÖVP was also able to achieve a monopoly on the Conservative wing by preventing the formation of a Peasant party as there had been in the earlier 1930s.

The 1945 election showed that the SPÖ would equally be able to defend a monopoly on the left. That was not by any means self-evident before the election. The KPÖ had expected to obtain significant parliamentary representation as the party of the liberators. In much of Europe this was indeed the case. Communist parties, basking in the prestige of the Red Army and in the general reformist, if not revolutionary atmosphere that followed the war, achieved substantial electoral gains until the onset of the cold war.

However, that was not the case in Austria, where the support of the Soviet occupation authorities was relatively limited, but even so represented the kiss of death which identified the KPÖ as the 'Russian party'.

The SPÖ was also able to achieve dominance in the other branches of the labour movement such as the unions and cooperatives. Even in 'red Vienna', it was the SPÖ and not the KPÖ that had control. As a result, both of the two large parties were of necessity broad churches with centrist, pragmatic policies and approaches. Indeed both were or rapidly became 'Volksparteien' – people's parties – and both achieved a large degree of freedom of maneouvre as they were not threatened by more radical parties of any significance to their left or right. This party structure could obviously have equally-well formed the basis for a different (and more competitive than consensual) political system as in the Anglo-Saxon democracies. As it was there were other factors in Austria which favoured the consensual approach.

In 1945, the fate of Austria was far from clear and in any event Austria was not a fully independent state. Her independence was limited to the parameters set by the Allied occupation authorities. Her government could not survive without the recognition of the Allied Council and indeed, under the First Control Agreement, all laws required Allied consent: under the Second Control Agreement some laws still required consent, while ordinary laws could be vetoed by a unanimous Allied Council.

More broadly, the future of Austria would be settled in a State Treaty as part of a wider settlement that would require the consent of the four Allied Powers. Room for maneouvre was limited and there were considerable inherent dangers in allowing internal discussions to predominate. These could only weaken the Austrian position in the view of the Allies, who would be able to exploit the differences. Above all, a failure to maintain a broad-based coalition would offend one or other Ally. Hence, the initial decision to include the KPÖ was inevitable. So the KPÖ was retained in the coalition and indeed remained over-represented, despite its mediocre electoral showing, even after the 1945 election. As it was, its departure in 1947 caused no ripple in relations with the Russians, but that could not have been foreseen in 1945. At the same time, a broad-based coalition was strong enough to impose the necessary political and economic decisions on the population, without the fear of any political unpopularity being exploited against them by the opposition.

The Grand Coalition thus became the norm. As its most immediate political origins receded, though they retained their basic cogency, new benefits flowed from the consensual approach to policy-making that the Grand Coalition engendered. Under the broad umbrella of the political coalition, a parallel and inter-linked social coalition, formalised in the Joint Commission (Paritätische Kommission), came into being. This served as a means of canalising and resolving economic and social conflicts and involving all sectors of the economy in decision making and planning in relation to the development of the economy as reconstruction moved ahead. This system envisaged a long term moderation in wages, costs and prices that was vital to the country's economic competitiveness.

This second or parallel socio-economic coalition, which is examined in greater detail in Chapter 6, is a vital and effective part of the Austrian political system and a key factor in the decision-making process.

A key element in the Austrian political system, and perhaps its most significant characteristic, is the permanent search for compromise, balance and involvement, through the broad participation and cooperation of all major political actors in the process. This is an approach, a mentality, that is difficult for others to understand. It is all-pervasive and can be boiled down to the view that all conflicts are amenable to resolution through compromise based on dialogue and on involvement in the political process. Every political and economic decision is thus the result of processes of compromise in which every partner has ceded some ground but has also gained enough to have a stake in the outcome.

This approach, born out of the bitter experiences of the inter-war period and the dire necessities of the first post-war decade, together with the pressures of occupation and the privations of reconstruction, has 'taken' and become almost the norm. It is as if the political parties still do not wish to exercise power alone, or allow unimpeded political conflict to emerge. Even during periods of one-party government, numerous shock absorbers remain within the system to deflect and canalise political conflict, not least the sense that the Grand Coalition can and perhaps should return, as indeed it did in 1987.

One should neither infer that conflict is totally excluded from political relationships, nor that compromise and consensus is always easily achieved. Political conflict in Austria is handled within certain consensual norms and forms have been developed to canalise and dampen conflict to the point where it can be resolved by compromise, as is considered appropriate. Meaningful political conflict is thus usually within a coalition or at least within some kind of consensual framework. The aim of political parties and their associated interest groups is to obtain or maximise their influence and leverage within the framework of consensual arrangements. Political expectations are based on this maximalisation of influence and on the necessity of compromise.

Even the ÖVP and SPÖ one-party governments were not exempt from these necessities. The ÖVP government could not ignore the necessity of compromise with the Social partners, which indirectly involved the SPÖ. Equally, during the long Kreisky era of one-party SPÖ government, Chancellor Kreisky was well aware of the fact that his absolute majority was in itself a coalition, part of which had merely lent its support to the SPÖ as the most credible reformist party. He was also attuned to the need to work within the Employers and Farmers Organisations (and even with the FPÖ and ÖVP), to ensure a broad base for his reformist plans.

What was important were the positions of blockage or leverage in the system that set the terms of exchange within a coalition or within the various consensual forums forming the Austrian political system. Elections do little more than distribute the bargaining chips at the start of the process or, since the process is on-going, redistribute them and hence create new possibilities for the actors in the process. Some of the chips are not distributed or redistributed by the electoral process but from the socio-economic power of organisations in the Social Partnership system.

In the very first election after 1945, there was little by way of a benchmark to work from since no one could predict how the parties would perform. As it was, the ÖVP absolute majority was unexpected and the KPÖ performed less well than most well-informed observers had expected. The outcome was within a range from which there has been little subsequent variation. Both main parties had established a basic level of support and the balance between them was close. Variations in support between elections were never massive; SPÖ absolute majority, ÖVP plurality or SPÖ plurality have all been actual outcomes and at any one election have been plausible ones.

Thus in 1945, the ÖVP obtained 49.8% and the SPÖ 44.6%. The 1949 elections, with large votes for third parties (WdU 11.67% and KPÖ 5.08%) saw the ÖVP at 44.03% and the SPÖ at 38.71%, the same proportions as in 1945. The elections of the 1950s were much closer, with the difference in vote reduced to 2% or less. The 1966 election gave the ÖVP an absolute majority with 48.3% to 42.6% for the SPÖ. The 1970 election was transitional, with no overall majority but an SPÖ plurality (48.42% to 44.69% for the ÖVP). The elections of the 1970s gave the SPÖ an absolute parliamentary majority, but never more than 51.03% of the vote. The 1980s have seen a gradual breakdown in the hegemony of the larger parties. The SPÖ retained its position as the largest party both in 1983 (SPÖ 47.6% to 43.2% for the ÖVP) and in 1986 (43.12% SPÖ to 41.3% ÖVP). Thus, for the SPÖ, the range (excluding the 'freak' 1949 election) lies between 42.12% and 51.03% and for the ÖVP 41.3% and 49.8%.

The combined share of the vote of the two largest parties has lain between 82.74% in 1949 (and 84.42% in 1986) and 94.40% in 1945. For most of the period it was over 85% and in the 1970s it was always over 90%. Thus, the limits of party competition were, in terms of electoral games, quite narrow. Both parties were certain of about 43% as a minimum and 51% as an upper ceiling. However, as we shall see, these margins left considerable room for maneouvre in terms of political strategy. The leverage of a party in the consensual bargaining process could depend on very small shifts in the relative share of the vote, even if there was no drastic change in the parliamentary situation. This was especially true of the first Grand Coalition period.

How did the Grand Coalition function? This is important for our understanding of the Austrian political process and for the working of the new Grand Coalition, which, despite some important new features, draws on many explicit or implicit references from the previous Grand Coalition period. Various formulae were applied, which went under the general term of 'proportz'. ensuring a proportional representation of both coalition parties at all levels of government and more widely in public sector appointments, and above all in the management of the large state industrial sector.

Austria is basically a parliamentary democracy. However, the 1929 Revision of the 1920 Constitution (still in force) attempted to introduce some quasi-presidential features into the system. The president was to be directly elected by the people and was to exercise some increased power over the functioning of governments, the appointment of senior public servants, the dissolution of the Nationalrat and the conduct of foreign policy. There were no direct elections of the Federal President during the First Republic and the first State President of the Second Republic (Dr Renner) was elected by the Nationalrat.

The president holds office for six years and may be re-elected once. The office has never achieved the importance intended for it in 1929. This has been demonstrated by its tendency to attract non-politicians (who have a certain political coloration but no active party political past), or elder statesmen figures. This model fits Karl Renner (SPÖ) (1945–51), Theodor Körner (SPÖ, 1951–57), Franz Jonas (SPÖ 1965–71), Rudolf Kirschläger (SPÖ, 1974–86) and even Dr Kurt Waldheim (OVP, 1986–). Karl Renner was perhaps the most politically influential of the Federal Presidents, being active in the talks preparing the State Treaty, but even he did not give the office much political clout. Theodor Körner is known to have blocked the inclusion of the WdU in the Grand Coalition in 1953. Dr Waldheim was initially reputed to wish to upgrade the political rôle of the Presidency, but the controversy surrounding him has excluded such an initiative, which probably would, in any case, have been ill-received even within the ÖVP.

Even in foreign policy, the President's acts are almost purely ceremonial or formal and must in any case be 'covered' by the counter-signature of a minister. The president's powers are exclusively negative. He can block certain proposals and if he has the political weight, influence coalition discussions, but only marginally. Normally, he can only act on a proposal from the Federal Cabinet, which forces him to work with the Cabinet and not against it. This even applies to the power of dissolution of the Nationalrat.

For much of the Grand Coalition, though elections were contested, the 'Red' SPÖ President was seen as a balancing factor to the 'Black' ÖVP Chancellor. This was never explicit, but was widely accepted. The elections showed the fine balance of public opinion, and the tendency of the pan-Germanic vote to favour SPÖ candidates. There was never, even in the 1950s, a clear conservative electoral majority in the country.

Despite the popular election of the president, Austria is not France. Presidential elections are not the central element in the political process. The conservative attempt to use the 1986 Presidential election for the purpose of building a conservative political majority was only partly successful as the rather different outcome of the later Nationalrat election was to show. The 1986 election seems unlikely to change the nature of the Presidency nor the essentially secondary nature of presidential elections. Austria remains, and will, remain a parliamentary democracy.

Executive political power is formally in the hands of the Cabinet (headed by the Chancellor and Vice Chancellor). It is elected for four years, and is responsible to the Nationalrat, but not the Bundesrat, the Chamber of the Federal Länder. The reality is often considerably more complex and the real focus of power is frequently elsewhere. Certainly, the Federal Chancellor has a key pivotal rôle in the system. That was true even before the extreme 'mediatisation' of politics from the 1970s onwards. Possibly the importance of his rôle goes back to the imperial tradition, where one minister, whatever his shifting formal title, emerged as the political leader of the emperor's ministry.

This tendency was emphasised by the changing nature of politics and the arrival of media Chancellors such as Bruno Kreisky and Franz Vranitzky who have understood the key rôle of the press and television in promoting a direct relationship with the electorate as a means of creating an effective image and 'selling' government policy and the Chancellor himself.

The parties now seek the Chancellorship, even in a coalition, less for the significance of the office in terms of policy making, than for its media significance. It is clear that the 'chancellor effect' – the popularity of a Chancellor such as Kreisky or Vranitzky – can give his party the edge in the elections and is cited by many poll respondents as either the reason for their vote or at least a major determining factor. It is also clear that the chancellor sets the tone and fixes the all-important 'image' of his government, which image is then propagated by the media. He leads his team and must always remember that, in the mind of the public, the old Harry Truman adage 'the buck stops here' applies to him.

The mediatic developments have created new complications in a coalition. The junior coalition partner always provided a Vice Chancellor, who thus acquired (to a lesser degree than the Chancellor), a roving brief which enabled him as the titular leader of his party to represent it in the upper circles of government over the whole range of policy (even outside his own portfolio) and to speak publicly for his party on broader political issues. Yet under modern conditions, which are the result of the Kreisky era (which inaugurated a whole new approach to government and media relations), the Vice Chancellor must also keep himself in front of the media and avoid 'being lost in the crowd' of ministers. He must keep himself, his party and their achievements (within the coalition) before the public.

Thus, in the present Grand Coalition, the ÖVP leader and Vice Chancellor Alois Mock has sought to present himself as a *primus inter pares* with the Chancellor and to promote the achievements of the government as due to the positive influence of the ÖVP on policy. The ÖVP, although it considers that it obtained 80% of its demands in the coalition negotiations, still remains behind the SPÖ in the polls. The 'personalisation' of politics has obviously been to the advantage of Chancellor Vranitzky (SPÖ) rather than Mock. The 'chancellor effect' is as powerful when both parties are in government, as when one of them is in opposition.

The Chancellor is the undisputed head of government. His position is reinforced by legal, political, and media/image considerations. He constitutionally nominates the other ministers for appointment by the Federal President. Naturally, in a coalition government, his freedom of manoeuvre will be less than in a one-party government.

In the 1987 coalition agreement, in the first appendix, the exact apportionment of ministers between the two parties is laid down, but each party is free to nominate people to the posts allocated to it. Chancellors (and in coalitions, Vice Chancellors), do not enjoy anything like total freedom of appointment. In the SPÖ, the Social

Affairs Minister is nominated from among ÖGB members and in the ÖVP the distribution of ministerial posts must respect a proporz between the organisations that make up the ÖVP and the various Länder.

Various posts, such as the Minister of Agriculture and Minister of Trade, usually fall to the ÖVP in coalitions and are almost filled with respectively ÖBB and ÖWB members. The Chancellor is nearly always the leader of his party. On rare occasions in both the ÖVP and, between 1986–88, in the SPÖ, the position of Chancellor and party leader has been separated for a short period. The experience has rarely been a success and has normally soon been brought to an end. The Chancellor as party leader has a pre-eminent political position in party and government. He also has a key pre-eminent position as the Chairman and hence coordinator of the Cabinet. This places him in the position of arbitrator between conflicting views, and makes him the court of last resort. In a coalition, he will be the ultimate negotiator (with his Vice Chancellor from the coalition partner).

The Federal Cabinet is the cockpit of Austrian politics – the ultimate coordination point. Yet, in many ways, it is a formal body that legitimises decisions taken or decided elsewhere by other participants in the political process. It is at the apex of a triangle, linking the government party or parties and their parliamentary parties.

The cabinet alone has the authority to table Bills and set the annual budget, as well as making important appointments. Its decisions must be unanimous, and formal votes are not taken. The cabinet meetings are often very short and merely endorse the proposals prepared by relevant ministers, and ironed out in the labyrinth of consultations with interest groups (the Begutachtungsprozess) and then considered in the parliamentary groups and in the 'preparatory meetings' (Vorbesprechungen) that precede each cabinet session. These sessions are held in two phases.

Ministers hold preliminary discussions in their own parties (when there is a coalition cabinet). Serious matters may involve the mediation of the Chancellor in a one-party cabinet or of the Chancellor and Vice Chancellor in a Grand Coalition. The formal cabinet session on a Wednesday is preceded by a long preparatory meeting which involves party leaders not in the cabinet. For example, during part of the SPÖ–FPÖ Cabinet and for the first year of the SPÖ–ÖVP Grand Coalition, Fred Sinowatz remained SPÖ chairman, but was not a minister. He attended these sessions. The formal cabinet session set for 11.00 a.m. is often delayed, and when it is held represents a continuation of the earlier meeting. It often only lasts fifteen minutes and is followed by an impromptu press conference with the Chancellor and other senior ministers. The press conference was an innovation of Dr Kreisky, with his flair for communication with the media. This press conference, held among a mêlée of journalists in the elegant room of the Ballhausplatz, then forms the centre-piece of the evening news. Even here, the 'chancellor-effect' is evident. The manner in which the cabinet functions is very typical of Austrian politics: an adroit mixture of ceremonial, informality and broad and demonstrable consensus building.

Coalition governments will begin with pragmatic agreements on both inter-partner relations and the substance of policy. In the old 1945–66 Grand Coalition, there was a policy committee (Koalition-sausschluss, and later Arbeitsausschluss) which was an unofficial inter-party contact committee which arranged deals that were then merely approved in cabinet. It was the 'real' cabinet. At the same time, there were only very general policy agreements. The government, and indeed parliament, could not act, as both parties were also bound together in parliament. This situation led to criticism of the old Grand Coalition in its last phase, for its immobility and its secret 'particratic' government that reduced the constitutionally responsible bodies to rubber stamps. In the SPÖ–FPÖ coalition there was a more detailed policy document agreed at the outset in 1983. However, FPÖ policy had little impact as the party was small and wholly inexperienced in government.

The new model Grand Coalition formed in 1987 could not be merely a new edition of the previous Grand Coalition. Times had changed. The criticisms made of the political class had increased, as the 1986 gains of the FPÖ and the Greens attested. Conditions had also changed. There was no easy consensus after almost 20 years of more-confrontational modes of political life. The external necessities that had forged an earlier coalition discipline were absent. A new generation had to learn the positive benefits of consensus and compromise. Nationalrat Deputies, like society in general, had grown more open, more critical and more independent. The new coalition had to permit more breathing space, more 'coalition free' space, in parliament.

The present Coalition Agreement provides for no coalition committee as such, as the cabinet is to be allowed to play its proper rôle.

However, there is provision for the 'negotiating teams' of the two parties to meet to resolve problems of a very severe nature. In practice there *is* a coalition committee, but it is much weaker than in the 1945–66 period. The two partners have committed themselves to ensure that government initiatives 'find a majority'. This clearly does not require one-hundred percent whipping in both parties on all issues, even those enshrined in the Coalition Agreement. There is room for independent positions by significant numbers of ÖVP or SPÖ Deputies, from issue to issue, and there is evidence of small scale negative voting and abstentions in the government ranks, especially on the ÖVP side.

Given the traditions of consensus and discipline, these cases will remain few, but the psychological effect of the possibility existing is seen as important to the 'image' of the coalition. Indeed, as yet there have been no votes without a coalition consensus. Only one opposition initiative from Dr Ofner, former FPÖ Justice Minister, has been taken up and passed, albeit somewhat amended; but it *was* a continuation of his work as a Minister and received an all-party consensus. The present Coalition Agreement is untraditionally and indeed almost absurdly detailed. It runs to seventeen policy papers as appendices and covers over sixty pages, dealing with almost all areas of policy in great detail. The main emphasis is on State finances, the nationalised industries, the reform of pensions and social security.

There is also a recognition of the greater activism of parliament. Even in previous parliaments, the share of legislative initiatives fell. Indeed, in the Small Coalition, it fell from 85% to 65% in the 1966–70 legislature. The coalition agreement provides for discussions between the Klub (parliamentary party) leaders on all new proposals.

'Agreed proposals', for which the Finance Minister certifies that appropriations are available, become 'coalition proposals' and a majority must be found. This financial veto is seen as important by the ÖVP to prevent new spending initiatives. However, the Finance Minister is from the SPÖ (Dr Lacina).

Other initiatives that have not been cleared are discussed between Klub leaders in order to reach agreement on the position to be adopted, and are examined for financial implications. No non-budgeted expenditure must be made. Where no agreement is reached, one party may not out-vote the other on matters declared by the other to be 'of importance to mutual cooperation' or 'occasioning non-budgeted expenditure'. A small amount of coalition free-room is created, within which initiatives can be brought to the vote and carried with the votes of the other parties (in practice only SPÖ + FPÖ or ÖVP + FPÖ majorities are arithmetically possible) against the other coalition partner. Again, the effect is probably more apparent than real, but offers a safety valve provided that the vital interests of one or other part are not at stake.

It should be remembered that, in recent parliaments, even with one-party absolute majorities, over 75% of all votes are unanimous (SPÖ, ÖVP, FPÖ) and over 80% of majorities have included the SPÖ and ÖVP. In the present legislature, the more competitive and populist FPÖ (under Jörg Haider), and the Greens, are breaking the pattern to a certain degree. In the first two sessions, unanimity fell to 39% in respect of all Bills. It is higher for government proposals (45%) and the share was still greater than the percentage adopted only with coalition (SPÖ and ÖVP) votes. Indeed, the percentage with three-party support rises to at least 61%.

This tends to confirm the view of the FPÖ parliamentary leadership that it is the Greens who have broken consensus. Even here, it is their lack of discipline which often prevents unanimous votes. 73% of Bills still obtained unanimous support or the support of one or more opposition parties. Even the Greens supported 51% of Bills, and have given support to the coalition on measures relating to the environment and the rights for foreign workers, whereas the FPÖ has only done so on economic issues.

There was no increase in censure motions. The Greens and the FPÖ have cooperated to meet the formal rules for tabling interpellations (twenty members required). There has been an increase in questions. Only about 40% of government proposals have remained unamended. Parliament, with the unorthodox tactics of the Greens (unfurling a Nazi flag in a debate on Waldheim for example), has become somewhat more lively and has attracted more attention. At the same time, the Nationalrat has been an additional consensus building institution between the coalition parties, from which amendments to the government's bill may arise. The change is, however, not fundamental.

The present coalition agreement provides for some measures to increase the effectiveness of parliament and its control of the executive. The electoral system is to be reformed so as to create closer links between voter and member and decrease the control of the composition of the Nationalrat by the party machines. A constituency system will be introduced for some 100 members and the remainder are to be elected from lists (with preference voting) to ensure proportionality, with a 3% threshold clause (compared with 5% in Germany).

Discussions are in progress to improve the rights of minorities in parliament. This may involve more open committees, the right of a minority to require the establishment of an Inquiry Committee and to provoke an investigation by the Audit Court, but above all easier access to tabling interpellations and the creation of a 'topical debate' period. The aim here, too, is to avoid the stifling effect of the old Grand Coalition in its last phase when no real debate, or opposition to an over-mighty coalition, appeared to exist.

In the new, model, open-marriage coalition, opposition need not be limited to the, at times, irresponsible and demagogic FPÖ and Greens. The SPÖ and ÖVP can continue their constructive competition and maintain their individuality in the coalition. Most participants and observers see no political alternative to a Grand Coalition, and see these kinds of measure as a corrective to the criticism that arose in the 1960s. All, however, recognise that this new type of coalition is difficult, especially after a gap of some twenty years. However it seems to be working, at least in the Cabinet and Parliament.

Parliament is the second key political forum of decision-making. As we shall see in the chapter on federalism in Austria, the Bundesrat – the representative chamber for the Länder – is significantly weaker than the Nationalrat. The Nationalrat is elected for four years by proportional representation, but may be dissolved earlier by the Federal President, as happened in 1971 and in 1986. However, the Legislature usually goes to its full term. The election of the 183 Nationalrat Deputies is relatively proportional and the element of proportionality was in fact increased in the electoral reform of 1970.

Each Land is now a constituency, with seats apportioned according to population. The basis of representation is the 'Grundmandat'. Only parties that obtain a 'Grundmandat' in that Land are admitted to the second phase of distribution. The Länder are split into two groups. The remainders (votes left from the first phase) are used to allocate the remaining seats proportionally to each of the groups. The aim is to ensure a close-to-proportional distribution of seats. The small parties that win no 'Grundmandat' because their vote is too spread (KPÖ or Greens in 1983) win no seats at all.

The Cabinet is responsible to the Nationalrat and can be removed by a vote of no-confidence, as can an individual minister. In this era of mass parties and one-party majorities or majority coalitions, such events are unlikely. Even in the scandalous case of FPÖ Defence Minister Frischenschläger, who was censured by the ÖVP for ceremoniously receiving a war criminal on his return from an Italian prison (1985), the automatic solidarity of the majority (SPÖ/FPÖ) was invoked to reject the motion, whose passage would have ended the coalition.

Pressure on the government and control is exerted through the government party and it is here that a loss of confidence in a minister can be expressed. The opposition speaks more to public opinion outside Parliament. Yet, even in these times of automatic majorities and declining beliefs in the value of Parliament in Austria as elsewhere, and in Austria where Parliament has never been highly regarded, the influence of Parliament is more than often thought.

Parliament and its Committee and Klubs influence legislation and the actions of the executive to an unexpectedly significant extent. This should not be exaggerated, but the present tendency is to over-minimise the importance of the parliamentary institution in Austria. Certainly, it is by no means the only forum of political decision-making, nor perhaps even the most important, but it does play a rôle that should be taken into account.

The Nationalrat has all the 'classic' parliamentary functions. It exercises legislative power and controls the executive through the usual mechanisms such as the motion of no-confidence, interpellations, questions and investigations through its committees, or through the Audit Court for financial matters.

Most ministers have been Nationalrat members, but a sizeable average of one-quarter of ministers in most cabinets are not parliamentarians; there is a tradition for the Justice Minister to be a non-party man. However, it is the Nationalrat that forms the cockpit of politics. The government must respond to its opposition and other critics in the Nationalrat, even though only some 2–8% of the public watch the televised proceedings of parliament. In recent Legislatures (Gesetzgebungsperiode, G P), the number of no-confidence motions has been fairly constant at eight (six ÖVP, one FPÖ, one ÖVP + FPÖ) in the XIV GP (1975–79), eleven in the XV GP (Seven ÖVP, three FPÖ and one ÖVP + FPÖ) and nine (all ÖVP) in the XVI GP. These motions are the heaviest parliamentary artillery.

Next come the interpellations (questions with debate) which require twenty members to table. In the XIII GP there were twenty-five, twenty-three in the XIV, in the XV the number rose to thirty-one and fell to the average of twenty-three in the XVI period. When the SPÖ was in opposition, it tabled thirty-one motions. Interpellations are the weapon of an active opposition and can serve many purposes: attack, seizing the initiative, controlling or investigating scandals, or provoking debate. They have dealt mostly with general political issues, the economic situation, the state industries, scandals. Questions can be asked in writing or for oral answer. The number of questions has increased from 379 in the X GP (1962–66) (the last period of the first Grand Coalition) to 2,365 in the XVI GP. The main adressees are the Chancellor, Finance Minister, Minister of Public Works, and the Minister for the Environment. Beyond that the spread is quite even between ministries. Parliament has seen the number of sittings rise sharply and the doubling of the number of hours per month of sittings. In the X GP, there were ninety-five sittings and thirteen hours on average per month, whereas in the ÖVP one-party government (XI period), there were 175 sittings and thirty-one hours per month. Parliament then settled to a slightly less frantic rhythm of 123 sittings and 28.1 sitting hours per month in the XIV GP (SPÖ majority) and 161 sittings but 26.9 hours per month in the XVI GP.

Another weapon of control is the increasing number of Government Reports, both written and oral (Foreign Policy, Security Policy, Agriculture, Arts, Education, Subsidies). There are also periodic oral reports on the economic and budgetary situation. Reports on these reports usually pass by consensus. Even in the XVI GP, 81% passed with support of all parties. The Finance and Agricultural reports were the most controversial.

The influence of parliament is greater than often estimated. Of course, there is no concrete measure of its influence on the preparatory phase of legislation, but it is considered to be significant. During the legislative process, its importance can more readily be traced.

As already indicated, the share of bills passed originating with the Cabinet has been falling. Already, in the XVII GP (1986–), the Greens tabled sixty bills. Most of these have no chance of passage, but do serve a demonstration purpose. The number of bills which pass unamended has remained roughly constant or may have declined slightly.

In the XI period (ÖVP majority), 49% of government bills passed unamended. In the XIII GP, only 38.5% passed unamended. In the later SPÖ majority GP, the figure was only about 47%; it was

45.6% in the XVI GP (SPÖ–FPÖ coalition). Most Bills were amended in committee rather than on the floor. Legislation is mostly passed by consensus. Indeed, much legislation is technical or routine and hence inherently uncontroversial, but about half the available parliamentary time is used on legislation. Only about 12% of bills are significantly amended, but again most bills are already broadly acceptable before they are tabled. In the ÖVP government 71% were unanimously passed and a further 14% obtained 'mixed' majorities.

In the Short Legislature (1970–71), where there was an SPÖ minority cabinet, 84% of Bills obtained the support of all parties and 16% that of mixed majorities. In the ÖVP XI GP, 80% received the support of all parties, or at least of the ÖVP and the SPÖ. In the SPÖ majority period, bills received 85% (XIII GP), 79% (XIV GP) and 75% (XV GP) unanimous support. Bills often received the support of either the ÖVP or the FPÖ. Only in the XV GP did a significant proportion (15%) of bills receive only SPÖ support.

In the Small Coalition, 80.1% obtained unanimous support. The influence of Parliament has been greatest on 'regulatory bills' and least on economic bills. Thus, 80% of Bills referred to the Trade Committee (Economic Affairs) remained unamended, whereas for the Education Committee the figure was 20% (XIII GP). Thus, the influence of Parliament is not negligible. The Nationalrat is another forum used for building and firming up consensus, a kind of second reading (after the broad preparatory consultation phases) within the executive and with the social partners.

The political parties in Parliament are a key element in the consensus building process. The process seeks consensus within the Klub and then between the Klubs. Almost 60% of Nationalrat members are civil servants or officials of 'Verbände', (that is organisations such as the Handelskammer, ÖGB, Landwirtschaftskammer or Arbeiterkammer). There is a close symbiosis between the Klubs and the organisations close to that particular party.

For the ÖVP, it will be members of the Handelskammer, or the ÖBB (the ÖVP Farmers Organisation) or the ÖAAB, the ÖVP 'Fraktion' (Group) in the Arbeiterkammer. For the SPÖ, it will be officials of the Arbeiterkammer of the ÖGB (Socialist group), cooperatives, state industries or party officials.

The FPÖ has only very small 'Fraktion' in the Arbeiterkammer. The FPÖ has larger ones, but still small, in the Handelskammer and Landwirtschaftskammer. Some of their Nationalrat members come from these Freiheitliche Fraktionen. The ÖVP and SPÖ also sponsor

other more specialised 'Verbände' for tenants, teachers and university lecturers, families, and so on. These bodies are also sources of
recruitment for Nationalrat members. In the ÖVP, electoral lists are
drawn up so as to respect 'proportz' between the three major
constituent organisations (ÖAAB, ÖBB, ÖWB). In the SPÖ, a set
proportion of winnable positions on the list go to the ÖGB-Socialist
group. Both parties allow for a Land and Bund Executive 'reserve'
(in the SPÖ, 20%) to place candidates which the party leadership
wants in the Nationalrat, such as 'independent' candidates for the
ÖVP in 1971. In the FPÖ, which has only a very weak local (Bezirk)
structure, lists are drawn up at the Land level subject to final
approval by the Bundesparteileitung (a mini convention).

In recent legislatures, as many as seventy-five members have been
direct-organisation or party officials. The most important symbol of
this close symbiosis was Anton Benya, the long-time Nationalrat
President (speaker) and ÖGB Chairman. The representatives of the
organisations also work closely with the Klub Committee sub-groups
to prepare the detailed legislative work in committee.

Klubs can be automatically formed by members (minimum five)
elected on the same list. Others can be formed only with the majority
approval of the Nationalrat. Floor crossing is rare and, indeed, has
not occurred at all in the Second Republic. Expulsions are also rare,
but there are examples such as Franz Olah, expelled from the SPÖ in
1964. He remained in the Nationalrat as an independent until 1966
and formed an independent party, but was not re-elected.

Klubs, and above all their leaders, dominate the work of parliament. Klub-Obmänner (chairs) work out committee seat allocations
on a rough proporz basis and each Klub-Obmann appoints 'his' own
contingent. The seats 'belong' to the Klub and would revert to it if a
member left or was expelled. Committee membership – those of
Finance, Public Works, or the Constitution being the most sought
after – is a disciplinary weapon in the hands of the leadership. The
Klub-Obmann is a member of the Präsidialkonferenz (with the
Nationalrat Speaker and his two deputies) which control the business
of the House and represents an important consensus building forum.
Klubs also decide which initiatives, questions, interpellations and
censure motions (when in opposition) to table and determine the
tactics to employ in response to other motions.

Formal sovereignty in each Klub belongs to the plenary Klub
meeting, and lengthy discussions sometimes occur in that forum,
especially in the FPÖ whose Klub has not had an Executive Committee (Vorstand) due to its small size. However, Klub decisions are

largely determined by the Klub leadership, composed of the Obmann and Vorstand, and then ratified by the plenary Klub meeting. The plenary Klub meetings take place before each Nationalrat sitting and once or twice each year in longer conclave strategy meetings. The plenary ratifies Vorstand proposals and receives reports from the Leader or Chancellor and other Federal Ministers, when in government, and from Committee Chairmen or spokesmen. Party Secretaries and press officers also attend, as do the members of the Party Executive (SPÖ) and (for the ÖVP) representatives of ÖVP Verbände. There are few voting sessions as decision-making is by consensus.

The Klub Obmann is now usually the Party leader. This was not always so, especially in the ÖVP and FPÖ. Recently, the posts were separated in the SPÖ as Chancellor Vranitzky was not, until 1988, Party Chairman. When this personal union does exist in the SPÖ, a 'working Klub-Obmann' is elected, on the proposal of the Party Executive. In the ÖVP, the Vice Chairmen represent the other two Verbände. The SPÖ Klub-Vorstand has about twenty members with several ex-officio members (Obmann, Party Leader, Whip, President or Vice-Presidents of the Nationalrat, Bundesrat Klub-Obmann, the Party Secretary). It meets before sittings to decide on proposals, amendments, tactics, speakers, etc. It makes appointments from the proposals of the Klub-Obmann. It works by consensus rather than a majority vote. The ÖVP Vorstand has about eighteen members, with a similar number of ex-officio members, and ten elected Nationalrat members chosen by the full Klub, but respecting the proportz between the organisations (three ÖBB, three ÖWB, four ÖAAB). Any ÖVP ministers are also ex-officio members. The FPÖ does not have a Klub-Vorstand as such, nor do the Greens.

The larger Klubs also organise their members in Committee Groups (Ausschussfraktionen) composed of the Klub's membership of a given Committee. These groups hear Ministers, officials of Ministries and representatives of the 'organisations' and prepare amendments and tactics in Committee and report to their Klub. In the ÖVP, appointments to Committee must respect the balance between the 'organisations'. However, the Social, Trade and Agriculture Committees follow a three-way party split between ÖAAB, ÖWB and ÖBB deputies. These 'Fraktionen' are very important and, perhaps, overshadow the full official Committees.

There are numerous contacts between Klub leaders even when there is no coalition. These take place in the more formal setting of the Committees, the Präsidialkonferenz and directly. When the

Grand Coalition ended, the need was felt for more, less-formalised, periodic discussions between the SPÖ and ÖVP leaderships, and those were often channelled through the Klubs. These talks, as well as the on-going contacts between the 'organisations' in the Social Partnership System, coalition or no, maintained the relationships and broad consensus between the parties and ensured that there was no dramatic increase in confrontation politics. As before, consensus was the first priority aim. Only where consensus proved unattainable at a reasonable price to all, was a conflictual, majority-against-opposition outcome accepted, reluctantly. The persistence of this consensus mentality throughout the period of one-party or Small Coalition government does much to explain the ease and, indeed, almost relief with which the Grand Coalition was revived in 1987, as if it was, in a certain way, the natural order of things.

Having looked at the various fora of consensus building (Cabinet, Coalition Committees, Parliament, with its Klubs and Committees and organisations – to which we shall revert in more detail in Chapter 6), we shall now turn to the key actors in all these processes, the political parties.

The Austrian party system is supposed to correspond to a three-lager structure of Austrian society, which has also represented a broader principle of social organisation, as in some other countries such as Belgium and The Netherlands. This has led analysts to describe its structure as 'verzuiling' and the resulting political processes as consensual. This had been a largely accurate view of Austrian society until the late 1960s, when the tight bonds of 'verzuiling' began to break down. In the First Republic there were three distinct and bitterly antagonistic lagers: the Socialist/Marxist Lager dominated by the SDAP (later the SPÖ), the Catholic Lager dominated by the Christlich Sozialpartei (later the core of the ÖVP) and the pan-Germanic Lager which contained two distinct trends: Austrian pan-Germanic Liberals and National Socialists. The Socialist block was more united, with only a small Communist Party (KPÖ) which did not threaten the dominance of the SDAP. The Conservative block was split into sharply antagonistic lagers and some periodic special interest parties (Peasants).

In the Second Republic, the SPÖ soon recovered total dominance of the Socialist Lager after a short period in 1945 when the KPÖ seemed to constitute a threat. The ÖVP rapidly assembled the old Catholic Lager, the farming vote and some of the former pan-

Germanic Conservatives who were not anticlerical. The almost 750,000 former Nazis were disenfranchised in 1945 and no party of the Third Lager was authorised at that election. An unholy alliance of some rightist industrialists and SPÖ tacticians pressed for, and obtained, the legalisation of a fourth party for the 1949 election. It was a rag bag, mostly dominated by former Nazis, running on the one touchstone issue for all the groups of the right: rehabilitation of former Nazis and the repeal of the de-Nazification legislation. Otherwise, the party had no clear ideological basis. The general programmatic thrust was close to national Socialist economic and social ideas without this, obviously, being explicitly stated. The party called the 'Wahlbund der Unabhängige' (WdU: but later the VdU) was successful beyond expectations with 489,273 votes (11.67% and sixteen seats and prevented the ÖVP from winning a second absolute majority. Yet, the party had not gathered much more than 60% of the potential, former Nazi vote, and had also taken some other votes. The integration of ex-Nazis was well underway and no long-term basis existed for a large or even medium-sized party based on the old pan-Germanic Lager. In the 1953 election the WdU vote stagnated (472,000 in a larger electorate – 10.95% and only fourteen seats) and fell back (by now it was named the FPÖ) to 192,000 votes (6.52% and six seats) by 1957. This was to remain the level of support of the FPÖ until the populist surge of 1986 when it achieved 472,000 votes (9.73%) and eighteen seats in the larger Nationalrat.

The KPÖ lingered as an unsubstantial minor party in the Nationalrat until 1959 when it lost its last three seats and fell back to 3.27% of the vote. From then on, its vote has been insignificant and has fallen below 1% in most elections. In 1986 it received 0.72% of the vote (or 5,104) mostly in Vienna, Niederösterreich and the Steiermark.

No new party emerged or sought to emerge until the arrival of the Greens/Alternatives in 1983. This movement has been beset by internal problems and splits and has not yet achieved a broad national structure or programme. The Green groupings both received significant votes in 1983, preventing either of them achieving representation in the Nationalrat at that election (3.3% in all). During the XVI GP (1983–86), the Greens gained seats in several Landtag elections and the Presidential election of 1986, where Mrs Meissner-Blau received 5.5% in the first ballot, was a launching pad for a more united campaign under her leadership in 1986. The list won 4.82% and eight seats. However, the Austrian Green party is by no means as solid a feature of the political landscape as the German Greens, and it remains to be seen if it will become a permanent, if unsubstantial, part of the Austrian political scene.

The party system can be described as a two or two-and-a-half party system. Even at elections, such as those in 1949 and 1986 where smaller parties succeed in achieving some impact, the two major parties still obtained over 80% of the vote and in 1986 retained 84.5%. In other elections their joint share has exceeded 90%. Even the populist Jörg Haider predicts that the two majors will together retain about 75% of the vote. In the first two decades of the Second Republic, the party system operated as a 'Konkordanz' or consensual model, with smaller parties excluded from political influence. The weight of the major parties relative to each other decided their leverage in the coalition. This gave way to a Konkurrenz or competitive model in the 1966-1983 period when absolute majorities either for the ÖVP or SPÖ parties were in reach. Now, few observers expect either party to be able to achieve an overall majority. Through the 1970s the SPÖ leadership under Dr Kreisky groomed the FPÖ to act as the additional balance-weight for the SPÖ, as it did in 1983. The logical evolution towards a German-style system with the small, third party performing a periodic 'Wende' to permit changes in government, was upset by the weakness of the ÖVP and the populist putsch in the FPÖ by which the Nationalist Jörg Haider wrested control from Vice Chancellor Norbert Steger (partly Jewish) and thus simultaneously broke the coalition with the SPÖ (returning the FPÖ to the political ghetto), and brought about the reconstruction of the Grand Coalition in 1987. Yet, as we have seen, it is not the same Grand Coalition as that of 1945–66. The political situation is much more fluid and open. The smaller parties are not inevitably or permanently excluded from all influence.

Down the road, an ÖVP–FPÖ coaliation is certainly possible, as some in the ÖVP already wanted in 1987. An SPÖ–FPÖ coalition also cannot be excluded for all time. The very moderate Austrian Greens could be a partner for the SPÖ, perhaps at first as an external supporter of a minority government. These are elements in the strategic calculations of the parties. Even now, the small parties exercise an indirect influence. The fact that ÖVP + FPÖ > SPÖ + Greens greatly weakened the negotiating hand of the SPÖ in the 1986 – 87 coalition negotiations and still does so within the coalition. The ÖVP has more strategic options, though it is smaller than the SPÖ in the Nationalrat. The aim of the SPÖ – and the polls point to this as realistic – is to remain larger than the ÖVP and to be in a parliamentary situation where SPÖ + Green > ÖVP + FPÖ and perhaps even where only ÖVP + FPÖ + Green > SPÖ. In that situation, the ÖVP could form no government without the SPÖ and the SPÖ could form alliances with the Greens or, on some issues, with the FPÖ against the ÖVP. A minority SPÖ Cabinet would be an option, or the Grand Coalition could continue. Within the present XVII GP, the 'Coalition free' areas can be an advantage to the ÖVP, as it can seek majorities with the FPÖ. This exerts pressure on the SPÖ, even where no actual use is made of this possibility. The ÖVP's goal is to retain the present parliamentary equation of ÖVP + FPÖ > SPÖ + Greens, but to exceed the SPÖ in size and see the FPÖ (a threat to the ÖVP for conservative voters) cut back. In such a situation, the ÖVP could claim the chancellorship (and hence the 'chancellor-effect') for its leader.

We shall turn now to look in more detail at the parties and their respective strategies. It would go well beyond the scope of this work to attempt a comprehensive history of the Austrian political parties. We shall attempt a profile of the parties, setting out their main characteristics and the differences between them, to develop a profile of them and their rôle in the political system.

Austria's largest party, the Sozialistische Partei Österreichs (SPÖ) is the pragmatic successor of the Sozialdemokratische Arbeiterpartei (SDAP), a Marxist–Socialist party that played a key rôle in the early period of the First Republic and was then suppressed in the civil war of 1934. The post-1945 party was an altogether more pragmatic animal, behind its facade of historical and ideological continuity. Much had been learnt by the old socialist leaders (like Karl Renner) and the 'new men' who emerged from the internal underground, and those who returned from exile such as Bruno Kreisky. The SPÖ has transformed itself from a party of the lager, confined in a political ghetto, into a broad church, capable of dominating Austrian politics and winning an absolute majority (as it did in 1975 and 1979), not only of seats but of votes as well, and emerging as the largest party (at least in votes) in eight out of thirteen elections as in every election since 1970. Some have argued that the SPÖ has become a mere centre-left 'Volkspartei', without clear ideological premises and principles. That would also be the criticism of the KPÖ, of the SPÖ's own small and uninfluential left wing as well as, from a different standpoint, of the Greens. However, the SPÖ and especially its supreme pragmatist Dr Kreisky, has denied this criticism and the

SPÖ attempted in its 1978 party programme (through the symposia and internal debates leading up to the adoption, in the Spring of 1986, of a new policy document 'Perspectives for the '90s'), to re-define its ideology and policy priorities in the light of its governmental experience and the new post-materialist thinking.

The SPÖ is a mainstream social democratic party which originated in the traditional worker's lager, but came to transcend it by broadening its base, to become Austria's only liberal and reformist party. Its success has been considerable. It has been uninterruptedly in government since 1945 (apart from the 1966-70 period), and has provided the Chancellor since 1970. It has achieved a vast reform programme in education, the legal system and health care, pursued an active and respected foreign policy, and kept unemployment and inflation low during the recession of the 1970s and the 1980s. It obtained an absolute majority of votes in 1975 and 1979, and remains the key to the political situation. Like the Swedish party, it has come near to becoming the natural party of government. As we shall see in our examination of party strategies, this has led the SPÖ to adopt considerable degrees of pragmatism and compromise which have made it very much a 'Staatstragende Partei'. Yet, it is still committed to the notion that in a mixed economy, there remains room for the predominance of politics over the market in the pursuit of the goals of the party, such as full employment or a strong public sector, as a balancing mechanism to the private sector. Most of its earlier objectives have been attained and yet there has been no fundamental transformation in Austrian society. The party is now faced with defining its mobilising objectives for the next generation (beyond a mere defence of its achievements and its strongly entrenched positions in all areas of Austrian public life and patronage distribution).

It has become and remains, like the ÖVP a mass membership party. Yet its structure is very centralised, in letter and even more in spirit. The party now has 698,000 members, more than the German SPD. Its peak membership was 727,265 in 1960. Its membership represents 30.6% of its electorate, exceedingly high by European standards, but much lower than the corresponding figure for the ÖVP. The degree of participation of members is usually low, but they are kept in contact with the party by the local 'Vertrauenspersonen' who collect dues. Many join a party merely to obtain the benefits of patronage, such as municipal housing or jobs. The Vienna SPÖ is dominant with 260,000 members. At its high point, Viennese members represented 43% of all members. Now Vienna (33%) and Lower

Austria (19.4%) are still dominant, but there has been some spread to other Länder: Oberösterreich (14.3%), Steiermark (14.3%), Kärnten (7.1%). Women represent 34% of members, and workers 31% as against 44% in 1960. The membership is also ageing: 18% are now pensioners, as against 11.5% in 1960, a trend that is set to continue.

In the SPÖ electorate, the share of workers is 30% (1986) as against 34% (in 1979) and 25% white collar workers and staff in 1986 as against 17% in 1979. The share of pensioners has risen from 25% in 1979 to 31% in 1986. These figures are a confirmation of trends that began in the 1960s, with the SPÖ becoming a much broader party, with some significant support in all social groups. In 1969, 68% of the SPÖ electorate was still composed of workers. The main areas of voting strength of the SPÖ are to be found (1986) in Vienna (52.4%), Burgenland (49%), Kärnten (47.2%), Steiermark (44.1%), Oberösterreich (42.4%) and Niederösterreich (42.1%). At its peak, in 1979, with 51.03% of the vote nationally, the SPÖ obtained an absolute majority in five Länder: Vienna (60.61%), Kärnten (56.23%), Steiermark (51.57%), Oberösterreich (50.25%) and Burgenland (52.95%). The SPÖ has also tended to do better in Land elections in these strongholds such as Vienna where, for example, it obtained 55.52% in 1985 and 54.92% in 1987 – above its Nationalrat performances. The same has been true in Steiermark, Kärnten and Burgenland. The SPÖ's vote has remained relatively stable over time. Only the elections of 1966 and 1970 saw very large direct losses and gains to the ÖVP. In the 1970-86 period its vote remained in the 43% (1986) – 51% range. In 1986, the SPÖ lost votes principally to the ÖVP (120,000 or + – 5% of its 1983 electorate) and gained some 60% from the ÖVP. It lost 130,000 votes to the FPÖ and about 50,000 to the Greens.

The SPÖ is deeply implanted in Austrian public life, at all levels, including the Federal where, until 1986, it always held the Presidency and, since 1970, the Chancellorship. Before 1966, it held the Vice Chancellorship and key Ministries such as Social Affairs and State Industries (as well as Foreign Affairs), for a considerable period. It provides the Landeshauptmann in three Länder, including Vienna. It has been present in all the Landtage since 1945 and in all the Land administrations since the war. It has been present in all but the most rural local authorities. Its 'faction' dominates the ÖGB and the Arbeiterkammer. It has a minority representation in the Landwirtschaftskammer and the Wirtschaftskammer. The proporz agreements have ensured its representation on the boards of the State

Industries. The party bears a deep responsibility for the governance of the Second Republic. It is no longer, as the First Republic, 'their' state. It rapidly abandoned its continual support for the Anschluss that had been a bone of contention among the exiled SPÖ politicians. Indeed, through the person of Karl Renner, first Chancellor of the Second Republic and then its first President, the party was, from the first, closely associated with the new State and prepared to make compromises in the interests of reconstruction.

The SPÖ was formed in 1945 as a fusion of the old SDAP and the small Revolutionary Socialists' party, on the basis of the 1926 Linz programme that combined Marxist and revolutionary strategies with more pragmatic democratic approaches (with a considerable degree of contradiction, which enabled this platform to be ignored in the reality of political and governmental life). However, there was no clear, new start in 1945. Continuity of organisation and personnel was the watchword, especially where (as in Vienna, Niederösterreich and the industrial areas of the Steiermark), the old pre-1934 structure was still intact and able to emerge from the underground. The 'new' men in Austria itself, associated with Karl Renner, were on the moderate pragmatic wing rather than following the more radical line of the pre-war leadership under Otto Bauer, who died in exile in 1938. This wing rapidly adopted coalition politics and abandoned the old uncompromising oppositional tactics. The new leadership was also strongly anti-Communist and democratic in outlook. Despite not preventing an ÖVP absolute majority, the new-look SPÖ gained ground in the first elections in November 1945 and was virtually equal (at times larger in votes) in size to the ÖVP throughout the years of the Grand Coalition.

It is a party with strong and long-serving leaders, with power located in the government leadership, not in the party organisation. Until the election of Bruno Kreisky in 1967, the party was dominated by the traditional Viennese organisation, heir to the pre-war 'Rathaussozialismus'. The party has only had five leaders since the war: Adolf Schärf (1945–57), Bruno Pitterman (1957–67), Bruno Kreisky (1967–83), Fred Sinowatz (1983–88) and Franz Vranitzky, the present leader.

In terms of organisation, the party remained very traditional. However, especially in the 1970s, real power left the party apparatus, which was reduced to an administrative – rather than a policy-making rôle. The basic unit of organisation is the 3000 or so Ortsorganisationen, where the Vertrauenspersonen are actively keeping in contact with membership. The Land parties are important, having a structure of their own, which include a functioning Executive and an annual Conference (Landesparteitag). At the Federal level, there is a Parteirat (Council) which forms a mini-conference, elects a fifty-four member Executive (Vorstand) composed of forty-four representatives of the Land parties and ten ex-officio members. This body chooses the eight member inner Executive (the Präsidium) which wields real power in the party together with the SPÖ–Klub (parliamentary party). It is the Parteirat, at Federal level or Land level, which approves candidates for election, especially for the 'Federal reserve' places on electoral lists.

An essential feature of the party organisation is the plethora of auxiliary bodies associated with the party: the Socialist fraktion in the Arbeiterkammer and in the ÖGB, the Socialist fraktions in the individual unions, the Freie Wirschaftsverein (the Socialist fraktion in the Handelskammer), the Socialist Agricultural Organisation, cooperatives, Bund Sozialistischer Akademiker (BSA) (for sympathisers in the universities and professions (15,000 members)), the Pensioners Association, the Sportsverein and a myriad of leisure bodies. All of these organisations, perhaps, no longer represent a 'cocoon', a separate party world, as they once did, but they extend the party's network and bring it vital contacts and expertise on which to build its policies. The party is now looking for new ways of opening its ranks and making party work less of a closed circle understandable only to a group of initiates. The SPÖ is seeking to open the party as Dr Kreisky did the SPÖ electorate in the 1970.

Until the adoption of the new programme in 1958, the 1926 Linz programme remained the official programme, though a 1947 Action programme had already established the party as clearly democratic and reformist, though committed to planning and to a large public sector. The new programme was a compromise between left and right, but in practice, enabled the leadership to continue its support for a mixed economy, tempered by intervention in the public interest. The elimination of the party's Marxist baggage was not yet completed and the new 'third way' was too indistinct when the 1966 election came. The ÖVP won an absolute majority and the Grand Coalition could not be continued.

In opposition, a process of renewal was undertaken. Dr Kreisky was elected leader in 1967 by 347 votes out of 497. The trade unions and the Vienna organisation were hostile, but he won the support of the other Länder. He initiated an intense period of policy review, based on the need to modernise and democratise Austria in all spheres. He mobilised non-party experts and created a new air of dynamism, determination and excitement: the so-called 'Genosse-trend'. The SPÖ was to be the party of the future, of the successful. These new policies offered concrete and effective alternatives to the ÖVP policies over wide areas. They bore the stamp of Dr Kreisky's pragmatic, liberal humanism, capable therefore of attracting support from well outside the ranks of the traditional socialist voters – the post-materialists and the new rising generation. Together, these groups formed the basis of the extraordinary SPÖ electoral successes in the 1970–85 period. Yet, the composition of the SPÖ electoral majority was a limitation on its freedom of action: the SPÖ's 51% was a broad coalition, not a mandate for radical change. Despite far-reaching reforms of the penal code, of abortion law, of the education system, of health care, social provision and an active foreign policy as well as strongly interventionist economic policies to correct the market, the SPÖ government sought, and by-and-large obtained, broad compromise on its reforms.

Now, with the general neo-conservative swell of opinion, the recession, and the loss of its absolute majority, the party has been placed on the defensive. First in the Small Coalition with the FPÖ and even more in the Grand Coalition, its reform programme had to be limited in the interests of compromise. Even without the con-straints of coalition, the party was running out of steam and needed to recharge its intellectual and political batteries. Some might argue that this could best be done in opposition, as in 1966–70, but that is neither a viable nor a responsible position for the largest party in Austria. The SPÖ, so heavily identified with recent policy, cannot merely 'escape' into opposition. In that sense, there is no serious political alternative to the Grand Coalition, but that fact does not mean that the party can dispense with the vital exercises of renewal in organisation, policy and strategy.

If the later period of the Second Republic has been dominated by the SPÖ, it was the ÖVP that held the dominant place in the first twenty-five years. It was in government, in coalition or alone, from 1945–70 and provided the first four chancellors, excluding of course the head of the Provisional Government, Karl Renner (SPÖ). The ÖVP was either the majority party or the largest party in the Nationalrat throughout this period, though it never equalled the feat of the SPÖ in obtaining a majority in votes, even in 1970. The ÖVP was formed immediately after the war as a broad-based centre-right grouping including both Catholic, Conservative and Peasant elements. For example, in the Steiermark, the party always had a less clear Catholic image. The foundations were already laid in 1944 in discussions led by the first ÖVP Chancellor Leopold Figl. The party took over many of the ideas and personnel of the Christian Social Party but deliberately sought to become a new and broader party. It was formally founded on 17 April 1945 and completed its organisation and a short fifteen-point platform by September 1945. The new party was built up from three basic organisations and its membership was indirect and through membership of one of these organisations. The three pillars were the Österreichische Arbeiter und Angestellten Bund (ÖAAB, the party's trade union wing), the Österreichische Wirtschaftsbund (ÖB, the economic/industrial wing), and the Österreichische Bauern Bund (ÖBB, the farmers organisation). These organisations have their own independent existence operating as 'parties' in their respective Kammer elections, and are represented at all levels within the party on a carefully balanced proportional basis.

The same balance is maintained in candidate lists, in the Cabinet and in ÖVP representation in Committees of the Nationalrat and other public bodies. Thus the post of Agriculture minister 'belongs' to the ÖVP and with it to the ÖBB. At the same time, the party has, from its foundation, had a tendency to accord wide autonomy to the Land parties and enable them to develop in their own images. Thus, the central party leadership was doubly weak, balanced as it was between organisations and the region. The party was able to develop and maintain a virtual monopoly of the Conservative, Liberal, Catholic and Peasant electorate. No competing parties emerged for the old lager. Yet, the ÖVP's very advantage, in terms of its broad based confederal structure, became a liability and reduced the flexibility of the party. Each Bünd, had, in the case of the ÖAAB and ÖBB, preceded the founding of the party, and the ÖWB came soon after. These organisations were 'overmighty' and came into conflict. The ÖAAB viewpoint was often in conflict with the ÖWB and the ÖBB. It was difficult for the party to define a clear line in economic policy. The social-market policy (known as the Raab–Kamitz Kurs) could not be as consistently followed as in Germany, as periodic populist or protectionist/monopolist tendencies emerged and those factions, in alliance with the SPÖ coalition partner, obtained temporary sway.

The party introduced structural reforms in its organisations in 1972 and 1980, which were designed to strengthen the central party-leadership (the Bundesparteiobmann, General Secretary and the Executive) against the component organisations and the Länder parties. The party became less confederal. The number of component organisations was extended to include the Österreichische Frauen-bund (ÖFB, the women's organisation), Youth (the Junge Volks-partei, JVP), and Pensioners (the Österreichische Seniorenbund, ÖSB). The principle of direct membership was also admitted for the first time. The party had nine leaders, rotating from the different organisations. The internal personal battles and conflicts over stra-tegy have largely been fights between the component groupings. It was, indeed, hard to hold the party together after the dramatic loss of power in 1970.

Like the SPÖ, the ÖVP is a mass membership party. Indeed, it probably has more members than the SPÖ. There are problems of double membership in several organisations. In 1986, the party had 1,168,221 members through its various component organisations. Eliminating double membership, 34.37% come from the ÖBB, 23.7% from the ÖAAB, 13.6% from the ÖWB, 13.38% from the ÖSB, 9.8% from the JVP, 6.66% from the ÖFB. 0.27% were direct members (a mere 3,168 but up from 361 in 1980). Of the ÖAAB membership about 40% come from the public sector. The member-ship was larger (approximately 750,000) in 1980. The ÖVP factions dominate the Landwirtschaftskammer (84.3% in 1985) and the Handelskammer (84%) and represent a respectable minority (36%) in the Arbeiter Kammertag. Like the SPÖ, the party recognises a range of 'associate' organisations (Österreichische Akademiker Bund, Österreichische Mieter, Siedler und Wohneigentumsbund (Housing)). The party also has a research and educational academy, as do the other parties. Membership is concentrated in Niederösterreich (39.8%), Oberösterreich (20.0%), Steiermark (15.2%). Vienna only provides 6.6% of membership. Membership represents a very high 42% of the party's vote. The total membership considerably exceeds that of the German CDU.

ÖVP voters are, by occupation, 14% workers (25% in 1973), 9% farmers (35% in 1969, 23% in 1973), 26% from independent profes-sionals (16% in 1973), 22% employees (34% in 1975). The largest group is pensioners (30%). Whereas more men voted for the SPÖ an exactly equal proportion of men and women (43%) voted SPÖ and ÖVP in 1986. For a conservative Catholic party that is, of course, an unusually low share of the female vote. The vote is most concentrated in the Western provinces and Niederösterreich, but the ÖVP is a 'people's party' with strength in almost all areas and in all professional groups and classes. In 1986, the party exchanged votes with the SPÖ gaining 120,000 and losing 60,000. It lost 130,000 votes to the FPÖ, but gained some 50,000 1983 FPÖ votes. It gained some 1983 Green voters but lost more to the Greens. Its overall share fell by 1.9% from 43.2% in 1983 to 41.3% in 1986, its second worst result in the Second Republic.

Given the ÖVP's nature as, initially, a composite block of local and organisational baronies, it has been very difficult to create a modern national party. The formal structures are there, but old habits and mentalities change very slowly. The party is organised at Gemeinde (province/borough), Bezirk (district), Land and Federal level. In theory, the structure is federal, with the subsidiarity principle, of responsibility being assumed at the lowest appropriate level. Each level has its own statutes. Each level has a parallel structure: an Obmann (leader), Deputy leader and Secretariat, an Executive elected by the Parteitag (conference), a Parteileitung (mini-Parteitag) elected by the Parteitag and a Parteitag meeting annually or every two years. At all levels above the Gemeinde, the Parteitag is a delegate body. Reality criss-crosses this neat structure: the Land parties are often very independent and national leadership involves itself in almost all issues: the corporatist origins of the party remain more powerful than the formal structure.

Policy issues have been even more delicate than the organisational problems. The ÖVP is a fragile plant and its unity has at times been precarious. Policy must of necessity be applied with a broad brush and general. The party is a 'Volkspartei', open to all areas of society. Inevitably, that has engendered a degree of pragmatism and fuzziness in policy formulation, and until the 1970s, a tendency to avoid detailed programmatic declarations. People knew what the ÖVP was; that was enough. It stood for reconstruction, for the Austrian State, for opposition to Communism and for the defence of the mixed economy against too much socialism. It was, above all, pragmatic and moderate. Policy-making was also the art of balance between the diverse interests making up the ÖVP, which in itself made for prudence, and moderation and inflexibility. Yet, ironically it was the ÖVP that began the trend of 'modernisation' in 1966, that was to overwhelm it later.

Thus it was not until 1972 that the ÖVP adopted a Programme – the Salzburg Programme – which is still in force today. It is a long term programme of broad principles: individual freedom, solidarity and independence, quality of life and efficiency and participation. On this basis more detailed manifestos such as the Zukunfts-manifest (Future Manifesto, 1985) have been issued. The party has been influenced by the neo-conservative wave from abroad and has some sympathy with these ideas, but cannot fully espouse them as they would split the party and appear too extreme for Austrian conditions. This may explain their reluctance to consider a coalition with the FPÖ which would, on the face of it, offer more chance of achieving the full-blooded 'Wende' that the ÖVP appears to want yet lacks the courage to espouse openly. The party claims, with reason, to have achieved over 80% of its aims in the coalition negotiations with the SPÖ. Yet the party remains behind in the polls and is seen as weaker than the SPÖ by public opinion. The ÖVP seems at home in a Grand Coalition, able to govern with a broad majority and able to go a long way in carrying through the ÖVP's priorities, albeit mitigated by the SPÖ. What are those priorities? They are: less State and more market; more choice; more flexibility in the economy; more direct democracy; lower taxes and some privatisation. Yet all these themes are to be pursued moderately and gradually. The ÖVP sees itself as a responsible party with a rôle to play in ensuring the stability of the State. It is therefore prepared to gamble that its voters who wanted change will remain patient. The Grand Coalition remains the best and perhaps the only way to achieve lasting reforms. For the ÖVP, Europe and a rapid full membership of the EC is vital as a goal, which can mobilise Austria to become more market orientated and competitive to prepare for membership. For most in the party, neutrality is not seen as a real obstacle and no Soviet veto is expected or accepted. EC membership is seen as the key political theme of the next decade. The ÖVP sees itself as a resolutely modern, European and moderate party, responsive to popular opinion and responsible in its approach.

The ÖVP has always had problems of leadership, with successive leaders tending to become 'burned out', and with its identity as a moderate conservative party. In the period before the formation of the Grand Coalition in 1987, the party had seemed to espouse a more populist neo-liberal position and for a significant part of its electorate, the Waldheim election and the later Nationalrat election in 1986 were seen as an opportunity to break the SPÖ power monopoly and end the policies associated with SPÖ government. In the coalition, the ÖVP has obtained a considerable part of its goals (the figure of 80% has been advanced), but it has been forced to compromise and adopt a moderate coalition style, rather than a populist, rhetorical approach. It has not been effective at selling its achievements in government. Though the SPÖ has sacrificed most in the coalition, was on the defensive in 1986 and has suffered from recurrent scandals, it is the ÖVP which has taken the severest losses in the Landtage elections in Lower Austria, Salzburg, Voralberg and above all Kärnten where, in March 1989, it fell back into third place. It is the ÖVP that has seemed to be weak and has often backed down in conflict with its partner.

The continuing electoral haemorrhage to the FPÖ made the change of leadership inevitable. Vice Chancellor Mock, leader since 1979, was no longer sure of obtaining the two-thirds majority required for a fourth term as Bundesparteiobmann. Thus Agriculture Minister Riegler became leader at the May 1989 Congress. This was no doubt necessary, but in itself did little to resolve the ÖVP's identity problems. It still has to develop a sharper policy profile, and update the 1972 Salzburg Programme, and must choose a strategy in relation to the threat of the FPÖ. Should it continue in the Grand Coalition until the elections? Beyond the elections? Should it consider a 'small coalition' with the FPÖ? The change of leader, (though he personally is more opposed to the FPÖ than Alois Mock), the election of Jörg Haider to the post of Landeshauptmann in Kärnten in May 1989, (with ÖVP votes), which would thus make it possible for a less controversial figure, such as former Secretary General Guggebauer, to lead the FPÖ at national level, may make an ÖVP/FPÖ coalition more likely.

One of the most serious criticisms of the old Grand Coalition was the absence of a significant opposition. This fact was made more serious by the *modus operandi* of the coalition which tended, certainly in its last phase, to stifle debate and criticism from within its own ranks, and was conducive to paralysis since it had run out of steam. The new Grand Coalition is, as we have seen, more open, and Parliament is more lively than under the former Grand Coalition. In this Legislature, there is opposition; indeed it is more correct to speak of 'oppositions' as the FPÖ and Grünen (Greens) do not constitute a united front, although as small opposition groupings they do have some interests (but not standpoints), in common. In the present situation where there is no external pressure to maintain the Grand Coalition, where other formulae have been tried including both minority government, Small Coalitions and one-party rule, and where voter mobility has totally broken down the lager mentality and hence the former 'Stammwählerschaft' (permanent electorate which could be taken for granted), opposition can be a much more potent force. Options and strategies are much more open and electoral outcomes much more uncertain. In the former coalition period, the WdU and then the FPÖ were small groups with no growth potential, no clear policy and no meaningful political strategy, beyond rehabilitation of the former Nazis and, later, entry in the citadel of political respectability, which also depended on the strategies of other parties, notably the SPÖ.

The populist FPÖ under Jörg Haider has a message of populist taxpayers revolt, anti-Statism and nationalism that has an appeal to voters well beyond the ranks of immediate FPÖ voters. Jörg Haider has a strategy: to render the Grand Coalition impossible to manage and create a clear, rightward 'Wende' in the ÖVP, making possible the creation of a clear conservative block, as an alternative to Socialism and to centrist compromise. The FPÖ threatens the ÖVP on its right flank and can create internal party debate less in favour of the FPÖ cooperation with it (though that strategy has its adepts), than for the more conservative stance that it embodies. The so-called economic wing of the ÖVP is influenced by neo-Thatcherite privatisation and de-regulation ideology, in which the FPÖ could be an ally. *Ad-hoc* cooperation with the FPÖ in the 'coalition free' area is also an option, which is still consistent with the general ÖVP distaste for Jörg Haider's 'irresponsibility'. The Grünen represent a second opposition, even smaller than the FPÖ. Again, they have a greater potential support and on many issues can find common ground with the FPÖ and segments of the SPÖ. As a more moderate and more classical political force than the German Greens, they have integrated relatively easily into the Nationalrat. Their aim is to develop a Green programme and Green alternatives to put pressure on the SPÖ, from whom they could gain voters, though the evidence is that Green voters have been drawn from all over the voting spectrum. Thus there are two lively and different opposition forces, both of which must be taken seriously by the coalition parties.

As we have seen, the WdU and subsequently the FPÖ were born out of the remnants of the Third Lager, the pan-Germanic Lager. The party has from the outset been an amalgam of diverse, competing and often contradictory tendencies which have alternated in controlling the party. Apart from its function as a pressure group for the former Nazis, which function was becoming redundant as early as 1949 when the party was formed, one can, at the risk of considerable but useful over-simplification, speak of oscillations between 'national' and 'liberal' poles, corresponding to different periods in the party's strategic development. Both of these terms are not unambiguous and are in themselves broad churches.

The party was founded in 1949 by two non-Nazi German Nationalists Dr Herbert Kraus and Viktor Reiman, both journalists in Salzburg, a key centre of nationalism. It brought together old Nazis, both those returning from the war and those expelled from former German areas in Eastern Europe. The party did not break-through in rural areas because the former Peasants political organisations were taken into the ÖVP. The party was therefore an urban party and even obtained a significant working class base at the Voest works in Linz, Vienna and Salzburg.

From the start, there were different tones in the leadership. The Kraus-Reiman group sought to develop the WdU as an anti-coalition and anti-proporz third force and yet work within the system, cooperating after the 1953 elections with the ÖVP after supporting the ÖVP candidate in the second round of the 1951 Presidential election. Fritz Stüber, the Vienna leader, opposed this moderate line and was eventually expelled in 1953, but he damaged the leadership. Internal pressure lead to the resignation of Kraus in 1952 and his replacement by the more conservative and nationalist Dr Stendebach who led the party until its fusion with the Freiheitliche Partei in 1956. This party had been formed in 1955 by Anton Reinthaller (the Nazi Agriculture Minister in the short-lived Seyss-Inquart Cabinet in March 1938), as a renewal of the National Lager.

After lengthy negotiations the FP and the WdU merged as the Freiheitliche Partei Österreichs (FPÖ). The founders of the WdU, Kraus and Reiman, refused to join, though most WdU members did so. On his death in 1958, Reinthaller was replaced as leader by Friedrich Peter, a former SS-man and member of an Einsatz-Kommando. He at first continued the old nostalgic line, but from his firm Nazi base, which inspired the confidence of the hard-line membership, he steered the party on a more middle course, which, though it did not increase its electoral strength, did increase its political influence.

The party entered its first liberal phase. As the Grand Coalition ended, new opportunities emerged for the new-style FPÖ. At first it flirted with the ÖVP, then supported the Kreisky minority cabinet, voting for its budget. Peter was defended by the prestigious and Jewish Chancellor Kreisky. Links with the SPÖ had begun earlier in their common opposition to the return of Dr Otto von Habsburg in

1963 and the strange diversion of trade union funds to the FPÖ by Franz Olah (the rightist SPÖ trade union leader), repudiated at the time by his party. The FPÖ was rewarded with an electoral reform in 1970 increasing the proportionality of the system. Dr Peter became a Vice Chairman of the Nationalrat and the FPÖ gave periodic support to SPÖ proposals.

A small coalition was already mooted in 1975 and was carefully prepared by Dr Kreisky in 1983 when the SPÖ lost its absolute majority. Meanwhile the fractious FPÖ leadership shifted to the right as its support declined and the party base propelled Alexander Götz, mayor of Graz (with ÖVP support) into the leadership. He attacked the SPÖ, but failed to dent their majority in 1979 and could only increase the party's share of the vote by 0.5%. His indecision over whether to remain mayor of Graz, his challenge to Dr Peter as Parliamentary leader as well as his poor leadership, led to dissatisfaction and his eventual surprise resignation. A young Viennese intellectual (born in 1944 and partly Jewish) from the new liberal wing and a social liberal, Dr Norbert Steger was narrowly elected in 1980 against the candidate of the National Wing, Harold Ofner. The party swung back on a more liberal line and the ground was prepared for the small SPÖ–FPÖ coalition in 1983, in which – showing the fine balance illustrated by the election result for Dr Steger – both Dr Steger (Vice Chancellor) and Dr Ofner (Justice Minister) served. The FPÖ was much the weaker partner and obtained only limited policy concessions while lacking government experience.

The government was weak, scandal ridden (Androsch, glycol in wine, Waldheim, ...) and indecisive. The FPÖ Defence Minister Frischenschläger made the double error of formally receiving former SS-man Reder on his return from an Italian prison, and then retracting. He satisfied no one in his party or wider public opinion.

The FPÖ had declined to a low point in the 1983 Nationalrat elections (4.98%) and later the Landtag elections showed no upturn: on the contrary (Oberösterreich, 1.5%; Salzburg, 4.5%; Steiermark, 0.5%; Tirol, 0.6%; Vorarlberg, 2.0%. Only in Kärnten, where Jörg Haider led a populist anti-Vienna line, did the party progress (+ 4.3%). The message was clear. The FPÖ faced political extinction unless it acted. Despite the adoption by unanimous vote of a new programme in 1985, which was true to the liberal and responsible image of a government party, a new conservative nationalist revolt was brewing. It found its standard bearer in the young dynamic Kärnten leader Jörg Haider (34) and erupted at the rowdy Congress of September 1986. Haider stood against Vice Chancellor Steger for the leadership and all attempts to find a compromise candidate failed. In a dramatic vote, with strong nationalist and anti-Semitic overtones, Haider defeated Steger with 57.7% to 39.2% of the vote.

What is the substance of the FPÖ and where does it draw its support from? The party remains balanced between a Deutsch-National party and a liberal party. That is most evident in its general political philosophy, but also in its economic positions. The early period emphasised the semi-corporatist, anti-modernist philosophy of the National Socialists and (more widely) of the Deutsch-National Lager. The party opposed the creation of an Austrian State and only reluctantly voted for the State Treaty. Successive programmes have referred to membership in a broader Germanic Community, even though the 1985 programme clearly recognises the nation's Austrian identity. The basic values of the party are now individual freedom and enterprise, the social market economy and support for Austrian membership of the European Community, which has replaced the Anschluss as a broader destiny – but ambiguities remain. The FPÖ stands for a 'success culture' rewarding an active and dynamic elite, which, in its view, creates progress. These developments towards a more modern ideology were seeded by the 'Attersee Circle', a pressure group for social liberalism in the party, from which Norbert Steger came to the leadership. Consistent with its historical roots, the party is a 'green party' supporting the ecological movement and opposed to soulless growth. It has also opposed nuclear power, as symbolic of that growth-at-any-price philosophy.

This modern development towards a form of social liberalism that would have been characteristic of main-stream European Liberal parties such as the FDP had it proceeded, has now come to a stop. The new FPÖ has become more nationalistic, more populist and more chauvinist. It opposes immigration and builds on antipathy towards immigrants, where the 1985 programme merely spoke against their integration. It has espoused the even more modern neo-conservative anti-Statist theories of privatisation and de-regulation and opposition to consensus.

It is therefore a demagogic and at times turbulent, but essentially irresponsible opposition. It seems to feel that the previous strategies developed in the period 1970–83 to groom the party for government, (for that was the central goal of Dr Peter and Dr Steger, with a view to gain a real political influence for what was otherwise a very small and seemingly declining party), have failed and required a radical antidote.

The FPÖ electorate is found in small towns, among self-employed and intellectual professions and older voters. Regionally it has been most successful in the traditional areas of German nationalism and post 1945 influx of Volksdeutschen: Salzburg, Kärnten, Steiermark and parts of Oberösterreich. In 1979 the FPÖ's best results were in Kärnten (10.0%), Salzburg (11.5%) Vorarlberg (10.7%). In 1983 its best results were still in Kärnten (10.7%, its only gain), Salzburg (8.0%), Vorarlberg (7.2%). By 1986, it could boast of significant results in several Länder: Kärnten (20.9%), Salzburg (15.9%), Vorarlberg (11.9%). In 1979, the FPÖ made significant gains from the ÖVP, but made a net loss to the SPÖ. At the 1983 election, the FPÖ made gains from the SPÖ, but lost to the ÖVP and Green lists, especially in Vienna, where only 39.6% of the party's 1979 electorate voted for it again. In 1986, it gained from both parties, but only held two-thirds of its 1983 votes, losing 19% to the ÖVP, though of course its net exchange with that party was very positive. The party's electorate is therefore constantly changing.

The FPÖ had entered a new nationalist phase and cashed-in the general alienation from the other parties, increasing its vote from a low of 4.98% to a new-high of 9.75% in the 1986 election, provoked by Haider's election as leader. The new leadership has different and much more combative points of view. It distances itself from the 1985 moderate platform, which is reduced to a long-term document. Consensus is opposed, as perpetuating outdated structures and consolidating the hold of outdated process and concepts on decision-making. Jörg Haider seeks to redefine these structures – in relation to such issues as social partnership, social security, taxation, state industries, privatisation, de-regulation. The aim is to control the government, draw in the new populist interests and, by the process of conflict, create a new climate in which the FPÖ could climb to about 20% of the vote, to put extreme pressure on the ÖVP to have the courage to form a conservative coalition. For Haider the failure of the Grand Coalition is inevitable and will create this new climate, if the alternatives are clearly and aggressively spelled out by the FPÖ.

The most recent developments – a series of electoral victories for the FPÖ in Landtag elections (Lower Austria, in September 1988; Voralberg, Salzberg and Kärnten in March 1989); and Jörg Haider's subsequent election to the post of Landeshauptmann in Kaernten – have tended to confirm that Haider's strategy was correct in-so-far as it went. The doubts of the more thoughtful and perhaps liberal members of the FPÖ remain as to where this approach is taking the party in the longer term. The very success of the FPÖ may cement the Grand Coalition for a new term. It is by no means certain that a coalition with the ÖVP would be good for the FPÖ in the longer term. The FPÖ's growth, based on populism and a floating electorate, can melt away. Austria has a tendency to favour stability and caution. The FPÖ has gone through previous cycles of rise and fall and of alternating liberalism and nationalism, which cycle can recur. Should a more moderate leadership, at least in Vienna, take charge and engineer a coalition either with the ÖVP or (yes, it is possible) with the SPÖ, the party system would be opened up considerably and Austria would move towards a more genuinely multi-party system. At this point, the FPÖ would have to abandon its anti-system tendencies. Does it wish to make this transformation? This is not at all clear.

The second opposition grouping is also in a phase of development and change, which makes evaluation uncertain. The Austrian Greens are not the German Greens. Their movement is weaker, less deep-rooted and more moderate than the Germans. Their future is uncertain, as they have no monopolistic lock on the green issues and they can as yet claim no permanent place in the political spectrum. In neutral and non-nuclear Austria (since the 1978 referendum), the emotional issues of peace and nuclear safety are less significant than in the Federal Republic. The Greens grew out of the various grass-roots movements of peace, women's rights, and the environment, and moved on to seek a degree of political expression. The post-1968 movement and the opening up of Austrian society during the Kreisky era created the pre-conditions for the movement and by the mid-1970s, several 'Burger-Initiativen' (Socialist moderates) and Alternative groups (radicals) were in operation in Vienna, Graz and Salzburg. It was a series of particular events: the Zwentendorf nuclear reactor referendum in 1978, the Hainburg reactor project in 1985 and the Waldheim election that gave the movement successive new impulses and took it into the political arena. Yet its progress has not been easy and has been fraught with conflict, divisions and splits. Even now, the Greens are still both organisationally and programmatically weak, and represent an amalgam of unassimilated tendencies.

In the late 1960s, the construction of Austria's first and only nuclear reactor had been authorised at Zwentendorf a mere forty kilometres from Vienna. By 1978 it was ready to go on-stream, but opposition was building up, from the FPÖ, in the Vorarlberg SPÖ, in the SPÖ Youth Movement, in sections of the ÖVP and through a well organised anti-nuclear lobby under the umbrella of the Initiative Österreichischer Atomkraft Gegner (IOAG) set up in 1976. With the vacillation of ÖVP leader Taus, the SPÖ faced the possibility of trying to push the legislation through alone, without a typically Austrian consensus. Yet, the leadership and the trade unions did not want to abandon the project. It was decided to hold a referendum. In the face of mounting opposition, Dr Kreisky sought to make the vote a matter of confidence in his government. This was a two-edged sword in a close vote (the government lost by a mere 30,000 votes). No doubt the 'yes' campaign was firmed up in Vienna, Burgenland, Kärnten, Steiermark and Lower Austria, in Eastern Austria where the SPÖ is strong, but given ÖVP opposition and the confidence issue, the black Western Provinces voted massively 'no' (Vorarlberg 84.4% 'no'; Salzburg 56.8% 'no'; Tirol 65.8% 'no'). The overall result was a close 50.5% 'no' and a major boost for the Green movement. Early Green lists tested the voters in Vienna and Niederösterreich in 1979 Land elections, but obtained less than 1% of the vote. More locally, Bürgerlisten, with Green characteristics, had achieved remarkable success in Salzburg and Graz.

It was a second power station, this time non-nuclear, which was to provide the second major push to the movement, after its relative failure in the 1983 election. Opinion polls showed that concern about the environment had climbed from 52% of voters in 1979 to 71% by 1983. Polls also showed a hard core of Green post-materialists of about 150,000–200,000 voters. These were, on balance, more conservative than the German Greens. Among new voters, as many as 14% (and among graduates up to 15%) indicated Green sympathies. They were drawn from SPÖ voters and ÖVP voters equally (30%), FPÖ voters (15%) and non-voters (25%). In Salzburg and Graz, Green voters came mostly from the conservative parties: in Vienna from the SPÖ. The two Green parties only began to develop their organisations in early 1983. The moderate, central VGÖ and more radical ALÖ both had internal problems and failed to unite. Neither obtained any seats, through the VGÖ came close to a Grundmandat in Vienna. Between them they obtained 3.3% of the votes. In Salzburg, they obtained 6.3% and in Graz and Vienna (inner city) 5.9%. These results perhaps cost the SPÖ its overall majority but this is not certain as Green votes come almost equally from the ÖVP and FPÖ as from the SPÖ. The Green Movement had made an uncertain start in electoral politics.

Then came Hainburg. The Donau Kraftwerk AG sought permission to build a hydraulic power station on the Danube in the nature reserve near the Czech border at Hainburg. After various legal processes at both Federal and Land level, the way was cleared. Both the government and the social partners supported the project. When clearing of the site was about to begin in December 1984, the area was occupied by Green demonstrators, and clashes with the police took place. In March 1985, court decisions and the establishment of a Commission put the project on ice where, following the Commission's report it still remains. For the second time, the combined weight of the traditional establishment was defeated and in this case it was defeated at a time when it appeared to be winning the battle, for between March 1984 and March 1985, support for the project rose from 39% to 43% and those wholly opposed fell from 27% to 23%. Even more significantly, over the whole period of the clashes, support rose from 39% to 43% and opposition fell from a high of 32% to 23%.

What happened here, in what protagonists on both sides saw as a highly symbolic battle between growth and ecology, material and post-material outlooks? The key lies in a closer analysis of the movement of opinion and the sources of opposition to the project. It is true that opinion was moving in favour of the government in a general way, but not in the key groups of the electorate who make and break majorities. At the outset of the conflict, the SPÖ and its smaller coalition partner, the FPÖ's voters, were not strongly differentiated from the overall state of public opinion.

For example, 28% of SPÖ voters approved of the anti-Hainburg movement, only 29% of floating voters did so. Yet, as the conflict evolved, opinion polarised and the SPÖ electorate hardened its support for the party's position, but floating voters, the Kreisky voters, young voters, educated voters moved to the opposite extreme anti-Hainburg end of the spectrum, as did FPÖ voters to a lesser degree. Green support rose to over 9% in the polls. The FPO fell to the danger zone of 3.3%. Forty per cent of the undecided voters supported the occupation. Thirty-four per cent opposed the project and only 26% supported it in March 1985 (down from 29% in November 1984) and only 41% of FPÖ voters (down from 46% in November) whereas the support of SPÖ voters rose from 47% to 57%. Among new voters, only 32% supported the project in March 1985, and only 29% of university graduates. The SPÖ was becoming isolated from the urban, young educated voters on which it depended and the FPÖ was in the danger zone. These reasons and not the position of the majority, nor the press campaign, explain what was a calculated tactical climb down. But it proved the strength of the Green movement even as a minority.

It was during the Hainburg occupation that the idea arose of a Green Presidential Candidate for 1986, and the active and respected ex-SPÖ member Freda Meissner Blau was the obvious choice. She was persuaded to stand, not so much for the Green cause or against Waldheim, but to oppose Dr Scrinzi, an ex-FPÖ extreme-right candidate. Her effective campaign, and the media coverage that went with it, as well as the 5.5% that she obtained in the first ballot, made her the obvious federator and leader of a Green parliamentary party. Her vote was an anti-politician protest vote, but also a vote for the environment. Yet, the Austrian Green movement is very hard to classify politically. On the second round 37% of her voters supported Kurt Waldheim and only 34% the SPÖ Environment Minister. This could hardly have happened elsewhere and perhaps eloquently explains the problems of welding the Green/Alternative movement into an effective and organised political party. At the 1986 National-rat elections, which took the Greens by surprise, in the process of organising, the list led by Mrs Meissner Blau obtained fewer votes than she did as a Presidential candidate, 234,028 (4.82%) and eight seats in the Nationalrat. Their gains came mainly in Vienna (+2.4%), Tirol (+3.1%) and Vorarlberg (+4.1%). Of 1983 Green voters only 55% voted Green in 1986. 25% went to the ÖVP, but net gains were made from all parties.

A single Green party as such did not exist, and is only now in the process of development. Freda Meissner Blau imposed an uneasy truce on most of the factions, to federate them into a single list. The Green Party is a federation of the Burger-Initiativen, the ALÖ (a less radical Vienna group), and 90% of the VGÖ. The federating force was the Burger Initiativen Parliament (BIP) led by Mrs Meissner Blau and other 'Promis' (prominent people). It has now adopted a strongly decentralised structure giving the Land parties almost complete autonomy. Theoretically, the party should exercise leadership and not the Nationalrat Klub, yet given the prior existence of the Klub and its easier access to the media, this remains difficult. The Green Klub is a mixed bag, like the movement itself: the elegant bourgeois Frau Meissner Blau, the 'alternative' Mr Wabl, Mr Srb, a Slovene, a handicapped member in a wheelchair, a lawyer (imposed by Frau Meissner Blau), and a member of the Salzburg Bürger

Initiative. Unlike the German movement, it has been electorally and parliament oriented. There is no mass organisation or alternative network in place. Hence, there has, say the alternative members, been no follow-up to the initial public sympathy. The FPÖ has formed a more radical opposition at times. The process of uniting the old Vereinigten Grünen (VGÖ) and the Alternative (ALÖ) is difficult. In Graz and Vienna the ALÖ still leads an independent existence and contests elections but the Meissner Blau movement is dominant. The movement must, Austria being Austria, remain very moderate. But a programme has been drawn up and an extra parliamentary wing is being developed from the Land level upwards.

The Greens in parliament have sought to keep debate on antifascism, green questions and social questions, open, and to act as the conscience of the SPÖ, placing it under pressure. The Greens have tabled sixty bills and asked 400 questions, mostly raising issues relating to dangerous-waste disposal, police brutality, the Slovene rights question, nuclear pollution from Tchernobyl, speed limits, energy saving, public transport, scandals. These correspond to the main themes of the Green electoral Manifesto: ecology, public transport, energy saving, an ecological economy, less intensive agriculture, more direct and local democracy, decentralisation, more democratic justice, cuts in defence spending, rights for minorities (Slovenes, Croats). A major issue for the Greens will also be opposition to membership of the European Community. It is demanding a referendum on the issue. Its grounds for opposition are both 'green' and 'neutrality'.

Recent electoral evidence is not conclusive, but would tend to suggest that the Greens are in the process of establishing themselves as a more permanent part of the political landscape, with continued representation to at least the present level in the Nationalrat, and in a majority of the Landtage. At the same time, the early chaotic period is ending. The seminal role of key early figures such as Frau Meissner Blau and other moderate greens is now over, and the inevitable conflict between them and more 'alternative' activists led to the whole moderate wing (such as Fuchs, and Geier, as well as Meissner Blau) leaving the party in some confusion. The new leader, Andreas Wabl, more clearly fits the profile of the German Green movement than did the early generation of Austrian green leaders. He has embarked the party on a more evident 'oppositional' course, without abandoning its parliamentary orientation. For example, much like his German counterpart Otto Schilly in the Flick Inquiry Committee,

Wabl has become a star and an effective performer in the Lucona Inquiry Committee, whose establishment he was instrumental in obtaining.

Party strategies have been an integral part of the political process. We have looked at the parties – the pieces on the political chess board and the various fora for inter-action – and the rules of the game. How have the parties operated? Strategy is a complex inter-action of goals, possibilities and means. This must be seen in the longer term. Parties interact with the broader development of Austrian society. They affect this development and are also affected by it. Policies and strategies can set autonomous changes in motion that alter the nature of society and undermine the position of those who initially set the changes in motion. This is true of the SPÖ whose modernising strategy of the 1970s eroded the party's electoral basis in the mid-1980s causing problems and dilemmas like that at Hainburg.

Another such development is the decline of agriculture, for the most part a conscious political decision, which has reduced the ÖVP base. Strategy must then proceed from a realistic appraisal of the positive and negative developments in society for the realisation of a party's goals. From that appraisal comes an analysis of possibilities and means. In the Austrian context, that has almost always, even for the oppositional FPÖ and Greens, been a pragmatic appraisal, based on realistic possibilities within a consensual framework, even during the period of absolute majorities. Strategies have sought to obtain or defend leverage in the system. Both parties have sought first to eliminate competition within their own electoral reservoir and, using dominance of their own natural constituency as a base, to bring non-attached voters into their orbit, as a basis for an absolute majority, or at least a relative majority, over the other main party. Thus, the ÖVP was at pains to eliminate the threat of the formation of a Peasant or rural party, such as had existed in the First Republic, by bringing the Farmers organisations into the ÖVP orbit, and in some Länder where this was possible (Steiermark for example), bringing former National Socialists and Liberals into the ÖVP at an early stage by giving the party a non-confessional image. There has though, been little tolerance for Länder differentiation. All parties, and especially the ÖVP and SPÖ have sought to set strategy centrally and limit Länder differentiation. Dissidence such as shown by the ÖVP over the stationing of Drakken fighters near Graz or in the Vorarlberg SPÖ over nuclear power, are rare and receive little toleration.

Austrian politics is very centralised in its mentality. Strong Land party leaders may acquire a position in their Land stronger than their party's Federal vote, but this confers little clout in Federal politics. Beyond control of their natural 'lager' and regional party organisations, the parties seek to use party organisations or factions as a means of extending party influence in the main social-partner organisations and professional bodies (liberal professions, cultural, sporting bodies). The multiform tentacles of party influence are ways of creating a favourable network for mobilising support and developing ideas. As we have seen, Austria has a very high level of party membership. SPÖ membership exceeds Labour or even SPD membership and ÖVP membership exceeds CDU membership. Ratios of members to voters are very high but members are not active and motivated. Many join parties for purely clientelist reasons. As a result, the traditional methods of party activity (based on local sections in the SPÖ, with a network of party workers regularly visiting members (70,000) to collect subscriptions) and the work of the constituent organisations (ÖAAB, ÖBB, ÖWB in the ÖVP) are now inadequate.

Strategy can no longer be aimed merely at captive groups whose opinion is already favourable. Modern methods of presentation, media communication, analysis of social trends and electoral sociology, are permitting parties to identify and address new social groups and marginal and floating groups of voters, who determine elections. Such 'political marketing' is not wholly new of course, but it reached new levels of both sophistication and dominance in the Kreisky era. However, the ÖVP were, perhaps more by accident than clear design, the first to notice the potential constituency for a programme of modernisation. The Action-20 launched before the 1966 election, brought in outside non-party expertise and gave the party a centrist 'modernising' image. It won an absolute majority and the Grand Coalition fell. Yet, the ÖVP failed to capitalise on this new and promising situation to draw in the 'liberals' and new unattached voters, only detaching itself from the unpopular Grand Coalition 'proporz' style of politics, with which the SPÖ could be identified. The strengths of the ÖVP, in becoming a strong people's party able to approach an absolute majority, were weaknesses in government. Compromise and indecision could be blamed on an unwilling coalition partner. Now that excuse was no longer available, and the fact that the ÖVP was forced to take decisions that divided it in areas that had traditionally been SPÖ competencies, gave the government an image of weakness. Proporz remained, but between the components of the ÖVP! There appeared to be no clear strategy.

As it happened, it was the SPÖ that saw and seized the opportunity of modernising. It accepted the challenge of opposition and the need to win initially a relative- and then an absolute-majority. It developed clear strategies, with considerable, but by no means total success. It used the years in opposition to remodel the party, to be more in tune with the trends of the times. It elected Bruno Kreisky, a pragmatic moderniser to the leadership in a bitterly contested leadership battle in 1967. He opened-up the party and established links to 'civil society' outside the party, involving 1,400 experts (many of them non-SPÖ members), in an exercise of broad policy renewal. The SPÖ became Austria's liberal party, the hope and home of progressives, willing to 'travel a bit of the way with the SPÖ', without being convinced socialists.

The strategy of the SPÖ in those years was aimed at consolidating support among three key groups: the old traditional SPÖ voters, the post-1968 post-materialist generation, and the modernising rising groups – perhaps what we would call 'yuppies' – success orientated groups. At the same time it kept the 'bourgeois' block divided. Structural reforms, education, social peace, long term growth, more democracy, a new cultural vitality, peace with the Catholic Church, an active foreign policy in the Third World – all served to cement these groups to the SPÖ. It was a judicious and balanced strategy. This strategy was remarkably effective until 1983. The main danger remained the threat of a 'bourgeois' ÖVP+FPÖ coalition.

Here, the SPÖ, and Kreisky in particular, followed a two-pronged approach. Firstly, the FPÖ was 'detached' from the 'bourgeois block'. As we have seen, the FPÖ was itself ambiguous in its line, swinging violently from liberal to nationalist tendencies. By seeking cooperation with the FPÖ in the 1970–71 Legislature when the SPÖ formed a minority government, in backing FPÖ leader Peter when his SS past was raised, in offering the FPÖ full rights in parliament as an Opposition (the chairmanship of the Audit Court, a vice chairmanship of the Nationalrat), thus preparing the way for the small coalition in 1983, the SPÖ sought to strengthen the hand of those in the FPÖ who wanted to transform it into a modern social–liberal party. The strategy worked partially, but in the end, the FPÖ was first upgraded, and then as a weak and inexperienced government party, broken, provoking the Haider rebellion in 1986 and provisionally ending such a strategy. However, the FPÖ has in a sense been returned to its earlier ghetto. It will be difficult for the ÖVP to work with it in its present form. However, the 'upgrading' and subsequent breaking the FPÖ has opened a Pandora's box.

The second prong was the attempt to divide the ÖVP, along the fault lines of its component parts. This was a plausible approach, based on the internal 'ständische' conflicts within the ÖVP and Bruno Kreisky's experience of Scandinavian politics, where the division of the bourgeois lager into (at least) two parties has ensured long dominance for the Social Democrats. In Austria, the main practical goal was to revive an independent farmers or Peasants party, such as had emphemerally existed in the First Republic. This approach was pursued through measures to try and detach the farmers from ÖVP dominated service organisations. It provided few concrete results in itself. As it was, the shock of the loss of power, the lack of credible leaders, self-generated internal conflicts over strategy, and the loss of patronage powers, was sufficient to weaken the ÖVP until 1983.

The opposition was able to recover a degree of initiative as the engine, as the moderniser, as the proposer, of new ideas. In the 1970s, the SPÖ had been careful to monopolise this function, even though it was in power. By the mid-1980s, it had lost momentum and was on the defensive, seeking to preserve the 'acquis' of the earlier reform period. This was especially true as the SPÖ, as a party, offered no clear alternative to the neo-conservative 'Wende', with which the ÖVP sought to identify. In the early period, the SPÖ and government itself performed the critical house cleaning rôle normally identified with the opposition. However, from 1980 with the Androsch scandal, the government lost its 'clean' image and a rôle for the opposition re-emerged. At the same time as the government lost its dynamism, the pervasive mood, that it was time for a change, took hold.

In the 1983–86 period, the ÖVP, unbroken, re-emerged as the main and, indeed, only parliamentary government and modernising reformer. The economic recession and the following weak 1983–86 government, led to a reversal of the earlier positive image with this modernising group of voters.

On the level of electoral sociology, the SPÖ lost its dominance of the three key voter groups. The old working class is in decline. It is pessimistic and defensive. It has, therefore, often shifted to conservative voting (ÖVP in Kärnten and the Obersteiermark for the FPÖ). The post-materialist 'Green' electorate, which potentially represents up to 20% of voters, became disillusioned with the SPÖ after the

Zwentendorf referendum and, above all, after the Hainburg dam affair, in which the vacillation of the SPÖ ended by satisfying no one. The conflict was real. Growth is central to the Social Democratic ideology, but the Hainburg movement opposes growth in any form. The 'success oriented' rising generation of floating voters only remained attracted to the SPÖ as long as it offered the image of economic success, a clean and efficient party.

The SPÖ, celebrating its hundredth anniversary in 1989, was therefore facing something of a mid-life crisis. It must throw overboard some ballast, without abandoning principles. It has fallen back into a defensive position, defending the gains of the 1960s and 1970s. It must seek a new vision, applying the party's basic principles to a new and more mobile society. It must not be afraid to propose more democratisation, de-bureaucratisation and de-regulation. The party must once again appear the party of the future, with a broader ideological vision, rather than providing the best administration of the present order. For too many voters, the SPÖ is seen as a bureaucratic and old-fashioned party. Although in present circumstances, the party seems likely to remain the largest party, facing two medium-sized 'bourgeois' parties (ÖVP and FPÖ) and the Greens, it should not rely for its position solely on the weakness of the ÖVP. It must recover its ideological substance. The 1978 programme is still an excellent basis. It requires updating. This is the aim of Perspektiven 90, Sozialdemokratie 2000 and the internal 'Glasnost' discussion launched by Party Chairman Vranitzky. The Sozialdemokratie 2000 will be a type of party work programme, elaborating the ideas contained in the 1978 Programme. The present Chancellor is seeking to modernise the party: he represents a bridge to a new era, untainted as he is by the past and by the past of the party. The SPÖ would hope to be well placed for a new reform era in the 1990s, after the end of the neo-liberal phase.

The immediate aim must be to maintain the Grand Coalition, with the SPÖ as its dominant partner, after 1990. Indeed, this can be reduced to the formula : SPÖ > ÖVP and SPÖ + Grünen > ÖVP + FPÖ. Thus, the SPÖ would be the key to the political situation and its bargaining power enhanced. It would have little to fear from any 'coalition free' votes in the Nationalrat. The party emphatically is not seeking a cure in opposition, which is equally rejected by both wings of the party.

For the ÖVP, the reverse is the case. It is seeking to draw ahead of the SPÖ and above all show that the 'Wende' and indeed the success of the government has come from ÖVP pressure. A key symbolic issue would be the move on an EC application. The ÖVP is very active in 'promoting' its rôle in government. As yet, it remains consistently behind in the polls and would not seem likely to obtain a majority with the FPÖ. However, much can change as the government's reform programme unfolds. The FPÖ is frankly divided abouts its future rôle. Jörg Haider does not seem to reason in a longer-term strategy context. His aim seems to end at making the FPÖ a 'middle-sized' party which can no longer be ignored by the larger parties. Others, especially those engaged in day-to-day parliamentary work, remain pragmatic and consensus orientated, as a constructive opposition, able eventually, perhaps without Haider, to enter government with either party. Jörg Haider's conflictual demagogic approach has hitherto paid dividends and so is not opposed. Those who are concerned about the party's long-term strategy consider that the question of alliances and policies cannot be ignored for long. The Greens' aim is to effect changes in the mentality of a significant part of the electorate and to organise the larger 'Umfeld' that is sympathetic to it, so as to create pressure on the other parties, especially the SPÖ, but without adopting a fundamentalist radicalism alien to Austrian political culture. These party strategies seem unlikely to lead to a fundamental change in the party or political system and seem to point to a continuation of the Grand Coalition, a seemingly appropriate form of government for Austria. The general conclusion must point to the successful development and adaptation of the political system already established in Austria, despite the new challenges that it has had to face.

5. Austro-Keynesianism: Politics Against the Market

By any standards, the Austrian economy has been a success since 1945. Reconstruction, modernisation and a successful response to the economic crisis of the 1970s can be ascribed to it. However, the 'Austrian Way' may need to be adapted to respond to new requirements and new challenges; some of its many successes – especially the large public-sector – have become the source of serious difficulties and may have been a root cause of slow adaptability.

Just as it was once fashionable to praise Austria (along with Sweden and other Scandinavian states), as a model of efficient, pragmatic social democratic welfarism and economic growth, in the neo-conservative climate of the 1980s it has now become especially fashionable to decry the 'Austrian Way' as the last vestige of the fossilised 1960s and to present the Austrian story as some sort of horrible cautionary tale of stubborn refusal to abandon state interventionism for the elysian fields of the ideology of the market.

The truth is that the record of the Austrian economy is excellent and remains so. Adaptation is taking place. However, Austria, including responsible conservatives, refuses to throw the baby out with the bath-water. We shall seek to look at the record of the Austrian economy and the structural features of the 'Austrian Model', before turning a critical eye on the policies and evaluating their capacity to adapt, (and thereby survive, and prosper in a changing environment), both internally and externally.

What are the main springs of the Austrian economy? Austria is a medium-sized landlocked state, at a high level of economic development and interdependence with her neighbours, vunerable to external influences in the wider European and world economy. Therefore, the Austrian economy is an open economy. In 1986, 66.9% of her imports came from the European Community and 60.1% of her exports went back to the EC. Her main trading partners are Germany (44.9% of imports and 32.7% of exports), Italy (8.9%

and 9.3%) and Switzerland (4.8% and 7.8%). 8.3% of imports and 9.6% of exports are from Eastern Europe, to which must be added 1% of imports and 2.3% of exports to Yugoslavia. Thus, 61.9% of Austria's imports come from her six immediate geographical neighbours and 55.5% of exports go to them. The main imports are food (23.3%), raw materials (22.3%) and energy. Her main exports are machinery, metals, steel and agricultural products. Tourism, and the provision of other services, is almost as important as trade in terms of her balance of payments.

Austria has significant heavy industrial capacity especially in the steel, oil refining, and machinery production sectors. The industrial areas are in Upper Austria, near Linz and in the Steiermark, as well as around Vienna and Wiener Neustadt. As we shall see, a significant proportion of Austrian industry is in the public sector. Agriculture is heavily subsidised and much of Austria's production is from marginal and mountain agricultural areas. There are three quite distinct economic traditions in Austria: heavy industry, of which the large firm VOEST AG Alpine is the flagship; agriculture and wine production in rural Lower Austria in the Burgenland and the Western Länder; and the tourist economy in the western part of the country.

Austrian economic policy has been a considerable success both in the immediate post-war reconstruction period and in the economic crisis of the 1970s when, unlike other European states, severe unemployment and economic downturn were avoided. Many argue that this result has had a significant cost, now being felt, in terms of the public debt, lower productivity and deficits in the public sector enterprises, and slow growth in the 1980s. To a considerable degree, these criticism of the 'Austrian Model' are exaggerated and in any case cannot alter the historic fact that Austria was spared the worst effects of the recession of the 1970s. What have been the results of the economic policy; what is the situation of the economy now and what were – indeed are – the features of the 'Austrian Way' in terms of economic policy?

The Austrian economy grew at an annual average of 5.7% between 1969–73, against 4.7% for OECD Europe. In the 1973–79 period, it grew 3% (OECD Europe – 2.4%) and in the 1979-85 period Austria grew 1.9% against 2.6% in OECD Europe. Over the whole 1969-85 period, Austria grew at an average of 3.2% against 2.5% in OECD Europe as a whole. In 1987, Austria grew 1.8% against 2.5% for the whole European Community, but some OECD states, such as

Denmark, showed lower or even negative growth. Real growth in Austria was above OECD Europe average levels every year since 1969, except 1973, 1984 and 1986. It has often been significantly higher, as in 1979 (Austria 4.7% against 3.3% in OECD Europe). Real wages have only shown negative growth in 1980 and 1984 and were rising significantly in 1986 (+3.3%) and 1987. GDP per head in Austria in 1987 was 190,000 ÖS. Real GDP per head has risen consistently every year since 1969, except in 1984. A very considerable degree of social peace has been achieved in Austria, with 2.9 minutes of strike per worker in 1980, 0.1 minutes in 1983 and 1984 and 3.9 minutes in 1985. Only Germany has a comparable record (2.7 minutes in 1980, 0.9 minutes in 1983, 125.1 minutes in 1984 and 0.8 minutes in 1985). For the UK, the figures were 249.9 minutes in 1980, 85.6 minutes in 1986, 613.2 minutes in 1984 and 143.1 minutes in 1985).

The Austrian economy has consistently maintained a low level of inflation since 1969 and, indeed, earlier. In comparative terms Austrian inflation has always been lower than the OECD Europe average and lower than most of her main trading partners. Austrian inflation rose to a high point of 6.8% in 1982, at which time the OECD average was 14.3%. Thereafter, inflation in Austria fell back to reach 3.2% in 1985 and 1.7% in 1986, and remained at that point in 1987. Her inflation rate was only bettered by Germany (−0.2%), the Netherlands and Switzerland in 1986. Over the whole period since 1980, only Germany and The Netherlands among OECD Europe states have had a lower inflation rate than Austria.

Unemployment has been moderate in Austria. In 1976, Austrian unemployment was only 2.0% and by 1981, it was still only 2.4%. By 1986 it has risen to 5.2% against 10.6% in OECD Europe. Austria was in fourth position. German unemployment was higher at 8.9%. Apart from Switzerland, only Norway and Sweden, both also with social democratic policies, had lower rates of unemployment. In 1987 and early 1988, the yearly average was falling again after an upward 'blip' in early 1987, and remained well below OECD and German average levels.

It has been said that the grip of the state in Austria is too strong and threatens to smother the economy. This may be only an impression or a matter of political psychology because the relevant statistical data do not seem to bear this out. The share of state expenditure in terms of the GDP was only 50% in 1984. It was 48% in

Thatcherite Britain and the growth rate from 1980–84 was 1.1% in Austria against 2.9% in Britain. Tax receipts as share of the GDP were 42% in Austria against 45% in France and the Netherlands. The German figure was 37.2% and the UK figure 38.5%. Austria does not appear as an aberrant case, diverging widely from the general European norm. In 1985, the public sector deficit was 4.4% of GDP, certainly higher than the German (1.2%), UK (3.0%) or French (3.3%) figures, but well below Belgium (10.4%) or the Netherlands (8.4%). Measured in ÖS per head, the deficit was 8,000. Again, Austria finds herself in a middle positon. The deficit has been stabilised and is decreasing.

From this summary and dry analysis of the performance of Austria's economy over the last two decades, several conclusions emerge. Austria is a modern, industrial and post-industrial society (with a high standard of living and a highly developed social system) standing at the top of the European league table. She has been an island of growth, low inflation, and moderate unemployment and excellent social provision during the recession of the 1970s. The pace of reform slowed in the later 1970s and early 1980s, but did not stop.

Austrian economic policy deliberately set out to counteract the effects of the world recession and isolate Austria from the effects of the recession on her economy, vulnerable as it is to outside influences because of her dependence on trade with her neighbours. The development of the Austrian economy is a success story on its own, and, by any standards, her economic policy has protected her from the chill winds of recession and rationalisation. And it has been achieved in a country that many doubted was viable on its own. It has been achieved by a conscious and determined policy, based on coherent choices.

What then are the key elements in what has been called the 'Austrian Way'? First of all, there is the general, almost un-ideological, recognition of the central responsibility of the state to provide a sense of coordination and impulsion to the economy and even to intervene directly on a permanent basis to provide a catalyst in a mixed economy.

The state is seen as having an obligation to set objectives and establish, through its own policies, a framework that will enable the mixed economy to function effectively. This has involved an approach and a series of specific policies, which have been called Austro-Keynesianism, based on the judicious counter-cyclical use of demand management, monetary stability and socio-economic reforms to achieve the objectives of growth and as near full employment as possible.

Industry and the Labour movement have cooperated with each other, with government and the political parties in building consensus and close cooperation into a central plank of the 'Austrian Way' through the system of Social Partnership. A major contribution has been made by the state sector of the economy. With over 20% of value added in industry, and considerably more in other sectors, and with strong involvement in the banking sector, the state sector has been able to exercise an influence on what is a genuinely mixed economy, with private, semi-private, cooperative and municipal, Land and Federal forms of enterprise in a spirit of co-existence and cooperation.

There has been a long tradition of active state intervention in the economy and state promotion of economic activity, going back at least to the time of Empress Maria Theresia in the eighteenth century. In the post-war period, the reconstruction of the country, especially under the four-Power occupation required a catalytic rôle for the state. Without denying that, economic policy issues have been a major source of divergence between the parties and, indeed, they involve divergences of principle. The major characteristic of Austrian political life, especially in the economic sphere has been its unashamed pragmatism. The Austrian translation of the German concept of the Social Market Economy, known as the 'Raab-Kamitz' line, was considerably more pragmatic, incorporating elements of state interventionism and a very much larger public sector than in Germany. This was inevitable. The foundation of Austrian policy was laid during the twenty-one years of the first Grand Coalition between the ÖVP and SPÖ, rather than, as in Germany, by conservatives alone.

Both parties were pragmatic and consensual in their approach and operated a certain division of labour between the coalition partners in relation to economic policy. Thus the ÖVP created the conditions for the Social Market Economy. The associated policies of a strong public sector, Social Partnership and an active social policy were overseen by Socialist ministers. Both parties readily accepted an un-ideological approach to economic policy and during this period divergences were relatively limited. Even in the 1980s, when both parties have attempted a certain 'retour aux sources' and in a more neo-conservative climate, the divergences were not so great as to prevent a renewal of the Grand coalition in 1987.

The ÖVP has always been a broad-based pragmatic 'Volkspartei', which easily accomodated itself to coalition with the SPÖ. The party did not adopt a full programme until 1972, after both the first Grand Coalition and the ÖVP majority government. The party had always adopted a pragmatic, consensual approach, based on experience in the day-to-day business of government.

The SPÖ was, of course, a more ideological party that had had practically no experience of government in the First Republic. It came to favour a pragmatic cooperative approach after 1945, as its experience of the practical problems of government increased.

During the period of allied occupation and immediate post-war reconstruction, there were often few choices in the decisions which needed to be taken quite independently of all ideological or political situations and attitudes. There was often only one obvious approach, dictated by the immediate national interest. For example, the Nationalisation Act of 1946 was necessary to keep former German property out of Soviet hands and to create the basis for a modern Austrian heavy industrial sector. On the other hand, the currency reforms and liberalisation measures associated with the 'Social Market Economy' approach was necessary for participation in the ERP (Marshall Plan). Both parties accepted these necessary compromises.

It was only in the mid-1950s that the ÖVP first raised the issue of privatisation in a limited and moderate manner. The first, limited privatisations, involved the sale of 40% of the shares in the Creditanstalt (CA) in 1957 and the sale of the Austrian subsidiary of Siemens to the German parent company in 1972. However, it was only in 1985, following the adoption of a new ideological manifesto 'der Zukunftsmanifesto der ÖVP', that the ÖVP drew up a more radical privatisation document, but even that was very hesitant, proposing only that some small and marginal holdings (<25%) should be sold and that the state should sell minority holdings in Austrian Airlines and the nationalised banks.

The characteristic of the Austrian parties has been their pragmatism, even in the more ideological era of the 1980s. Even the more liberal FPÖ failed to raise the issue of privatisation (or a roll-back of the state) during the small SPÖ–FPÖ coalition of (1983–86). However as we shall see, the new neo-conservative thinking reached Austria in an attenuated form which influenced all three political parties and the programme of the 1987 Grand Coalition. Even then, the basic outlines of the 'Austrian Way' have been attenuated rather than radically altered. The positive rôle of government remains a key element in Austrian economic policy today. The SPÖ have made concessions to the harsh realities of the 1980s and to the prevailing neo-conservative ideological wind, but the impact of these new directions has, unlike the situation in a number of other western countries, been moderated precisely by the strength of the SPÖ and the caution and moderation of the ÖVP.

What are the main-springs of the economic policies pursued by active and interventionist Austrian governments over the past two decades? Austria was a backward society, with considerable ground to catch up, especially in the eastern part of the country that had been in the Soviet zone before 1955. Austria recovered well from the war and the four-Power occupation. Yet, at that time, her productivity was low; her GDP per head lay some 25% below EEC average levels. Lying as she did on the periphery of Western Europe, faced with the threat of isolation from the coming Common Market, she did not seem well placed to take-off and enter the economic fast lane. Yet she did so, as a result of an active and interventionist government policy, in which social and structural reform was seen as an integral and central point of the modernisation drive.

When it came to power in 1970 as a one-party government, the SPÖ sought to mobilise the need for reform and modernisation in all corners of Austrian society; in the legal system, education, the rights of workers, social policy, women's rights – indeed, right across the board. It was, as in Québec, a 'Quiet Revolution'. It was a process of dynamic, but democratic and consensual change, releasing the forces of progress and dynamism in society.

The goal of modernisation of Austria that was central to the SPÖ policy platform of the 1970 and 1971 elections, was not specifically socialist. It was democratic, progressive and liberal. It was a broad enough message to sweep up new social groups from outside the traditional lager and bring the SPÖ an absolute majority that was to last until 1983 and, indeed, the relative majority that the SPÖ still retains. It brought an almost Gramscian intellectual dominance to the agenda. The SPÖ was the party of change, the party of movement, the party of competence and efficiency, the party of modernisation. It sought, successfully, to build a broad coalition that would make the SPÖ the naturally dominant party in Austria. The new classes, created by the cultural revolution of educational reform were taken on board by the SPÖ. These groups were, in the phrase of the time, 'prepared to go some way down the road' with the SPÖ, despite there never being a socialist (as distinct from a liberal) majority in Austria. Bruno Kreisky was a moderniser who symbolised the new, pragmatic SPÖ.

The Kreisky reform era was the basis of the later economic policies. It liberated energies and created a modern society that was to be 'Europa reif', ready to belong to the wider European ensemble and able to stand the competition. The main emphasis in this modernisation programme lay in the creation of modern infrastructures in education and training and in wide-ranging social reforms.

A modern society must be based on a modern system of education, training and research. Reforms in these fields have been key elements in Austria's quiet revolution. The schools budget rose twice as fast as the budget as a whole in the 1970–85 period and has continued to rise. Education took only 0.81% of the state budget in 1955, 1.77% by 1965 and 8.2% by 1987. This represented 0.22% of GDP in 1955 and 0.69% in 1965. The education explosion began in 1955. By 1960, there were 27,000 students and 41,000 by 1970, 100,000 by 1980 and some 150,000 by 1985. Socialist school policy was to create a basic comprehensive type of school for children aged ten to fourteen and to open up education to a broader cross-section by building more schools, colleges and universities, grants, free books and travel. The curriculum was modernised and more closely integrated with the needs of the economy. The aim was to make higher education more accessible and relevant. Scientific education and training was greatly expanded.

Research and Development expenditure rose from 0.61% of GDP in 1970 to 1.27% in 1986. Here, Austria was in the middle, in comparative European terms. In 1980, a Ministry of Science and Research was set up to integrate science, technology and education. A rolling research plan was established in 1980. Recent priorities are energy policy, structural changes and the environment. Austria has thus built on a long cultural tradition to create a modern education system, which has gradually been democratised.

A more open, equal and fair society was also not only an end in itself, but part of the modernisation drive of the 1970s, in which reforms of the legal system played an important part. Much of Austrian civil and penal law went back to the early 19th century. The aim of modernisation was to create a more open and more equal society. For the SPÖ, legal reform was an instrument of social reform and change, promoting or at least permitting change in society. However, in a typically Austrian manner, the long serving SPÖ Minister of Justice, Dr Christian Broda (1970–83), though he had clear goals deriving from the party platform of 1969 and 1978, sought and obtained a considerable degree of consensus with the ÖVP for his reform programme. The main areas of legal reform were in civil and family law, more liberal forms of penal law, a thorough reform of the Rent Acts, the enactment of the first extensive consumer protection legislation and legislation providing forms of judicial redress in labour and social disputes.

By the mid-1980s, Austria had been equipped with a modern legal system, though the major problems of the slowness of the administration of justice and its bureaucratic character had not been resolved. Certainly, the SPÖ principle of greater access to justice for all, and the use of law as a compensatory instrument in favour of weaker individuals or groups in society, had found considerable practical expression in the work of legal reform.

Social policy was also a key area of reform and modernisation. There, several distinct phases can be identified in the development of policy. Above all, the process of reform and improvement did not, as in many other European states, come to a halt or go into reverse in the economic crisis of the 1970s. Of course, new priorities were set and it became necessary to make more difficult choices, but the process of reform continued. Indeed, in 1985, with 15.4% of GDP, spending on social services had not declined and Austria was well placed on the European scale of social spending; the real value of social benefits was 50% higher than in the early 1970s. This is very far from a reversal of the push towards a better 'social net' of protection for all citizens.

In the first period down to 1970, the first significant basis of a modern social state was laid, with a number of measures introduced after 1955. In that year, the first Comprehensive Social Insurance Act, covering all areas of social benefit, was passed. The subsequent amendements increased coverage and upgraded benefits. The first breakthrough in working conditions came with the forty-hour week in 1969, now reduced to thirty-eight hours. SPÖ pressure was instrumental in achieving the breakthrough. Important extensions of the rights of workers through their Works Councils was also achieved. In 1968, an important measure was adopted for the promotion of an active labour-market policy that was to prove extremely valuable in the period of rising unemployment of the later 1970s and 1980s.

During these periods, it was possible to achieve progress by broad consensus between the parties – even with the FPÖ – and the social partners. This proved true, both during the Grand Coalition, and, for the most part, during the ÖVP one-party government (1966–70).

With the SPÖ government, the process of reform certainly accelerated, but the search for a broader consensus than the SPÖ majority in the Nationalrat was maintained and continued for all aspects (except the most controversial), of social policy. For the SPÖ, the 'insurance' or in German 'Leistungsprinzip' was less important than the criteria of need and the promotion of hitherto disadvantaged social groups. Social progress was less a luxury product of economic growth for the SPÖ than for the ÖVP. Hence the strong determination to maintain at least some of the momentum during the period of economic downturn.

Labour legislation saw significant reforms in the form of improved rights for the Works Councils (1971); three-weeks legal minimum annual holiday (1971); codification of conditions of work (1974); real increases in social benefits and pensions (1973); and changes in rules on contribution records, to qualify for benefit to cover periods outside the work force or in training, were also introduced. Measures to assist those made redundant or put on short time were enacted (1973). Already a degree of conservative backlash was evident, arguing that these measures had created an excessive 'social net' that was too expensive, that undermined competitiveness and reduced individual initiative.

The 1976–81 period was affected by those critical accents that were also heard in SPÖ and ÖGB circles. However, the general thrust of social policy was maintained. Despite the more difficult economic climate, a significant number of reforms were realised. At the same time, the worsening economic situation made it necessary to balance the need for budgetary savings, not least in order to retain a degree of flexibility for the continuation of anti-cyclical measures that were required to meet the number one priority of fighting unemployment. The SPÖ opposed a pause in the work of social reform, but recognised the need for budgetary prudence, as pension fund deficits and hospital costs rose alarmingly. Yet, a fourth week of legal holiday was enacted, and social benefits were upgraded in 1976 and 1978; also, early pensions for farmers, widows' pensions and anti-poverty measures were all introduced in this period. Absolute priority was, however, given to measures to fight unemployment, and to defensive measures to deal with the deficits in the pension system. These measures reduced the share of the Bund budget for subsidising pension schemes from 8.1% in 1975 to 5.4% in 1981. Savings of 8.1 billion ÖS and 9.5 billion ÖS were achieved in 1985 and 1986, respectively.

In the period since 1981, those accents have become more marked. Growth has been slower, full employment has not been achieved and the budgetary situation remains serious. Social reforms have not been given priority. The upgrading of benefits was postponed and, especially with the new Grand Coalition in 1987, the insurance and personal responsibility elements promoted by the ÖVP and FPÖ (and some inside the SPÖ) have made a greater impact on policy. There have been few reforms (5 weeks legal holiday), but no halt or reversal to the improvement of the 'social net'. Austria remains one of the leaders in terms of its welfare state, and has not reacted to the recession by social regression as in the USA, Britain or Germany.

Structural reform, more democracy, a more open, educated and mobile society with greater equality of opportunity for all, has been a major element in Austrian economic policy. This has contributed to the creation of a modern economy which, despite its relatively high international vulnerability, has resisted the effects of the recession quite well.

Another key structural element in Austrian policy has been effective exploitation of the existence of a very large public sector. Until 1985, the state sector was the flagship of the economy and was able to play a central counter-cyclical rôle in resisting the recession, and a pivotal rôle in modernising the economy. The public sector's sheer size is the first important and impressive point. This critical mass has enabled it to play a positive rôle in economic policy-making.

Let us plunge into the world of the Austrian state sector, warts and all, and then turn to look at its contribution to the development of economic policy in Austria and its rôle in the 'Austrian way'.

The state sector, in its various forms, represents 25.2% of all industrial production and, for the top 50 Austrian firms, it rises to 70.2% of production and 69.2% of exports. Austria's largest company in terms of both turnover and employment (69,719 employees) is Voest-Alpine (steel) and the second largest is VEW (17,259 workers). The third largest company is the Viennese energy company, Weiner Stadtwerke, with an annual turnover (1986) of 18.1 million ÖS and 15,376 employees. The fourth largest company is Linz-Chemie with a turnover of 19.1 billion ÖS. In the 'direct' Bundadministered sector, the Federal Railways employ 70,961 and the Federal Post Office 58,002 workers. The total industrial state work force, re-grouped in the state holding ÖIAG, is 96,000, with a peak of 131,000 in 1960. The state sector thus represents almost one-fifth of Austrian industrial production and some 6% of total GDP. ÖIAG represents some 18% of total Austrian exports and 20.6% of industrial investment (1986 figures). Earlier in the 1980s, these levels were even higher. Private Austrian capital represents 35% of industrial turnover; foreign capital 18.7% and the state sector 26.2%. The state sector therefore represents a powerful, and potentially catalytic, element in the industrial economy. This sheer size has been a key factor in explaining the greater importance of the state sector in Austria than in other equivalent societies.

There are, however, other factors going beyond the mere size, critical mass and, indeed, dominance of some heavy industrial sectors such as steel, metals, oil refining and other energy related industries. Those other factors relate to the historical and political context of the Austrian state sector. The state sector has not, until recently been a political football. It was created in 1946–47 (by the first ÖVP/SPÖ Grand Coalition) in the national interest, and has been perceived as a key national asset, with a positive and leading rôle in the economy.

Certainly, as in almost all else in modern Austria, the exact extent of the state sector was a compromise between the two parties. The SPÖ wanted to nationalise not only mining, energy, metallurgy (also accepted by the ÖVP), but also cement, sugar, vehicle building, banking and insurance, and food processing – in all some 125 enterprises and possibly a further 110 enterprises. Both parties agreed that a degree of nationalisation was necessary.

There was general agreement that in the inter-war period, Austrian heavy industry played a negative rôle. There was fear of the possibility of new foreign domination. (From 9% in 1938, German control of Austrian industry reached 57% in 1945). For the SPÖ, there were important economic and employment arguments, and, above all, there was agreement on the fact that only the state could recapitalise these heavy industries, which had been destroyed in the war. Most important of all was the need to keep these industries, mostly German-owned, out of the hands of the Soviet occupying power. In a series of Nationalisation Acts in the 1945–47 period, over 70 companies in the energy, mining, metallurgy and banking sectors were taken into public ownership. In the event, many of these enterprises could first effectively be taken over after the State Treaty was made and the settlement with the Soviet Union over German property had been concluded.

The most important political debates about the state sector arose about its control and organisation, rather than the extension of privatisation, though this issue did arise from time-to-time. There was competition for control between the coalition parties. At first the Ministry of State Property and Economic Planning, set up under an ÖVP minister in 1946, oversaw the nationalised industries. After an SPÖ election victory in 1949, the new Ministry of Transport and State Industries took over all industries, except the nationalised banks, under Karl Waldbrunner (SPÖ). This arrangement was reversed after an ÖVP election victory in 1956, where timid re-privatisation had been raised as an issue. A public holding company was set up under the supervision of the Chancellor's office, with a complex system of parity of board members for both parties and a mutual veto. After the next election, the state industries were placed under SPÖ Vice Chancellor Pitterman and so remained until the end of the Grand Coalition, but following ÖVP gains in 1962, a control committee was established with representatives of both parties.

The ÖVP government carried through the partial privatisation of Siemens Austria, the sale of 'popular shares' in state banks, and established an arms-length holding company for the bulk of the industrial state industries, the ÖIAG (1970). In 1986–87, the ÖIAG was restructured to increase the 'arms-length' approach. Administrative sector boards were set up under the superstructure ÖIAG holding-board. The complex 'proporz' system, of balanced ÖVP and SPÖ appointments to the boards (Aufsichtsräte) at all levels, was abolished. The ÖIAG Board has been given real powers of direction, planning and coordination, without direct political interference. It is required to operate in accordance with basic market principles. Those measures are in part a response to the deep crisis of Voest in 1985, but had earlier and deeper roots. They aim at a de-politisation of the state industries.

In the meantime, considerable reorganisation and many mergers took place at the industrial level, with the aim of creating large, but decentralised conglomerates under the ÖIAG holding company. In the period following the State Treaty, those former Soviet (USIA) undertakings that had been nationalised were incorporated (with difficulty and at the cost of modernisation subsidies) into the overall structure, adding some 28,000 workers. The Danube Steamship

Company (DDSG) was placed directly under the Transport Ministry. In 1963, a Restructuring Act cut the number of firms by half, through mergers. The 1970s saw the creation of the 'monster' steel conglomerates Voest-Alpine and VEW. Both had already absorbed smaller companies in the restructuring process. In 1973, Voest and Alpine, as well as two smaller undertakings (Böhler and SBS) were merged into one single giant state steel company (Voest–Alpine) and in 1975, the two special steel subsidiaries were linked into the Voest wholly-owned VEW company, all of course under the ÖIAG umbrella.

What was the economic rôle of this large, and in some sectors, dominant (steel 98%, coal 96%, iron-ore mining 100%, oil refining 74%) state industrial sector? The state industries played a major part in the post-war reconstruction, on a planned basis. Special sector plans were drawn up and Marshall Aid funds injected. Thus, by the late 1940s, the best pre-war year production levels (1929) had already been surpassed.

The state sector was also a pioneer in creating modern working and social conditions for the growing work force, which rose from 56,000 in 1946 to 109,000 in 1960. Raw materials were made available to Austrian private industry at very low prices, up to 40% below average European levels, which represented a vital advantage, for example to the machinery industry. Research and development expenditure reached 2 billion ÖS per year and investment has been 80% self-financed. Dividends of 3.6 billion were paid to the State in the 1970-80 period.

In the 1970s recession, the state industries sought to play a counter-cyclical rôle. They made a major contribution to employment and regional policy and to maintaining social conditions during the recession. As Dr Kreisky put it, debt was preferable to unemployment. The state sector was able to maintain a high level of investment and, indeed, in the critical year 1975, when private investment fell drastically, saw its share of total investment rise from 29.1% to 32.2%.

Employment levels were kept up during this period and rose by 0.9% in 1975, whereas private sector employment fell by 5.1%. In 1980, employment by state industries fell by 2.7% against 3.1% in the private sector. In the whole period 1973-80, public sector employment as a whole rose by 2%, as against a 7% fall in the private sector (and 12% in Germany). The state sector has, by deliberate policy, made a contribution to fighting recession and defending employment. However, such a policy could not, in an open economy where subsidies were much lower than with competitors – contrary to what most critics of the Austrian state sector think (steel subsidies were only 491 ÖS/ton in 1981-87 compared with an EC average of 809 ÖS/ton and a British level of 441 ÖS/ton) – continue over a long period without a major impact on profitability and even cash flow. The failure of the recession to lift, and the continuing crisis in the steel industry, led to a major crisis in Voest in 1985. Ironically, it was less losses in the basic industrial activities of Voest and VEW than failure of diversification and above all speculation in oil futures – areas where management had little experience or expertise – that the heaviest losses occurred. Yet, it was the longer-term threat of downturn and the problems of obtaining permanent state operating subsidies (as distinct from investment subsidies) that led to those measures being attempted.

By November 1985, Voest's situation was very serious. The accumulated losses were thought to be at least 5.7 billion ÖS for 1985. In fact, they were closer to 11.2 billion ÖS. The losses of Intertrading, involved in the oil speculation deals, were 4.2 billion ÖS. At the same time VEW also suffered losses of 1.3 billion ÖS and overall ÖIAG production fell by 15.7% in 1985. However, in 1986 four of eight ÖIAG subsidiaries obtained positive results, but the group still produced heavy, if smaller, losses than in 1985.

Despite the fact that Austrian state industries have received smaller subsidies than in most other countries (little before 1981, and for the period 1981–87 an amount of 59 billion ÖS) and that they remain relatively successful in the traditional areas of production, the dramatic nature of the losses of 1985, in addition to other scandals and a certain alienation from the political system in general, were a severe blow to the credibility of the state sector.

The ÖVP had just unveiled an economic programme which proposed less state intervention and, by British standards, mild privatisation measures. The crisis of 1985 was grist to the mill for the ÖVP privatising wing and to the internal FPÖ opposition, which, led by Jörg Haider, unseated party leader and Vice Chancellor, Norbert Steger, in 1986. There was a moderate (this was Austria!) 'Wende' in the air. The new managerial SPÖ Chancellor Franz Vranitzky met the criticisms of the state sector at least half-way and so deflected the ÖVP if not the FPÖ. The ground was laid for the new approach enshrined in the Coalition Agreement of January 1986. It was agreed to accord the restructured ÖIAG a 'final subsidy' which in June 1987 was set at 33 billion ÖS and to require it to reach profitability by

1990. Recourse to the private capital market and joint ventures with the private sector, as well as some privatisation, forms part of the agreed therapy. More job losses, perhaps another 10,000 at Voest, will also be required by 1990 and more may well be needed. The degree of privatisation is unspecified. It will certainly not be total, or even a majority privatisation, though some enterprises which do not have a clear place in the overall structure are to be totally privatised.

Even after these changes, the Austrian state sector will remain larger than in most equivalent countries, and its influence on the economy will also continue to be very considerable, though its room to act as an instrument of macro-economic policy, as a force of 'politics against the market', will now be severely limited, though not eliminated. Past experience shows the real, if time-bound, value and limitations of such an approach as part of an overall alternative economic strategy which does not merely resign itself to market forces.

Another structural aspect of Austria which has been of great significance to the development of a distinct 'Austrian Way' in economic policy, has been the system of Social Partnership, which is dealt with in detail elsewhere (Chapter 6). Suffice it to say here that it is a system of originality and stability. It has ensured social peace, bound together the consensus of social and political forces, and mobilised support for more moderation as part of an anti-recession strategy. It has enabled coherent and coordinated macro-economic strategies to be worked out and implemented.

Political consensus, Social Partnership, a large and active state sector, modernising reforms have all been elements in the economic strategy that has been called 'the Austrian Way' or Austro-Keynesianism. What were the specific components of that strategy? First, the strategy had certain clear and limited objectives. It put full employment first and subordinated it to all other goals of economic policy, though some of these goals were compatible and complementary. That is, in particular, true of measures to increase the rate of growth, and, contrary to the general view, measures to restrain inflation have also been supportive of employment. There was a readiness to use all the instruments available to the state in a coordinated and directed way, as part of a coherent strategy for achieving the main goal. At the same time, economic policy has been marked by almost total pragmatism as to means, if not as to ends. The maxim 'if it works, use it' has been much in evidence. However, the basic aim of tempering the impact of market forces by political action has been a central element, as has been the belief that there is an alternative to just bowing before those market forces.

The rapid growth – above OECD average levels – low inflation and low unemployment, gave Austria an excellent basis from which to meet the recession of the mid-1970s head-on. As we have seen, important structural reforms had been introduced such as the free trade agreement with the EEC (1972), the tax reform, the new competition laws, the restructuring the state industries (1973 and 1975), the increased emphasis on research, education and training, above all, in new technologies. Yet, despite all those positive developments and favourable signs, it is clear that Austrian policy was already more sceptical about the continuation of growth than most other equivalent economies, which scepticism made a rapid and positive reaction to the recession, psychologically easier to achieve in Austria than elsewhere, and gave Austrian policy its original character.

When the crisis hit in 1975, the reaction was to increase the budget deficit by 155% – as a counter-cyclical measure. A planned cut in income tax was advanced. A two-hour cut in the working week was introduced (+6.5% cut in working time in 1974–81, that is, double the German reduction). An expansionist demand policy was pursued. Rationalisation was delayed via the Social Partnership system and in the state sector. No monetary targets were set and inflation was dampened down through the Social Partnership system's moderation of wage and price increases. A hard currency policy, which closely linked the Schilling to the Deutschmark, was turned to advantage.

Employment increased in the state industries and the service sector. The direct employment effect of government policy was 0.5–1.5% of total employment. Austria was able, contrary to the usual IMF recipe, to maintain the strength of its currency by introducing measures to tax imports, promote exports and dampen-down demand.

Structural policies were promoted by key import substitution industries such as micro-electronics and the car industry. The reduction of the deficit was gradual and undertaken in parallel with renewed growth after 1977. Yet, the second oil price shock and American interest rates after 1981, threatened this recovery and opened up a vulnerable flank. Capital liberalisation measures had made it impossible to continue the policy of ÖS–DM linkage with constant interest rates. The National Bank was forced to bring in a restrictive monetary policy and hence raise interest rates.

The defence of employment then relied further on fiscal policy, which became expansionist again after 1982 and continued in 1983, contrary to what was happening in Germany, France and Britain. This expansionist policy took the form of special employment plans, special labour-market programmes (loans, relocation grants, early pensions), a youth employment scheme and a 6.3 billion ÖS stabilisation scheme in 1983, and a scheme for 8,000 public utility jobs in 1984.

The length and intensity of the recession made it difficult to maintain such a policy over the longer term, as debt servicing rose from 6.8% of GDP in 1975 to 15.6% in 1984. Measures to reduce the net deficit had to be taken but even then more prudently than elsewhere, and with full regard for the need to minimise the multiplier effect of this consolidation. Increases in revenue were preferred to expenditure cuts, and aids to export-industries and to investment (as well as an active labour market policy) were maintained. The process of budget consolidation has been accelerated under the Grand Coalition after 1987 and cuts in expenditure have been introduced, giving policy a more 'classic' accent than was the case earlier, with the aim of reducing the deficit from 4.0% of GDP in 1987 to 2.5% in 1992.

Thus, during the 1975–81 period, unemployment was kept down by a policy of Austro-Keynesianism and after 1981 to a lesser extent by what can be called 'rationalised Austro-Keynesianism', in the sense that, in this second phase, fiscal policy was less active and monetary, and currency policy was fully linked with surrounding international developments, whereas in the first phase it had screened them out to a large extent. As a result, the impact of the recession worked through, but slowly, in a weakened form. Unemployment rose to 4.6% and then continued to rise before stabilising in 1987. Thus, the policy was able to provide a considerable degree of protection against both unemployment and inflation, even for such a small and dependent economy as Austria.

While it is impossible completely to isolate a small, vulnerable economy such as Austria's from unfavourable developments as strong and prolonged as the 1970s and 1980s recessions, Austria has remained an effective example of a special kind of post-Keynesian economic strategy, in clear opposition to the monetarist supply side and anti-statist economic theories which have provided the ideological underpinning for government policy in much of the western world in the 1980s. Post-Keynesianism and its Austro-Keynesian variant seeks to act directly on imbalances caused by external shocks, through specific and short-term policy measures. That is not to say that such theories are not concerned with longer-term changes in equilibrium in areas such as industrial structure, energy policy or technological change. Indeed, by providing a degree of stability, they aim to promote such positive change, as an analysis of Austrian modernisation has shown.

Austro-Keynesianism is therefore not a mere counter-cyclical fiscal policy – though this has been an important element – but a broad-based policy mix, containing several elements in balance.

Fiscal policy has been a key element both with some direct measures to increase demand, via tax cuts, and also indirectly through incentives for investment and subsidies to building and construction. These measures have also been used to promote desirable structural changes and re-equilibrate markets. The state sector has been an important source of liquidity in these policies. To a degree, those measures have been partially self-financing in terms of additional taxation and the social benefits saved through job creation.

Austria has adopted a hard currency monetary policy, joining the DM zone, keeping the Schilling in close relation to the DM. The economy contains sectors which are exposed to foreign competition and some less exposed sectors. The exposed, export oriented sectors can only survive by adopting a price policy based on low costs, not on demand factors. This has required low inflation, maintained by a double mechanism: a low price and wage policy and dampening of import prices by a hard currency policy, which involved a revaluation against the US dollar, which limited the inflationary effects of the oil price shock and of increased import prices generally. This policy now is no longer seen as a re-valuation policy against the dollar, but as a linkage to the DM, which can, and mostly does, have a similar effect. The specifically Austrian component has been the use of 'flanking' fiscal measures to partially counteract the possible negative effects on employment of the rigid monetary policy or higher interest rates that this policy requires.

As we have seen, the Social Partnership system has been a key element in ensuring price stability domestically, through a moderate wage and price policy. The system has also enabled effective policy planning and cordination with all the key economic actors, a vital and specifically Austrian institutional aspect of Austro-Keynesianism.

As we have seen, longer term structural reform has been a vital element in the Austro-Keynesian strategy, as has the existence of a large and active public sector, able, for shorter periods at least, to operate counter-cyclical policies and slow down rationalisation during recession.

Many of the factors involved in Austria are perhaps specific to that country's institutional and political make-up. Yet Austria exemplifies the fact that expansionary policies can have positive and long-term effects on employment, without causing inflation or preventing structural change while increasing productivity. Indeed, Austrian productivity increased faster then in Germany in the 1973–81 period.

However, as the increasing unemployment up to 1987, the rising public sector deficit, the crisis in the financing of social benefits, the serious difficulties in the state industries and the general loss of confidence shows, the 'Austrian Model' has, inevitably, limitations on its staying power alone in a world in recession. Its short and medium-term success has been manifest, but the relay must be taken up by action elsewhere in the world economic system. Indeed, in the longer term, even compensatory fiscal policies, coupled with monetary policy and structural measures, will lose their effectiveness in a small, open economy. At the same time uncertainties about growth and new ecological concerns are undermining confidence in the growth-oriented strategies. Even more importantly, technological developments are uncoupling growth from employment. As a result, growth alone cannot guarantee full employment to the same degree as before. As a result, the strategy must be augmented with new labour-market policies, such as greater work-sharing measures.

Yet, all in all, Austro-Keynesiansim has been a success, and in a renewed climate of confidence could, with some adaptation, still give the lie to the view that 'there is no alternative' to acceptance of the impact of market forces.

It should be noted that the Austrian economy exceeded growth forecasts in both 1988 and in 1989. Unemployment has started to fall again. The coalition medicine seems to be working, as the economy shows itself to be adaptable to changing circumstances without abandoning the central postulates of previous economic policy. The model is adaptable and durable.

6. Social Partnership

One of the most important elements in the 'Austrian Model' is the system of Social Partnership which came into being in the 1950s and has survived all the political and economic changes that have occurred since. To some, on both sides of industry, the system involves too much compromise in the interests of consensus. Yet, for the majority it is the most durable and successful part of the 'Austrian Model'. It is the economic counterpart of the political 'Grand Coalition' and the proporz system. The Social Partnership is a para-coalition, which parallels the party coalition at the political level. To go further, the system of Social Partnership has been the cement of the political consensus and has played an important rôle in maintaining the essentials of consensus, even during the periods of one-party government or 'small coalition' government. Thus, the ÖVP government (1966–70) and the SPÖ or SPÖ-led governments (1970–87) took no measures which would undermine the system of Social Partnership. On the contrary, they saw it as an important stabilising mechanism, especially during the one-party rule periods.

The system of Social Partnership is especially Austrian both in its conception and in terms of the values which make it work. It can only be understood against the background of the situation which brought it into existence. A number of special features, in the structure and organisation of the Austrian economy and in the Austrian situation, have contributed to the success of a system of Social Partnership (SP) or, to put it another way, have been essential pre-conditions to its creation. These include a tradition of corporatism and state intervention in the economy, and a large State sector. The post-war situation in Austria, with the need both for reconstruction and to present an internal united front towards the Allied Powers of Occupation, was an added factor of considerable importance in the equation. Furthermore, this reconstruction mentality lasted longer than in almost any other European country and in any event at least until October 1955 when the State Treaty entered force, and even beyond.

At the same time, there is a deep interlocking between the main political parties and the social forces which are involved in the Social Partnership process. The ÖVP is made up of the Christian trade unions, the Employers Organisation and the Austrian Farmers Federation. The SPÖ has very close links with the ÖGB (Trade Union Confederation). Indeed, the president of the Nationalrat has traditionally been an ÖGB leader, as has the Social Affairs Minister.

The corporatist structure of Austria is built around the elected representative chambers, of which the three most important are: the Arbeiterkammer (Workers Chamber) which is organised on a federalised basis, with a national umbrella organisation (Arbeiter Kammertag); the Bundeskammer der gewerblichen Wirtschaft (Chamber of Commerce); and the Landwirtschaftskammer. Those chambers are established by law and membership is obligatory. Delegates are elected every five years by the membership. These bodies, with the ÖGB, make up the Social Partnership system. Each party (ÖVP, SPÖ, FPÖ) has its own 'fraktion' or group in each of the three chambers and in the ÖGB, though the dominant force varies from one chamber to the other. The SPÖ dominates the ÖGB and the Arbeiterkammer. The ÖVP dominates the Landwirtschaftskammer, with a significant FPÖ influence and the ÖVP also dominates the Kammer der gewerblichen Wirtschaft. These political 'Fraktionen' are then, in turn, represented in the national and party organs, creating a structure of mutual influence and interlocking membership between the parties and the organisations. These bodies are, as we shall see, also involved in an institutional way in the system of government.

Austria also has one of the largest public sectors outside the Socialist Block. Some 26% of industrial production derives from socially owned enterprises of one type or another. Heavy industry, such as steel and chemicals; the energy sector and banking are the main areas of state industrial concentration. There is also a tradition for the state sector to be actively used as a tool of economic policy. The political parties and associated social partners are also directly and proportionally involved in the management of the state sector. There has thus been a climate of opinion in the Austrian Second Republic which has been favourable to the broad involvement of the social partners in the consensual resolution of economic problems and a high degree of cross-fertilisation between the political parties, government, the social organisations and the state sector of the economy. Another important factor was the relative balance in strength between the two lagers: neither side was fundamentally weaker than the other, which was an essential element in the stability of the system of Social Partnership.

The present structured system of Social Partnership was, surprisingly, not established immediately after the war and was thus not, as might perhaps be expected, an immediate result of the formation of the Grand Coalition. However, the formation and durability of that coalition was a basic pre-condition for cooperation between organisations which, in, a historical perspective, had been at least as antagonistic as the political parties. Gradually, cooperation was established between the various representative organisations. These relations, vital to ensuring non-inflationary economic reconstruction and depolitisation of the economic distribution debate, were then institutionalised in a series of five wages and prices agreements between 1947-51, which established the framework for wages and prices in the coming period.

The unions renounced the use of the strike weapon, but obtained recognition and plant-level bargaining, which had been difficult in the First Republic. These agreements were reached in an Economic Commission in which the four organisations were represented. In 1951, following a period of industrial unrest in 1950 mainly fomented by the KPÖ, it was considered appropriate to reinforce the institutionalisation of the system. To that end, a law was passed establishing an Economic Directorate which, chaired by the Federal Chancellor, involved Federal ministers, representatives of the National Bank and the four organisations. It was to come to exercise wide powers of direction of the economic policy. However, doubts about the constitutionality of an arrangement which appeared to transfer powers from the democratically elected Nationalrat and Cabinet, to this new Directorate, soon arose and in the event, the law was declared unconstitutional by the Federal Constitutional Court. The passage of such a law indicates just how far governmental opinion was prepared to go in involving interest groups in consensual economic decision-making.

It was then that the system took on its present structure. A voluntary, rather than a statutory system was established, without formal powers. The effect was the same, but the Constitution was formally respected. Thus in 1957, the Joint Committee (Paritätische Kommission) was established, together with a series of subordinate bodies, with specialist tasks. The Joint committee is chaired by the Chancellor and the government is represented by the Ministers of Trade, Agriculture and Social Affairs. Each of the four organisations (ÖGB, Arbeiterkammer, Präsidialkonferenz der Landwirtschaftskammer, Handelskammer) send two representatives. The Plenary

Joint commission meets to resolve important problems and arbitrate issues that have not been resolved in its sub-committees. It must be unanimous, but government representatives do not vote. Its meetings are held in private, behind closed doors. The media are only informed of its decisions and not of its internal discussions. The government members do not have voting rights in the commission and all its decisions must be taken by unanimity, which means that a consensus of all the organisations involved in the process is required for any decision to be taken.

The Joint Committee has two key sub-committees; one for wages and one for prices. The same organisations are represented in these sub-committees, but not the government. The wages sub-committee is seized of wage claims and must determine whether they are in conformity with the general economic situation of Austria. The individual wage agreements are not decided in the wages sub-committee itself. The Austrian system involves the negotiation of sector wage agreements on a nation-wide basis, between the relevant section of the Chamber of Commerce and the relevant union (fifteen make up the ÖGB). These agreements contain clauses on minimum national wages levels and conditions of work, and permit locally negotiated increases on the minimum wages, within certain margins. These negotiations can only be opened with the approval of the wages commission, seized by the ÖGB, which will have in turn been seized by the member union concerned. Here too, unanimity is required. The chair of the sub-committee alternates between the Handelskammer and the ÖGB.

The Prices Sub-Committee contains representatives of all the four organisations and the government. The Minister of Trade and Industry takes the chair. The agreed rules of the Prices Sub-Committee involve acceptance by the Chamber of Commerce that price rises for goods, not otherwise subject to legal price control, will be submitted for prior approval in the Commission. The procedure is voluntary, but indirect legal sanctions do exist for non-compliance. Apart from imported goods and fashion articles, where a control is excluded, the system appears to be broadly respected. The aim of the system, which has been largely achieved, is to ensure that only the necessary cost increases are passed on in the form of increased prices. Of course, the Committee possesses no means of investigation of claims at a deeper level and has been limited to moderating and delaying increases. At the same time, the organisations have from time-to-time carried out some 'package dealing' trading approval of some price demands for wage increases. Some products, in particular food and energy, are subject to official price control, in which the three chambers have an advisory rôle. Where unanimity cannot be achieved in a sub-committee, the question is put before the full Plenary Joint Commission.

The full Joint Committee usually meets once a month, though special meetings to discuss important issues are called from time to time. As already indicated, the meeting is chaired by the Federal Chancellor; each of the four organisations has two representatives and the government up to seven non-voting members. However, the most important organ is the 'pre-meeting' of the presidents of the three chambers and the ÖGB, at which the work of the Joint Commission is prepared by behind-the-scenes compromises. The chairmen personally take part in the Joint Commission sittings. The full Joint Commission discusses matters referred up from the sub-committees, and more general matters of economic policy. It is here that its most vital influence lies.

At each meeting, the Chancellor introduces a discussion on the economic situation. From time to time, more detailed discussion-meetings (on the economic situation) are held. The President and the Vice President of the National Bank and the Director of the Institute for Economic Research both attend and, with the Finance Minister, give an introductory report which serves to launch the discussion. Thus the key decisions made on exchange rate policy, the introduction of anti-cyclical investment promotion measures, and the more recent measures taken in the state sector, have been carefully discussed in the Joint Commission before firm decisions were taken by the Cabinet.

In order to enable the Joint Commission to participate effectively in the process of economic decision-making and to provide a good technical input, it was decided in 1963 to create an Advisory Committee for Economic and Social Questions. This Committee is composed of three experts from each of the four organisations and has established a network of sub-committees with experts coopted from the Chambers' own staff, from ministries, the private sector and universities. This committee, which has over the years coopted the best elements of the rising élite, has played a key rôle in the socialisation processes and in promoting a style of consensual coope-ration and decision-making. The Advisory Committee has established sub-committees to look at a wide range of questions in the economic and social sphere: prices and wages, productivity, the construction industry, regional policy, migrant labour, periodic budget forecasts and proposals to strengthen the capital markets.

The basic work on reducing working hours was also developed in the Advisory Committee. Initially, the Advisory Committee appeared to be solely a technical body, but it soon became clear that its studies included political recommendations which could exercise considerable influence. As a result, the studies are submitted to the full Advisory Committee, and most importantly, to the Presidents of the four organisations, for approval before publication. By this procedure, the authority of the reports is considerably increased.

The Joint Commission and its offshoots clearly represent the summit of Social Partnership, but there is a broad-base organised cooperation which underpins it. There is the chamber system and alongside it, voluntary representative bodies, which are involved in consultative and cooperative procedures. The chambers are in a special category, in that they are established by law. Their leadership is elected by the membership and they have the legal right to be consulted on legislation which concern them; to provide services for their members; and to be represented in the management of the social insurance schemes and other advisory and management bodies. These chambers are a very special Austrian institution. Membership is compulsory and the resources of the chambers are such as to enable them to develop considerable and respected expertise and a large support staff. There are in all 13 such chambers, of which the Chamber of Commerce, the Arbeiter Kammertag, the Präsidialkonferenz der Landwirtschaftskammer are the most important and the only cross-professional chambers with a broad function. All chambers are decentralised. In addition to the Federal chambers, there is a chamber in each Land. For important pieces of legislation, up to forty-three bodies are consulted, outside the Federal and Land governments.

The Chambers of Commerce are the earliest and their roots go well back into the nineteenth century. The first Vienna Chamber of Commerce was established in 1848 and the first national body in 1850. The law of 1868 established the chambers on the basis that is recognisable today. The tendency towards breaking the chamber up into separate bodies for different sectors was introduced and its coordinating character retained, which was to be a major ingredient in the success of the Social Partnership.

In the First Republic, the Chamber of Commerce was divided into sections for Trade, Artisanal Production and Industry. In 1937, the geographical decentralisation into Land chambers was added. In 1946, following the war, the chambers were re-established, with six sections (Trade, Industry, Artisanal Production, Finance, Credit, Insurance), each with sub-sectors by branch.

The organs of the Federal chamber are elected at a local branch level and then, through indirect election, the sections send delegates to the Land and Federal assemblies. Political groups have been formed in the chambers: Österreichische Wirtschaftsbund (ÖVP), Freie Wirtschaftsbund (SPÖ), Ring Freiheitlicher Wirtschaftstreibender (FPÖ). The Österreichischer Wirtschaftsbund has a dominant position (84% in 1985).

The Arbeiterkammer were a later creation. The 1867 Constitution opened the way to the legal establishment of trade unions. The first Austrian Trade Union Congress was held in 1893. Membership was small, a mere 88,818 (1.3% of all workers) but by 1913 membership had risen to 500,000. The workers movement was long ambivalent about the creation of the Arbeiterkammer, though the demand was discussed from 1872. The Hainfeld SPÖ Congress in 1888 did not propose the creation of such chambers and, indeed opposed it, seeing the fact that the idea had liberal support as an indication that it was intended as a device to avoid universal suffrage.

After the First World War, the situation was radically altered and in 1920, Arbeiterkammer were established, with the rights to be consulted on legislation, to be represented in public bodies, to provide services to workers. After 1934, the chambers lost their free and democratic character and were subordinated to the State Trade Union. The chambers were re-established in 1945, and in 1954 the umbrella body at the national level, the Arbeiter Kammertag was given legal recognition. The organs of the nine Land Arbeiterkammer are elected for four years by universal suffrage of all workers, and the Land Chambers send delegates to the Arbeiter Kammertag (ÖAKT). The ÖAKT has fifty-nine members (fifty delegates and ex-officio the chairmen of the nine Land Chambers) and a nine member board. Each Land Chamber has an elected Assembly and a Board. The assembly meets twice yearly, elects the chairman and Board members, votes the budget and fixes the chamber's policy aims. The Boards can establish policy-making committees, with coopted members to assist it. The Vienna Chamber Board has, for example, established seventeen committees. The chambers have a right to be consulted on all Bills and regulations and to prepare Bills themselves. They send representatives to a wide range of public bodies such as the Food Code Commission, the Pensions Board, the Labour Market Policy Advisory Board, the Monopolies and Mergers Commission and the Board of the National Bank, a total of over one hundred memberships. The full range of the involvement of the ÖAKT in public policy can be exemplified by a few other random examples: the Timetable Commission of the Federal Railways, the Bus Licensing Commission, the Commission on Approved Medicines, the Agricultural Management Committees. The Chambers are also entitled to appoint members to Social Security Tribunals. The ÖAKT sent a basic statement of its economic, social and educational demands to the government in the form of a memorandum in 1985, which was updated in 1987, with emphasis on full employment and the protection of social standards.

The Assemblies contain political groupings. All chambers, and as a result, the ÖAKT, are dominated by the Socialist (SPÖ) group. The SPÖ has 64% of the seats in the Arbeiterkammer, with 31% for the ÖVP, 3% for the FPÖ and 1% for the KPÖ at the most recent elections.

In the Landwirtschaftskammer (Chambers of Agriculture), the ÖVP has a dominant position of 84% with 10% for the SPÖ, 2% for the FPÖ and 4% for non-party lists. As agricultural policy is largely a Land matter, the Kammer are organised on an even more decentralised basis than the other Chambers. However, a national umbrella body – the Präsidialkonferenz – has been established and takes part in the Joint Committee and is the body that is consulted by the Federal Government.

The Präsidialkonferenz has set up a number of Committees which have responsibility for particular areas, such as mountain agriculture, women in farming, trade questions, wine, dairying, machinery, tourism in rural areas. Agriculture was one of the most important sectors of the Austrian economy (and even today still occupies 9% of the work force), and it remains the backbone of the economy of the more rural Länder such as Burgenland (14.3%), Niederösterreich (13.3%) and Steiermark (12.4%). The sector is characterised by a high degree of cooperative organisation in production, marketing, distribution and banking, and considerable state intervention through marketing regulations, the milk and grain industry stabilisation funds, guide prices, quota systems, import levies, forestry premiums and measures to support mountain agriculture. The aim of policy is to guarantee food supplies and mountain agriculture. The Land Chambers of Agriculture and the Cooperative Movement (Raiffeisenverein) make up the Präsidialkonferenz, which is involved in defending the interests of the industry at Land and Federal level in relation to government. A key aim of the Chambers in the Social Partnership is to promote the fair distribution of prosperity between agriculture and industry.

Social Partnership was vital in keeping social peace and in ensuring orderly development of the economy in the post-war reconstruction phase, and played a key rôle in the Austro-Keynesian policies of the 1970s which kept Austrian unemployment and inflation below that of other developed economies. It is worth recalling that, in the period of most acute crisis in Western Europe, unemployment in Austria remained at an average of 1.95%, well below German levels (1975–81). In more recent years, unemployment has risen to 5.2% (1986), still below levels in other Western States, but is now falling again. The rate of growth was 5.7% between 1969–73 (OECD 4.7%) and 3.0% between 1973–79 (OECD 2.7%) only falling below the OECD level for the 1979–85 period with 1.9% (OECD 2.6%). Inflation was always well below OECD averages, with a high point of 6.8% in 1981. At the time of writing inflation is at 1.7%. For the most part of the period 1966–1986, real growth in Austria lay above the OECD level, being below average only in 1973, 1978 and 1984. The average number of 'strike minutes' per worker in Austria was a mere 2.9 in 1980; 0.1 in 1983 and 1984 and 3.9 in 1985. Even Japanese and German figures are higher, and British figures – even in the Thatcherite era – are, of course, dramatically higher. Indeed, the strike is rare and virtually an exception in Austrian industrial relations. These bare figures suggest considerable success in managing the Austrian economy, even during the periods of world recession. Social Partnership has, by common consent, been an essential element in that success.

Earlier, we pointed to certain factors which have made the system of Social Partnership possible and effective, such as a highly centralised and developed system of organisational representation, a large state sector and an interventionist tradition, close inter-penetration between political parties and the Social Partnership organisations, and a consensual style of political decision-making. Above all, Social Partnership and the associated consensual style of politics is a state of mind, which permeates Austrian society. The bitter experiences of the inter-war period generated a desire to avoid conflict or sublimate it into institutions and negotiations.

In the early years of the Second Republic, there was a conscious movement to break down barriers between the lagers, to work together across the barriers of class and interest. It was an individual and collective movement, leading to greater understanding and compromise. Spheres of influence were fixed and balances struck, of which the Social Partnership system is one, and perhaps the most important, example. It is a permanent para-coalition, existing at times in parallel to its political counter-part, the Grand (ÖVP/SPÖ) Coalition and at other times without it. All governments have nurtured Social Partnership and it has flourished equally under ÖVP or SPÖ one-party government, SPÖ one-party government Small Coalition (SPÖ-FPÖ) and Grand Coalition. Indeed, it represents a guarantee that whatever the type of government in power, the major economic interest groups and the political parties behind them will have at least an indirect involvement in economic and social policy making.

During the ÖVP government (1966-70), the Arbeiterkammer and ÖGB retained their influence and during the SPÖ government (1970–83), the Handelskammer and Präsidialkonferenz (Agricultural Conference) retained their influence in decision-making. Thus, in the broadest sense, there has always been a consensual system with solutions emerging after broad-based negotiation, which the Cabinet and Nationalrat, often unanimously, endorsed. A government has rarely acted against the consensus of the social partners, or even against one or other of the organisations. Indeed, it would not be too exaggerated to speak of a system of mutual veto in which key decisions can only be taken with very broad consent. Naturally, there have been shifts in the balance of forces from time to time, especially with the election of a series of SPÖ governments in the 1970s, but even then, the system has operated as a shock absorber, limiting the degree and pace of change in the balance of power within the system. However, there are also areas, such as problems of society, the reform of the legal system, educational policy and cultural policy, which lay outside the sphere of Social Partnership and which could be given a new direction through the political process. The basic result of the system has been to ensure a balance between interests, to guarantee their minimum influence and to maintain their 'acquis'. Change would be gradual and balanced and irreversible. Most opinion has therefore been favourable towards the Social Partnership system, though recognising its limitations.

Its very success has led to criticism. It has been essentially conservative in its tendency to absorb change and produce stability, which was, after all, its initial objective. Criticism has come from several different perspectives. Indeed, Social Partnership has not escaped the recent questioning of the pillars of Austrian society, which questioning has become more and more prevalent in recent years. Yet the system is seen to have considerable powers of adaptation, which should be adequate to ensure its continuation, which majority opinion certainly seems to consider desirable and, indeed, necessary to the future stable development of the Austrian economy, especially with the problems of re-orientating the economy in a more competitive direction and restructuring the state sector in preparation, among other things for the internal market, whether as a full member of the Community or in some other closely related status. For most of those involved, there seems no serious alternative to Social Partnership and more rather than less cooperation seems to be called for.

However, a new critique of Social Partnership can be heard, in line with the generally more critical tones that can be observed in Austrian society generally over the last few years. They key question must be whether those critical accents seriously threaten the basis of Social Partnership, or merely entail a degree of adaptation, which the system can take in its stride quite easily without its advantages – admitted by almost all – being lost. Whatever may be the criticisms levelled at the functioning of the Social Partnership system, one is struck by the fact that few see any alternative to it, most expect it to continue, perhaps with a degree of greater flexibility, and most seem to find that a both natural and desirable situation.

One line of criticism is that the system required very particular historical circumstances to develop, which can no longer prevail. The argument is, that although the Social Partnership system may have been appropriate in the period of post-war reconstruction, it is no longer appropriate, because its conservatism could only be successful if it could impose constraints and restrictions on Austrian society that are no longer desirable in changed circumstances. The most essential of these conditions is the consensus mentality, which has required the effective sublimation of social and political conflict into institutionalised negotiating machinery.

The para-coalition system presupposes a broad-based consensus, with recognition of spheres of legitimate interest between the two camps (Red and Black) and acceptance of a system of *de facto* mutual vetoes on both agenda and outcome. Of course, and here the adaptability of the system is illustrated, the Social Partnership has survived the period of 'Grand Coalition' in the old form. All of the

ÖVP, SPÖ and SPÖ–FPÖ governments were careful not to damage the system, though there may have been criticisms of their handling of the partnership during their tenure. Indeed, it may be argued that in periods without a political 'Grand Coalition', the Social Partnership structure is even more important, as it then constitutes the only institutionalised bridge between the two camps.

The system has been criticised as requiring a too centralised and, indeed, authoritarian structure in the participating organisations if it is to continue to function. Both in the unions and among the business community, there has been an increasing criticism of the Vienna bureaucracy, which in this context is not the bureaucracy of the state, but of the organisations involved in the Social Partnership. If the system is to work, power must be concentrated in the hands of a few decision makers who have achieved each other's respect and confidence, and who can 'deliver' the full support of their organisations.

In periods of increasing competition between firms and increasing conflict between small and larger firms, between old and new technology industries, this centralisation has become difficult on the employers side. On the Trade Union and Arbeiterkammer side, the same conflicts arise in other forms. Generalised support for wage moderation, rationalisation and the introduction of new technology, has come into serious conflict with the interests of workers in the threatened heavy industries in the Upper Steiermark and Oberösterreich. The conflict has also become characterised by the same East/West cleavages as we see in the debate about federalism. The interests of the Western Provinces, turned towards the Southern German economic space and rapid modernisation and flexibility, may differ from those of the Capital and the industrial East (Oberösterreich, Niederösterreich, Steiermark).

More radical criticism has been directed at the system on the grounds that it presupposes, or at least has entailed, a too close a relationship between the political class and the organisations, with the parties being colonised by the organisations or the organisations being colonised by the parties. It is argued that the organisations are not able to act primarily as the representatives and defenders of their members' interests, but are appendages of the political parties that dominate their lager. At the same time, government and parliament are considered to have too little real independence from the organisations.

The Social Partnership system, and above all the Joint Committee, has been seen as the real focus of economic decision-making rather than Cabinet and Nationalrat, which are then mere rubber stamps, endorsing decisions taken elsewhere. There may be some truth in this at various periods. Yet, there have always been important and conflictual areas of policy where the writ of Social Partnership does not run. These may also be affected by the existence of a political Grand Coalition or consensual habits in the political arena, but that is another issue.

This line of attack has come above all from small business and from the political right of the ÖVP and the FPÖ. The FPÖ has accentuated its, at times, demagogic attacks on the 'system' under the leadership of Jörg Haider since 1986. The FPÖ was always an 'out' party until it became a junior partner in government in 1983–86. Nor does it have significant influence in any of the Social Partnership organisations. It has strongly criticised the system as over-bureaucratic, as unresponsive and undemocratic, as creating privileges for the political class and for organisation bureaucrats which the FPÖ argues have become over-concerned with preserving the system and hence the consensus and mutual concessions and, like business monopolies, the exclusion of new forces from the system. Thus, for example, the FPÖ proposed to end compulsory membership of the various chambers as a means of reducing their power and resources.

Other ideological criticism of the Social Partnership system has come from the left in the SPÖ, from the KPÖ and the Linksblok (left block) in the Arbeiter Kammertag and the ÖGB. Here, the central objection is that the acceptance of Social Partnership by the SPÖ and the ÖGB represents an implicit acceptance of the *status quo* and the effective abandonment, however mitigated it already was in reality, of class struggle with, as its goal – however distant – a radical change in the nature of society. Social Partnership is seen as a non-ideological approach, owing more to Catholic social teaching – that there are no unbridgeable conflicts in society.

Modern socialist leaders and thinkers have argued that Social Partnership does not entail the abandonment of conflict of interest, but merely its pursuit by other methods – as Renner called it, 'the class struggle of the green baize table'. Indeed, they ask, would the Labour movement have been able to gain more by a more conflictual strategy. Critics argue that the Social Partnership method has systematically reduced the militancy of the Labour movement and its ability to mobilise for conflict should that be required at some time in the future. The Social Partnership system then clearly implies acceptance by both sides of the *status quo* in terms of the ownership of industry and the broad distribution of property and income. It is a recipe for stability rather than radical change, for social peace rather than social conflict. This is seen by its critics as an emasculation of the workers movement.

Yet, in a period of weakening of trade unionism elsewhere, it should not be forgotten that the restrictions are not one-sided. The Social Partnership system is not a one-way street. The employers' side and the state are bound into a system which imposes obligations on them. These involve recognition of the formal equality of the 'other side' of industry and an acceptance of a moderate, consensual approach to wages and conditions of work. This implies that no attempt will be made to break the power of trade unions or reduce real wages.

The state and employers have also accepted the rôle of the state industries and the Welfare State. Furthermore, whole areas of economic policy have been removed from the dictates of the market by their politisation within the para-coalition system. Here, decisions depend on the balance of political forces and bargaining within the para-coalition, with considerable advantages for the workers' side. These matters have become, through works councils, through Arbei- terkammer and the national mechanisms of Social Partnership, matters of political co-decision, rather than being subjected to the arbitrary authority of the employers' side or the vagaries of market forces. The advantage of this should be measured against the situation of the trade union movement in Britain since 1979. Further- more, the main conservative party (the ÖVP and the social organisa- tions in its orbit), and the Association of Industrialists all accept these basic premises, which represents a very significant guarantee for the future.

A basic pillar of the system has been an agreement on basic economic goals, specifically economic growth. This agreement gave the system coherence and stability and avoided sharp conflict about distribution. Growth as an economic goal is increasingly contested in Austria, as new post-materialist values emerge, and has led to 'Green' critiques of the Social Partnership system. Between 1980 and 1984, environmental protection rose to overtake job security in voters' minds (in 1980 it was identified as 'urgent' by 52%; it was 80% in 1984) as the most salient issue. Survey evidence has shown a fall in the number of 'pure materialists' from 38% to 10% in the 1976–86 period and has identified a potential of 11% post-materialists and a hard core of 4% pure post-materialists, with concentrations as high as 21% in Vorarlberg and Tirol, and 15% in Kärnten and Steiermark.

The credibility and cohesion of Social Partnership has been weakened by its difficulty in adapting to the emergence of new lines of cleavage, to which it is ill adapted: the economy/ecology cleavage or materialist/post-materialist cleavage. It has supported both the Zwentendorf nuclear power station in 1978 and the Hainburg power station project in 1984–85, and in both cases found itself on the losing side, unable to mobilise support for the projects. It was almost as if this 'establishment' support from the Social Partnership apparatus was perceived by many as a negative factor.

Many problems threaten the Social Partnership system. As in other areas of Austrian life, its very success in achieving its original aims may have prepared the ground for a more flexible, less centralised and less hierarchical society, more open to new ideas. The new tendency towards political de-alignment, of a reduced identification with a 'lager', declining political participation – though party membership remains high – structural changes in society (which may reduce union membership as has happened in other advanced post-industrial societies), and the trend towards non-materialist values, may all undermine the old system of Social Partnership.

Yet the tradition of Social Partnership and with it consensus-building is now so strong in Austria – to the point of being a reflex. Paradoxically, there was great public support and pressure for a new Grand Coalition in 1987. Few want to abandon Social Partnership, although many recognise that the changing structure of the economy and the emergence of new political values will make the adaption of the system at the same time both necessary and difficult. Contesting the growth ethic as a basic goal will sharpen the distribution issue and make it increasingly difficult to maintain a broad political consensus. However, the advantages of Social Partnership remain real for everyone involved.

Possibly the system can be maintained in those strictly limited areas of incomes policy and related issues, while its broader functions are abandoned, although to many this would be regrettable. The authority of the system, until now virtually uncontested, may become more difficult to maintain. More positively, on the Socialist and trade union side, the missing ideological underpinning for the system may be developed. This would entail seeing Social Partnership as a form of embryonic economic democracy and co-determination, which must be built upon. This would enable the Socialists to resume their leadership rôle – it is from their side that almost all initiatives have come – without fear of ideological embarrassment.

The most likely development therefore is that the system of Social Partnership will continue in its present form (or close to it), while making some necessary adaptations to changing circumstances and with a much less absolute authority than before.

7. Democratic Reform: Federalism and Direct Democracy

Democratic reform is a very wide-ranging concept and is variously understood in Austria. For some, such as the Greens it means a radically different approach to the very processes of government. In this view limited institutional changes, though perhaps useful, cannot suffice. More openness and more political conflict, less consensus- and less coalition-mentality would be required. For others, such as the FPÖ's new Aufsteiger or Quereinsteiger generation voters (yuppies) what is needed is more room for individual initiative, less corporatism, less parteibuchwirtshaft (party membership-card economy), less privilege and patronage for the political class and more control of government. For others in the political mainstream, these issues are more a matter of degree, and limited institutional reforms are seen as useful. Thus, largely at the initiative of the ÖVP, the 1987 coalition agreement contains a section on democracy, which covers federalism, direct democracy, electoral reform and parliamentary reform.

An important area of renewal in the Austrian Model over the last decade has been the renaissance of Austrian federalism. Certainly Austria has been a federation since its creation in 1920. However, during the First Republic and indeed during the early years of the Second Republic, there was little real interest in federalism as a living concept. Particularism was a form of provincialism, rather than a real form of federalism.

In much more recent years, there has been a renewed interest in federalism as a means of expression of regional differences, of ensuring a wider political debate and a wider form of pluralism, and as a countervailing force against consensual centralisation, which has been seen as having gone too far.

Federalism is now increasingly seen as a means – alongside the other elements of the 'Austrian Model' – of injecting a greater degree of variation, flexibility and responsiveness of government and engendering a greater sense of participation and responsibility in government. In this way, federalism is not in contradiction to the 'Austrian Model', but rather represents an adaptation and enrichment of it.

What has federalism meant in Austria? What are the existing bases on which the new federalist consciousness can build? Modern Austria has nine Länder or Provinces: Vienna, Lower Austria, Upper Austria, Salzburg, Tirol, Vorarlberg, Kärnten, Steiermark and Burgenland. Vienna has the largest population, but is contracting (1,771, 000 in 1939 and 1,489,000 in 1985). The smallest is Burgenland with a population of 268,000 in 1985. The rate of population growth in the Western Länder is considerable. The population of Vorarlberg has doubled from 158,000 in 1939 to 309,000 in 1985.

The present boundaries of the Länder were laid down in the peace settlement of 1920. Several of the Länder then lost population and land area to the successor states. Lower Austria lost small areas to Czechoslovakia. The Steiermark lost both Slovene and German-speaking areas, including the towns of Marburg, Petten and Luttenburg to Yugoslavia. The Province of Kärnten ceded the Kanaltal to Italy and the Rosegg, Ferloch, Valkermark, Bleiburg and Miestal districts to Yugoslavia, but retained Klagenfurt. The southern part of the Tirol, including German-speaking areas, was ceded to Italy. On the other hand, the new Burgenland Province was created from Western Hungary, an area, which was mainly German-speaking, around the Neusiedlersee. However, when Austria sought to take control in 1921, the Hungarian resistance led the Allies to order a plebiscite in Ödenburg, which was eventually awarded to Hungary.

Despite these recent territorial changes, minor for the most part, the present Länder can be said to correspond to long-standing traditional regions, with a common past stretching back into the Middle Ages. Vienna is, like the German Länder of Hamburg and Bremen, a city state.

The Burgenland is rural, isolated and has a character of its own. The Western Länder have shown the strongest economic dynamism in recent years, and the difficulties of the state's heavy industries are mostly concentrated in Lower Austria and the Steiermark.

Traditional political differences, which divide 'red' Vienna from the 'black' Western Länder, are coupled with resentments created by the centralising tendencies of the capital. These divergences were increased in the ten-year occupation after the Second World War. At first, there were serious difficulties in communication and misunderstandings between Vienna, Burgenland and Lower Austria, which were isolated in the Soviet zone, and the Western Länder. The Länder in the Soviet zone also fell behind in the process of reconstruction. Even in a country as small as Austria, there are very real regional differences in terms of history, traditions, political outlook, culture and economic structure which make federalism meaningful.

Despite the strong central Habsburg administration in the Monarchy, the Länder had survived as units of administration with a real sense of identity. When the Constituent Assembly was drawing up the Constitution in 1920, there was a confrontation between two tendencies: the Social Democrats opposed federalism and argued for a single-chamber National Assembly in a centralistic state, while the Christian Socialists in the Länder argued for the exact opposite – a very weak central Parliament, nominated by the Landtag and with only limited powers of coordination. The German nationalists, the 'third force', held to a middle positon, favouring neither extreme centralisation or excessive particularism.

Although the Socialists did not have a majority in the Constituent Assembly, the compromise enshrined in the 1920 Constitution leaned more to the Socialist view. This arose in part because the strong man of the Social Christian Party, Dr Ignaz Seipel, was a Centralist. He considered that a state, as weak and economically vulnerable as rump Austria, required a strong central administration. Furthermore, he was confident, with good reason, that the political right would obtain and maintain a permanent majority in the State.

As a result, the 1920 Constitution established a federal state, but limited the power of the Second Chamber (Bundesrat) to one of delay. The powers of the Länder are limited, and their financial and administrative autonomy restricted. The reality of the 1920 Constitution is more unitarist than federal. Until the 1970s, the trend of reforms to the Constitution has been in the direction of even greater centralisation. The Western Länder were never reconciled to this, which was an unfavourable compromise in their opinion.

In the spring of 1921, Salzburg and Tirol organised unofficial plebiscites on union with Germany, which showed massive majorities for union. Voralberg had sought to initiate discussions with Switzerland before the conclusion of the Treaty of St Germain, as to whether she could join Switzerland. However, the Swiss reaction was unfavourable. These early divergences were the basis of the later conflict between 'Red' Vienna and the countryside, leading to the installation of an authoritarian regime after 1934. The long-term suspicion of federalism in the SPÖ was founded. Until relatively recently, only the ÖVP was interested in promoting greater federalism.

The 1920 Constitution was amended in 1925 and 1929 in the direction of greater centralisation and twenty-nine competences were removed from the Länder and given the Bund. The most important of these were water, policing of foreigners, police and communications. In the Second Republic, these centralising tendencies continued, at least until the mid-1970s.

The transfer of competences has numerically been less significant, but probably substantially more serious, education, macro-economic policy and the nationality laws. The more recent trend in the other direction, which we shall analyse in greater detail, is by no means a one-way street. Whilst competences have been transferred back to the Länder, other competences have also been transferred to the Bund.

Austrian federalism is constitutionally and politically weak. This can best be understood by looking at the respective competences of the Bund and Länder, the system of administration which involves the Bund and Länder, the financial arrangements, the rôle of the Länder in federal law-making, the system of constitutional amendment, and the political balance between the Federal and Land governments.

As we shall see, in virtually all these areas, the Länder are weaker and the rights and powers that they do have lack substantial protection from incursions by the Bund. Indeed, it is not unreasonable to assert that, of the nominal federations in the western world (Germany, Switzerland, USA, Canada, Australia), Austria is in fact the least genuinely federal and the most centralised.

The general residual clause in the Constitution, article 15(1), appears to accord a broad competence to the Länder, in that it lays down that any competence that is not expressly attributed to the Bund belongs to the Länder. However, in reality the Constitution has been successively amended to reduce the areas left open to the Länder, by attributing new competences to the Bund. Furthermore, the Nationalrat alone, without the approval of the Bundesrat or of the Landtag, could amend the Constitution and hence attribute new competences to the Bund. The Constitution offered no protection to the Länder against such amendments, except that a two-third majority is required in the Nationalrat.

Over the long periods of Grand Coalition between the ÖVP and SPÖ, this has been easy to obtain, once the Cabinet had agreed on a measure. With one-party governments or the several SPÖ–FPÖ coalitions, it has been possible to amend those competence articles, in 1974 and 1984, for example.

A first bundle of competences is fully given to the Bund, for both legislative and implementation purposes. This covers matters such as constitutional questions, foreign relations, trade, customs, border security, money, banking, interest-rate policy, private, civil and family law, maintenance of public order, competition policy, patent law, industrial policy, transport policy, health, labour law, water utilities, defence policy and population policy. This is already a not inconsiderable total federal competence, to which must be added education, for which the Bund is, with some exceptions, also almost exclusively competent since the 1960s. In addition, the Bund has legislative authority, with implementation left to the Länder, in a further range of areas such as internal shipping, housing, citizenship law. In a series of other matters, the Bund has competence to establish framework laws covering land reform, electricity provision, and insofar as it does not fall under industrial policy (a full Bund competence), some aspects of labour law.

The Bund and Länder are permitted to make agreements on reciprocal delegations of powers and duties. Where the Länder fail to exercise their responsibilities in those areas where they are charged with the implementation of Federal law, the powers can be exercised by the Bund in their default. Therefore, the Länder only retain exclusive competences in areas such as planning, building regulations, protection of the countryside and waste disposal. Of course, the areas of shared competence also allow the Länder a real degree of autonomy on detailed implementation and actual local variations.

The Länder, however, lack real financial autonomy, as the Bund has virtual pre-emption rights over the most productive taxation sources. Under the constitutional law governing the financial relations between the Bund Länder and local authorities, it is, of course, the Bund which determines the level of contribution (Ausgleich) to be accorded to the Länder, by Federal law, and the classification of taxes between exclusively Federal and Land taxes or shared revenues.

In addition, each level of government is responsible for the expenditure that it incurs, but the Länder and local authorities have little margin for increasing revenue. The Bund has pre-empted taxes on companies, income tax, excise duties on beer, wine and spirits, customs duties and sales taxes. The Länder can only raise much smaller taxes not pre-empted by the Bund, such as entertainment taxes and licence fees for hunting and fishing. In practice, though they have no legal right to a negotiated settlement, the Länder, acting collectively through a Centralised Coordinating Committee (Verbindungsstelle), negotiate the 'Ausgleich' with the Bund and the resulting agreement is then enacted into law. As a result, in a typically Austrian consensual but extra-constitutional way, the Länder obtain at least a degree of influence over the resources that the Bund puts at their disposal. The Bund however, spends about 60% of public expenditure, and the Länder only about 19%, as the local authorities spend slightly more than the Länder.

As to the administrative and organisational autonomy of the Länder, it is certainly more considerable than their financial autonomy, but even here the Federal Constitution places considerable restrictions on their freedom of action. Certainly, each Land has its own constitution, but that constitution cannot deviate from strict, federally determined rules. These rules deal with the electoral system, the organisation and powers of the Landtag, the powers of the Landeshauptmann (Governor/Prime Minister) and the Land governments as well as financial and judicial organisations. This leaves the Landtag only a limited degree of autonomy in constitutional matters. This is in part justified by the fact that the Land governments have a dual function: that of the autonomous exercise of the legislative and executive competences of the Länder; and the exercise of executive competences as agents of the Bund. In the latter rôle, the Landeshauptmann and members of the Land governments, though elected by the Landtag and responsible to it, are subject to federal jurisdiction and to instructions from the Federal Government.

Much of the work of the Land administration involves these 'agency' functions. This again is the reason why certain Land officials, especially in the police, have to be approved by the Federal Government.

Judicial power is exclusively a federal matter. All courts are federal courts. Even the Supreme Court, to which a number of judges are appointed by the Federal President on a proposal from the Bundesrat, is a Federal Court whose perspective is federal. A major demand of the Länder has been for a greater influence in the judiciary.

The political institutions of the Länder are the Landesregierungen, led by the Landeshauptmann and the elected Landtag, which in its turn elects the Landeshauptmann and exercises legislative power. Vienna is a special case in that it is both a city and a Land. The Bügermeister exercises the function of Landeshauptmann and the

Magistrat the function of the Land Cabinet. The City Council exercises the power of a Landtag. The Landtag must be elected by universal suffrage and by proportional representation.

Given the clear, relative dominance of each Land by one of the parties and the small size of the Landtag, as there have usually been one or two parties in the Landtag one of them will clearly dominate. Thus, the Landtag in the Länder of Vorarlberg, Tirol, Salzburg, Kärnten and Burgenland have only thirty-six members and those in Niederösterreich and Oberösterreich have fifty-six members. Only the Vienna Landtag and City Council are larger, with 100 members.

In 1987, there were two parties represented in Burgenland, Niederösterreich; three in Kärnten, Oberösterreich, Salzburg, Tirol, Vorarlberg and Vienna (ÖVP, SPÖ, FPÖ), and four parties in the Steiermark and Vorarlberg (ÖVP, SPÖ, FPÖ and Greens). However, the largest 'small party' representation comprises the Greens in Vorarlberg and the FPÖ in Salzburg. In no Land does a small party or even all the small parties hold the balance between ÖVP and SPÖ. Thus, one large party has an absolute majority in every Landtag (Burgenland, and Vienna are SPÖ and the other Länder are ÖVP). The formation of the Land government is based on consensus and proporz and not on these majority positions. The Federal Constitution lays down that the Landeshauptmann, and the members of the Land government are elected by the Landtag on a proportional basis. Except in Vorarlberg, at least one member of the Land government will come from the second largest party in the Landtag (always either ÖVP or SPÖ). Thus, the Land cabinets are always Grand Coalitions and have never included FPÖ members. Recent more volatile election results could alter this situation but only to a small degree, as the smaller parties would require very considerable gains to obtain a share in the executive power as now in Kärnten.

It is an essential ingredient of real federalism that the second tier governments, in the Austrian case the Länder, should have entrenched rights and competences and a degree of involvement in the processes of federal government. Here too, Austrian federalism has been weak, to the point where it has been arguable whether the system was actually genuinely federal in character. However, a change, of both a formal and an informal nature, has been set in motion in this area, which will probably lead to a real re-equilibration between the Bund and the Länder. However, much of the problem lies in the centralising tendencies in Austrian political life and governmental and party practice, which the successive periods of

Grand Coalition and Vienna-based SPÖ government, as well as objective exigencies of the occupation down to 1955, had entrenched very strongly in the mentality of those involved in decision-making. Here, the best constitutional provisions are powerless, but the pointers that attitudinal change is taking place, are significant.

The Second, or Federal, Chamber of the Austrian Parliament (the Bundesrat) is intended to be the chief vehicle of influence for the Länder. It has simply failed in that respect. It has never achieved the significance of its German namesake, though in both concept and powers it is quite similar.

The Austrian Bundesrat has sixty-three members, distributed as follows among the Länder: Vienna twelve, Lower Austria twelve, Upper Austria ten, Salzburg four, Tirol five, Vorarlberg three, Kärnten four, Steiermark ten and Burgenland three. There have always only been ÖVP and SPÖ members in the Bundesrat. The members are elected by each Landtag, following new elections, by proportional representation. The Constitution also specifies that at least one seat must be allocated to the second largest party in the Landtag. This provision is also a 'proporz' element in that it ensures both ÖVP and SPÖ representation in the delegation of every Land. It might be needed to ensure SPÖ representation in some of the smaller western ÖVP dominated Länder. Frequently, the Bundesrat has had an opposite political majority to the Nationalrat. This was the case for the last phase of the 1966–70 ÖVP government and also the case for much of the SPÖ government from 1970–83 and for the period of the SPÖ–FPÖ Small Coalition (1983–86).

The constitutional powers of the Bundesrat are stated as sharing the legislative and the control functions with the Nationalrat. Political reality places the Bundesrat in a position of inferiority: even in constitutional law it does not enjoy equal status with the Nationalrat. First and foremost, the Cabinet is not responsible to the Bundesrat, though it can ask questions, table resolutions and exercise the other normal instruments of parliamentary control. The Bundesrat may amend or reject legislation, but this action is only a delaying power, which can be over-ridden by a further vote in the Nationalrat. The Constitution does not even (as with the House of Lords in the UK) specify the length of the delaying power. That, in essence, is up to the Nationalrat. In the early period 1945–73, the Bundesrat only objected to thirty-two bills and in the 1953–56 and 1959–66 periods, none at all. Twelve were raised during the one-party ÖVP government (1966–70) when the SPÖ controlled the Bundesrat and a further three came in the 'short' legislature of 1970–71, against Bills passed by the ÖVP+FPÖ against the wishes of the SPÖ minority cabinet. Nine came in the 1971–73 period, when the ÖVP had gained control of the Bundesrat.

In the one-party period, and later in the Small Coalition (SPÖ/FPÖ), the opposition used the Bundesrat and was overruled by the coalition majority in the Nationalrat. However, during the coalition period, the Bundesrat vote more often reflected second thoughts and was not overruled. Only three cases showed any reference to protection of the interests of the Länder as a motive for the objection. There were four cases in the first SPÖ majority legislative and fourteen and thirteen in the 1975–79 and 1979–83 legislatures. With the 'Small Coalition' and the breakdown of the previous ÖVP/SPÖ consensus, despite periods of one-party rule, there were no less than forty-seven objections (out of 109 in all) during 1945–86. Of these, forty-four led to an override decision by the SPÖ/FPÖ majority. The others were amended and then approved. Only one Bill was wholly abandoned. Over the whole period, ninety objections were overridden out of the 109. No Bill which had received ÖVP support in the Nationalrat was subsequently objected to by the Bundesrat.

These figures show eloquently that the Bundesrat is a political body and is used as such by both the two main parties. It does not operate as a body protecting the interests of the Länder. Its positions are defined by the central party leadership. Its members are not necessarily members of their Landtag and, indeed, are often not. They may well be ex-Nationalrat members, demoted to the Bundesrat or awaiting re-election to the Nationalrat. Hence, both because of its limited powers and its character, the Bundesrat has never been seen as a forum for the defence of Land interests, though the Länder have argued for an increase in its powers. The Länder have, as a result, looked for other means of promoting their interests in relation to the Bund.

The Länder have established a Coordination Committee which prepares negotiation positions with the Bund, both in their periodic catalogues of demands and in the Finanzausgleich discussions. Federalism is not just a matter of formal governmental structures, but can permeate Austrian public life in every area. All the political parties have a federalised structure, with separate Land parties having their own decision-making bodies. The Kammer system (Arbeiterkammer, Handelskammer, Landwirtschaftskammer) is also federalised, with federal coordinating bodies. Voluntary interest groups, such as the Industrialists Organisation and the Trade Unions (ÖGB), have a federalised structure for the most part.

Where is the debate about federalism going and what are the main demands of the federalists? How do the political parties stand on the issue? For the ÖVP, with its philosophy of subsidiarity, federalism has always been part of its basic doctrine. Its base in the Western Länder and its long period in opposition have increased its support for federalism and the FPÖ has, as a small and uninfluential party on the federal scene, also seen advantages in federalism. For the FPÖ and the ÖVP, greater federalism would weaken the hold of the central state and would enable Länder to determine their own development. In this view is implicit the belief that the state could to some extent be rolled back in the process.

The SPÖ, on the other hand, has always been considerably less favourable to the idea of increased federalism. A reformist party, the SPÖ has sought, with success during the Grand Coalition and the SPÖ government of the 1970–1986 period, to use above all the machinery of central government to push through reforms aimed at increasing welfare, equality and freedom on a nation-wide basis.

Federalism, which would in the Austrian situation have meant freedom for ÖVP Länder to opt out of reforms, was not an acceptable approach. With the rise of neo-conservative thinking, with the inevitability of a degree of retrenchment in public spending and power-sharing first with the FPÖ and then with the ÖVP, the attitude of the SPÖ has begun to alter perceptibly. In the 'Perspektiven 90' Socialist Programme adopted in 1987, there is a much more positive expression of opinion in favour of federalism. Federalism in favour of the Länder must also be accompanied by decentralisation to the local communities and must not threaten the right to general high standards which are guaranteed centrally. There was thus a much closer basis than in the past for agreement on more federalism when the 1987 SPÖ/ÖVP Coalition Agreement came to be negotiated.

At the same time, the new social movements at the grass-roots represent pressure for more localised and 'burgernahe' decision-making, which in turn has its impact on the political parties. Thus, the Vienna SPÖ programme is now much more positive towards greater federalism and seeks greater direct cooperation with its neighbour Lower Austria, without federal involvement. A 1980 initiative Pro-Vorarlberg put a ten-point programme of federalisation to the electorate in Vorarlberg and obtained a 70% vote in favour. The Tirol Landtag supported these demands and the 1985 Länder programme took up many of the same ideas. The leading Vorarlberg newspaper, the Vorarlberger Nachrichten, took up the theme and organised a Day of Action for Federalism in June 1987 with many prominent speakers including Chancellor Vranitzky. The tone of the discussion was that Austria was seeing a renaissance in federalist consciousness, to which the political system must respond.

Federalism can also be a response to the new social movements, such as the Hainburg protest movement, and the Green and Alternative groups, in so far as there would be greater scope for new and more local initiatives and variations in policy according to the wishes of local inhabitants. However, like many in the SPÖ, the Greens fear that there could also be negative consequences from greater devolution to the Länder, but support a greater degree of devolution to the inhabitants of communities to take their own decisions.

The issue was an important agenda item in the negotiations for the formation of the Grand Coalition in 1987. Yet, the Länder have increased their pressure for reform since the late 1960s, with successive Länder Programmes of Demands (Förderungsprogram), leading to significant constitutional changes in both 1974 and 1984, without reversing the basically centralised nature of the Austrian State. The most difficult areas have concerned the rights of the Bundesrat, the distribution of powers between the Bund and the Länder, financial powers and control over the Land administrations (which, it should be remembered, have many 'agency' functions). On all these issues, some of the demands of the Länder were met in the 1974 and 1984 reforms and in other more piecemeal changes. Yet the Bundesrat still remains weak, and the financial legislative and administrative powers of the Länder remain limited and powers are still flowing towards the Bund (especially in relation to the protection of the environment) as well as to the Länder.

The SPÖ/ÖVP Grand Coalition appointed a State Secretary in the Chancellery (Mr Neisser, ÖVP) responsible for Federalism. That is in itself a major innovation. Mr Neisser himself sees in this a major change in attitude in the SPÖ. Indeed, there are signs that the SPÖ is prepared to relax its earlier opposition to more federalism and indeed that the powerful Vienna party has begun to argue a federalist case in Vienna and to devolve power to the local districts within the city. It was therefore possible to reach a measure of agreement on the issue in the coalition negotiations.

The latest Länder programme in 1985 builds on their earlier demands from 1964, 1970 and 1976. The aim is to make Austria a genuine federal state. The new catalogue established the priorities of the Länder for the coming period and in this responded to a request from the Federal Government to review its earlier positions.

The first area relates to the extension of the competences of the Länder. The main demands cover housing, rent control, slum clearance, electricity supply (apart from the country-wide high tension network), and civil laws.

The second area concerns the right of the Länder to be involved in appointments to various joint bodies which exercise judicial or administrative control such as the Supreme Court, the Administrative Courts and the Court of Auditors. The Länder also want greater discretion in areas where they act for the Federal Government, and direct control over all police and security bodies.

Thirdly, the Länder demand that the consent of the Bundesrat be required for treaties which would impinge on areas of Land competence. The Länder also demand a greater financial autonomy and independent taxation competence, with the division of revenues being the subject of negotiations and approval by the Bundesrat.

In the Coalition Agreement, a number of statements about federalism are made. On a general level, a review of the distribution of competences and revenues is proposed. Housing policy is to be decentralised and air pollution is to become a coherent federal competence. Action has followed on some, but by no means all of the areas of priority for the Länder and the new coalition. Indeed, some, especially the financial demands, raise serious problems. However, the responsibility for housing policy has been transferred to the Länder as from January 1988.

The government is working on a review of the constitutional provisions on the distribution of competences. The draft was discussed in a joint committee with the Länder on seven occasions and was in broad terms approved by the June 1987 annual conference of Landeshauptmänner. After consultation with the usual network of bodies that have a right to be consulted on legislation, it was approved by the cabinet. The proposals would create a guaranted Land nationality, transfer competence for air pollution control and for garbage disposal to the federal level, while some educational competences would be given to the Länder. The Länder are to be relieved of certain requirements of federal authorisation in their adminstrative functions. The Länder are also to be given the right to be consulted on the appointment of Heads of the Security Forces in their Land and would be given the right to propose nominees for up to one-third of the members of the Federal Administrative court; the Bundesrat members would be given the same right of challenge of the constitutionality of Bills as the Nationalrat members. The most significant change would be to give the Länder (with the consent of the Federal Government) the right to conclude treaties with Austria's neighbours, on matters within their competences. This would enable the Länder to pursue a limited foreign policy, even with Eastern European states. Treaties which are concluded by the Federal Government in areas of Land competence would require the assent of the Bundesrat.

The overall impact of these and the earlier changes may appear quite limited and are far from reversing the centralisation of the past ten years, especially as the financial arrangements have not been finalised. However, a new attitude is evident which will bear fruit over the years. The new, looser federalism will provide a partial antidote to the recreation of the Grand Coalition and criticisms of centralism and uniformity.

The new thinking in some of the Länder is interesting in this context. The whole debate about an independent capital for Lower Austria was revived in the 1970s. This was, in itself, an indication of a new federalist spirit. Lower Austria split from Vienna in 1921 but the administration stayed in the city. Prior debates about a capital ended inconclusively. The new debate had broader aims: providing opportunities for people in the Land; decentralisation within the Land; establishment of a university, (possibly a Danubian University linked to Central Europe through the idea of a Danubian Cultural Festival based in the new Land capital). Five hundred million ÖS have already been appropriated for over 100 regional projects to spread growth and development in the Länder. After a referendum in 1985, a political consensus finally emerged, leading to the declaration of Sankt Pölten as the new Land capital in the mid-1990s.

The Steiermark is also an example of regional consciousness. The Land government is actively examining how the autonomy of the Land can be increased both politically and economically. The Steiermark is an ÖVP Land that, by its industrial structure, should be SPÖ. The ÖVP in this Land has always been a liberal rather than Catholic party and has often, as in the affair of stationing Drakkar fighters near Graz, been opposed to the national ÖVP. Yet, the dramatic episode of Steiermark ÖVP Nationalrat deputies tabling a censure motion on the ÖVP Defence Minister, has only highlighted the weakness of the Länder and increased feeling that the Steiermark needs greater autonomy and has a distinct southern Austrian destiny.

These are interesting examples among others of the new federalism in Austria, which can be expected to develop strongly in the coming period.

It is, of course, not only mere institutional reforms that can alter the consensus mentality and improve parliamentary control and promote open political debate, though both are desirable as a counterbalance to the mechanisms of consensus inherent in the Grand Coalition (but which have also existed during periods of single party rule). However, to some degree, institutional reforms can help.

The coalition agreement proposes a reform of the electoral system, to provide for greater direct influence by voters over who is elected to the Nationalrat and hence a corresponding increase in accountability and a reduction in the influence of the central party machines. The specific reform proposed in the coalition agreement would involve the creation of some 100 single member constituencies, in which members would be elected by the first-past-the-post system, and additional members elected from Land and national lists to ensure proportional representation of all parties gaining at least three per cent of the national vote. It was also agreed that discussions should take place, with all parties represented in the Nationalrat, to increase the rights of the opposition parties to control the government through interpellations, questions and inquiry committees.

Another area in which there has been a considerable amount of new thinking in response to the need to adapt the over-centralised and elite-dominated 'Austrian Model', had been the debate about direct democracy. Pressure for a more direct democracy, or at least to give reality to provisions for direct democracy long enshrined in the Constitution but effectively a dead letter, have come from various apparently contradictory sources: the ÖVP and FPÖ, the Western Länder and from the 'Basis-Demokraten' and new social movements which became the Green Party. Their target is the same – an over-mighty, centralised, élitist Vienna-based political and bureaucratic system of decision-making – but, of course, their positive aims, and the type of direct democracy that they would wish to introduce, vary considerably.

There are also elements of direct democracy built into the Constitution, and they have been there since the Constitution was originally drafted. Recent laws (1972 and 1973) have regulated the application of these general principles. For what is called a 'Gesamtänderung', or global revision of the Constitution, a referendum is required. This provision has never been invoked, but there is no clear view of its legal impact. It is usually accepted that a revision which affected basic constitutional principles such as federalism, subsidiarity, representative pluralist democracy, the separation of powers and basic rights, would be a 'global revision'. Other amendments can be put to the people if one-third of the members of the Nationalrat or Bundesrat so request. This has never happened, and given the propensity for all changes to be taken by consensus, including naturally the SPÖ and the ÖVP (well over 80% of Nationalrat seats), it seems a provision without much value, but it could be agreed that its mere existence forces the parties to seek very broad compromise.

Outside the constitutional field, a Bill can be put to the people in a referendum where the Nationalrat so decides. This provision has only been used once in the matter of the Zwentendorf nuclear power station. It cannot be invoked against the Nationalrat or by a minority in the Nationalrat.

Provision is also made for the Volksbegehren or popular initiative, whereby 100,000 voters, or one-sixth of the voters in at least three Länder, can petition Parliament to consider a draft Bill, which the petitioners present. The Parliament is bound to consider this Bill, no more and no less. This provision is much newer. To date, there have been seven popular initiatives, covering such diverse items as reform of the State Broadcasting System, an anti-nuclear bill, opposition to the building of a UN Conference Centre in Vienna. The number of signatures obtained has varied from 150,000 to 1,360,000. All were rejected by Parliament, but since 1975 a report must be presented to the full House within six months to prevent the initiative simply being shelved in a committee.

Initiatives and referenda are more developed in the constitutions of the Länder and indeed, several Länder such as Vienna and Lower Austria introduced these provisions in the late 1970s or early 1980s. The provisions in force in Salzburg, Burgenland, Steiermark, Upper and Lower Austria and Vorarlberg include the right to demand the revision, abolition or adoption of laws. The other Länder have more general provisions similar to those at the Federal level. The number of signatures required vary from 10,000 to 85,000 and in some cases 5% of qualified voters. In two Länder (Burgenland and Lower Austria), local authorities may also promote initiatives. In Salzburg, Lower Austria and Vorarlberg a specific text of a Bill need not be presented to the Landtag which is elsewhere (as at the federal level), a formal requirement of the validity of the initiative.

Most importantly, in Salzburg (10,000 voters), Vorarlberg (20% of voters) and Steiermark (85,000 voters), a referendum on the bill must be held if the Landtag refuses to act. In all Länder except Upper Austria, a referendum can be demanded to abrogate Land laws passed by the Landtag. In some, the Landtag or a minority itself can call a referendum on a bill before promulgation into law. At the local government level, similar provisions have been introduced since 1962. Again, a given proportion – often as high as 25% of electors – can present an initiative, demand a referendum on it (should the local authority fail to act upon it) and also require that decisions taken by the local authority be subject to a popular vote.

The key issue remains – especially at the Federal level – the right to force a referendum. Here, political divisions are quite great. The pressure for referenda, both at Land and Federal level has come from the ÖVP and to a lesser extend from the FPÖ (until it entered government in 1983), which were for the whole period from 1970 in opposition. Following the ÖVP inspired initiative against the UN-city project in Vienna (which collected 1,360,000 signatures in 1982, but which was ignored by the SPÖ controlled Nationalrat), the ÖVP has favoured an automatic right for a referendum for initiatives which collect at least 500,000 signatures. In 1979, the FPÖ had proposed that any initiative which was rejected by Parliament should be subjected to a referendum, yet when part of the Small Coalition, the FPÖ voted against the ÖVP proposal in 1983. The negotiations for the Grand Coalition did not lead to significant agreement. The ÖVP saw the referendum and intitiative as important adjuncts to parliamentary democracy when in opposition and as a response to criticism of the Grand Coalition – that it stifles opposition. The SPÖ remained opposed to any automatic right to invoke a referendum against the majority in Parliament, but in its 1986 election platform, it indicated its readiness to facilitate the use of initiatives and introduce the 'Umfrage' (questionnaire) on important political issues. The ÖVP proposal for automatic referenda both if 500,000 voters had signed an initiative and if the Nationalrat had not acted within a year, was, however, not acceptable to the SPÖ. The Coalition Agreement emphasised that respresentative democracy was to remain the basic constitutional principle. It limited itself to proposing measures to simplify the presentation of initiatives which would in future not have to propose a fully drafted Bill, but merely a proposal in general

terms, with the proposers of an intiative having the right to participate in the work of the Nationalrat Committee to which it was
referred. The 'Volksbefragung' will also be introduced. Thus, the
ÖVP did not make significant progress. The debate is far from over
and will continue and be strengthened by the very existence of the
Grand Coalition with its tendency towards conflict avoidance and
consensus.

8. A Summing Up

Where does our excursion into the various aspects of Austrian history, society, economic and political life and foreign relations, leave us?

Austria is not a popular cause at present. For many, Kurt Waldheim is, by association, Austria. For many, his attitude of bland unconcern, of apparent ignorance of what the issue is, his bureaucratic references to merely 'having done his duty' represent the quintessential Austrian attitude to her recent past. He is, for too many, the typical Austrian figure, indeed so much so it was argued that the majority elected him and a larger majority still support him. Even his opponents, at least those of a pragmatic stripe such as the present Chancellor Franz Vranitzky, hope that the problem will in time disappear and do not wish it to interfere with Austria's reputation or with other pressing business for his coalition which includes Waldheim's party, the ÖVP.

For many Austrians of almost whatever standpoint, the issue has gone on long enough and is largely now only of interest to foreigners. This fact can and has been exploited politically both by the ÖVP and the less cautious FPÖ under Jörg Haider. Yet for those who seek to judge Austria from the outside, those attitudes, so to say, compound the felony. It may well be that the permanent and almost excessive exercise in Vergangenheitsbewältigung that is indulged by the German media, politicians and opinion-formers is no more sincere than the attitude of Austrians towards the past, yet it is so much better public relations. The issue cannot be ignored in any assessment of Austria today.

There is no direct link with the other prongs of criticism launched against Austria. The 'Austrian Model' or the 'Austrian Way' – so often associated with Bruno Kreisky, but which, in many of its key elements, long preceded him – is declared dead. Dead, because it could only moderate and not reverse the effects of an ongoing long-term world recession. The bar was set very high indeed if that was the realistic criteria by which success was to be judged. For many others, the model could not succeed and was doomed to fail. Indeed, their own political attitudes positively required it to fail. It opposed or denied far too many of the current neo-conservative nostrums: it

173

believed in a positive rôle for a large state industrial sector; it believed in high public spending; it believed in social engineering, moving forward by consensus and involving the social partners on a broad front of economic policy. It was pragmatic, not doctrinaire. To its critics on both the right and left, almost all these aspects, and above all the pragmatic consensual approach, were far from virtues.

There is, of course, no direct link with Waldheim, yet the subconscious view is that a society built on too much pragmatism and too much compromise is built on moral shifting sands and hence the wine scandal, the Androsch affair and other financial scandals, and indeed the largest scandal of all – Dr Waldheim – are the products of such a society and such a system.

The third prong of the attack is against yet another pillar of the 'Austrian Model', her permanent neutrality. In the 1950s, this was seen as a creative and imaginative way out of the impasse in which the talks about the State Treaty had run. However, with Austrian membership of the new European Community being debated, the old question of 'Is membership compatible with neutrality?' is being stood on its head and re-posed by high standing personalities in the community such as Leo Tindemans in the form 'Is neutrality compatible with membership?.' Neutrality for many is again seen as synonymous with provincialism and lack of principle, as a product of pragmatism and compromise so characteristic of the Austrian system.

Provincialism, pragmatism, compromise, absence of open debate about key political issues, coupled with a weak ethical climate in politics have all been seen as major and unfortunate characteristics of Austrian public life. It is, for example, striking that there are so many political scandals in Austria, involving corruption or misuse of political office. This is striking both because it could suggest that there is a rather low standard of ethics, which is mutually tolerated by the political class, and because it has become such a dominant feature of public debate. Political issues as such have tended to be crowded out. Press and broadcasting media tend to concentrate on personalities and scandals, rather than substantive questions. Certainly, the scandals are serious, but they seem at times an alibi for deeper debate and criticism. Indeed, in the end the constant revelations seem to have a numbing effect on public opinion and undermine the political class as a whole, rather than those specifically guilty. In fact, the welter of scandal, covering a very wide field (such as for example: the cost overruns and corruption in the building of the AKH Hospital in Vienna; the building scandals in Vienna in the 1970s; the tax evasion – and moonlighting as a tax advisor – of former Finance

Minister Hannes Androsch; the case of the sinking of the Lucona – loaded with machinery for treating nuclear material – and the subsequent frauds and cover up, which has involved former Foreign Minister Leopold Graz and Interior Minister Karl Blecha; and the tax fraud and evasion of the SPÖ and certain leading party officials that caused the resignation of the Party Secretary in 1988, to name but the best known) have created a form of immunity through overkill. That is the case for the prosecution.

Yet most of those characteristics were formerly much praised. Austria was seen as an island of stability in a troubled world. Many outside, and as we have seen, some inside now question the success of the model and, even if there has been undeniable success in many areas, argue that the price has been too high. These questions were asked in the introduction, but they were looked at through the external observer's end of the telescope.

Our excursion through the 'Austrian Model', as it was and is, has been aimed at presenting the Austrian's eye-view: that is the sense of the subtitle 'In defence of Austria'. It is not a complacent view, nor a passive defence. There are as we have seen, sceptics and critics of the model (and of every aspect of it), in Austria itself. There are questions about the durability of the model and about its present appropriateness. Yet the defence case can rest on two aspects that have emerged from our metaphorical journey. Firstly the facts speak for themselves: the success of the 'Austrian Model' is there, on the record and that success is not a twenty-year old, past success – it is real and tangible today. Secondly, the broad consensus of opinion seems to be that, despite doubts and concerns, the 'Austrian Model' can and should continue. How should we give a judicial summing-up as between the two cases that can be made?

Some credence should be given to the opinions of key Austrian decision-makers themselves. Their confidence in the future of the model, especially as they tend to admit the need for some adaptation, merits careful consideration, not least because the system itself rests, in large part, on mutual confidence and trust between the actors in the system. Without fundamental confidence and self-confidence, the system would cease to function. It is here, at the level of the maintenance of confidence that both internal criticism and the opinion of outsiders can play a rôle, by undermining belief in the system.

Yet, at present, with the Waldheim affair on the back-burner, with the favourable rating of the coalition up from 57% in 1987 to 70% in the autumn of 1988, with several difficult reforms carried through, and above all with the economy taking-off again, the solidity of the system seems much more assured. Of course, these positive factors could all go simultaneously into reverse. The very fact that so many of the positive or negative elements which influence the evaluation of 'image' of Austria are short-term and reversible in either direction underlines the modish nature of much recent excessive criticism of the 'Austrian Model' and suggest that longer-term trends should be looked for. Almost all actors and observers regard the 'Austrian Model' as having a positive balance-sheet and expect its main features to be replicated and to continue, but perhaps with a more flexible and rapid capacity for adaptation to new situations and challenges. It is important to note that even among the 20–29 age group, only 23% are dissatisfied with the functioning of the system and express a favourable judgement of the political parties by a margin of 48% to 34%. One might add that with inflation remaining at no more than 2.5%, growth rising beyond forecasts to 2.5% in 1988 and unemployment falling (5.4% in 1988) for the first time since 1980, even among young people, only a minimum sensitivity towards more democracy and more transparency and to new social trends, such as post-materialist values of environmental protection, or shorter working hours, is all that is necessary to prevent serious problems of governability and legitimation emerging.

It may well be that those organisations that had so successfully performed the function of social integration in the early years of the Second Republic, but which without doubt had become less capable of reacting to new emerging needs and trends by the late 1970s, have learned serious lessons from that experience and are once again prepared to carry out the dual function of integrating and educating people in the necessities of the Austrian situation. These functions have for strategic reasons fallen largely to the SPÖ and the Social Partnership system. Certainly, the ÖVP played a major and vital rôle in the early phase of reconstruction, and again at vital points in the evolution of the Austrian society, by integrating the greater part of the conservative electorate into a constitutional party committed to building an Austrian nation. The SPÖ, too, played a major part in that integration process. It brought the Austrian working class out of the political ghetto and brought it into the process which enabled a major programme of reconstruction and then reform to be achieved by democratic and peaceful means.

Austria, initially a creation of the Allied Powers, first in 1920 and then in 1945, has now taken. The attempts by Jörg Haider to re-open the 'National' debate have fallen on barren soil. Austrians accept, and indeed see it as a positive asset, that they belong to a wider German-speaking cultural community, but that acceptance in no way undermines their belief in Austria as their country. Indeed, 87% now identify themselves as Austrians; a mere 9% identify themselves as Germans or German-Austrians. Only 5% consider that Austria is not a nation. As was commented to the author, Americans and Australians speak English, but no one would think they were British.

The process of nation-building is virtually complete. The East-West situation is so much improved that Austria can 'think the unthinkable' in terms of its neutrality and EEC membership. Dr Kreisky has even argued that if the détente process continues, the whole question of neutrality could be seen in a different light and re-evaluated. The present Grand Coalition is seen by 70% as doing a good job. The degree of political alienation is not increasing. Economic growth is rising again and unemployment is falling. Once again, Austria can point to a success story. Her institutions and parties have shown flexibility and adaptability, enabling them to react positively to criticism and to integrate new trends, even though the monolithic character of these institutions and traditions has had to loosen-up in the process.

The only question is the price for those successes. Certainly, in at least two respects, there has been a price. The Waldheim affair, and the uncomprehending attitude to outside reactions that has frequently been evoked in Austria, is symptomatic of the whole Austrian approach to the past. Designated as 'the first victim' of Nazi-aggression in the Moscow Declaration of 1943, required by the Allies to assume an Austrian nationhood that many initially rejected and occupied for ten years (with measures against Nazi war-criminals being a 'reserved' Allied responsibility), it is perhaps not surprising that most Austrians came to prefer to ignore the past. Furthermore, anti-Nazi laws were enacted in 1945 and at the 1945 election, all former Nazis were disenfranchised. Yet the problem of integration of these almost 800,000 former Nazis into the national community was real, and failure could threaten the nation-building and reconstruction efforts mandated by the Allies as much as by the Austrians.

An Austrian nation could only be a German-Austrian nation. Its frontiers had been consistently threatened in the South. This perhaps helps to explain the hostility of many to the various minorities and especially to the Slovenes in Kärnten. Yet Austria has fulfilled her obligations to the Slovene minority under the State Treaty. One may perhaps conclude that there was no alternative to this form of collective amnesia; in many ways there was a considerable excuse for it. Yet a more rapid realisation that, by 1986 when the Waldheim affair broke, the issue was real and should be laid to rest by a genuine national debate, would have been appropriate. The national reaction to reject such a debate, with some noteworthy exceptions, can perhaps be explained by a subconscious feeling of fragility of the Austrian edifice and the dangers in this as in any area, of open debate and conflict. This is surely over-cautious.

The second 'price' has come in the form of a pragmatism, which can at times be seen to border on the unprincipled, and a provincialism or narrowness of vision. Pragmatism and compromise are a necessary part of the Austrian system and cannot be dissociated from it. Certainly, political conflict has been subdued and neither left nor right have had full room to manoeuvre. In the light of the civil war and insurrection that marked the First Republic and the stiff uncompromising positions that prevented any constitutional evolution of the Monarchy in its last 50 years, this is certainly a good thing. Until the system itself was robust enough to have a capacity for survival, excessive conflict could only be dangerous.

Austria is a small country, her foreign policy options limited by the geographical proximity of the Eastern Block and by her neutrality. It is not surprising that provincialism and a cultural nostalgia for the Empire, with its wider vistas, should be strong. Yet, as perspectives open up in the wake of *glasnost'*, Austria is there to take advantage of these new situations.

The Joint Vienna-Budapest application for the 1995 World Fair is a potent symbol. The debate on Mitteleuropa is increasingly drawing-in participants from Hungary, Yugoslavia and Czechoslovakia. Austria has shown quick adaptability to the threat and possibilities of the EEC's internal market. Neutrality has been used as an asset in developing an active foreign policy and not a restriction. Indeed, her neutrality may be an important asset in the evolution of Eastern Europe. As the Gorbachev reforms develop the need for change in Central and Eastern Europe, the 'Austrian Model' (and the Finnish model) could be examples of how respect for legitimate Soviet concern about her security can be combined with a free and open society.

In fact, the 'Austrian Model' has shown itself to be adaptable. Austria has shown itself capable of reacting rapidly to the external challenge of the 1992 single market. The crisis in the state industries is on the way to being mastered. The economic situation is favourable and business and the work-force remain optimistic about the future. New thinking about relations with central Europe is developing. Austria is often accused of being a rigid and closed society, but the Green movement was very quickly effective: Austria rejected nuclear power in 1978 and the Hainburg project was not built. The persistent scandals are seen by many as a relic of the rapid post-war reconstruction period. They are typical of a transition period and may fall to a less-remarkable level in the near future. The adaptation to a looser, more open, less unreflectedly consensual society, more able to accept hard and bitter truths and to benefit from the positive catharsis of open democratic debate, is underway. The problem is to ensure that the process of change does not destroy what was positive in the old model. To date though, these changes have been set in train without creating the double-figure unemployment and inflation that characterised the early Thatcher years in Britain. The process is slow and uneven, but the conclusion must be that the 'Austrian Model' will prove itself capable of adaptation and hence be able to build on its very considerable earlier achievements.

Further Reading

2 From Empire to Nation

History

Louza, Radomir
Resistance in Austria, University of Minneapolis Press, 1964

Schonsberger, N.
Oesterreich: Der Weg in der Republik 1918–1980, Graz, Leykom 1980

Mamatey, Victor
The Rise of the Habsburg Empire 1526–1918, Krieger, New York 1980

Brueckmueller, E.
Sozialgeschichte Oesterreichs, Wien, Herold 1985

Andics, H.
Oesterreich 1804–1975, four volumes, especially vol 4, *Von Moskauer Deklaration zur Gegenwart*, Moldenverlag, Wien 1976

Bled, J. P.
Francois-Joseph, Fayard, Paris 1989

Kitchen, M.
The Coming of Austrian Fascism, Croom Helm, London, 1980

Steger, G.
Rote Fahne, Schwartzes Kreuz: Die Haltung der Sozialdemokratische Arbeiterpartei Oesterreichs Zu Religion, Kirche und Christentum, Von Hainfeld bis 1934, Bohlau, Wien 1987

3 Austria in the World

Occupation to State Treaty

Bischoff, G.
Die Bevormündete Nation: Oesterreich und die Allierte 1945–49, Haymanverlag, Wien 1988

Rauchensteiner, M.
Der Sonderfall: Die Besatzungszeit in Oesterreich, 1945–55, Verlag Styria, Graz 1979

180

Cronin, Audrey — *Great Power Politics and the Struggle over Austria*, Cornell University Press, Ithaca, 1986

Haas, H. (*ed*) — *Oesterreich und die Sowietunion 1918–55*, Wien 1984

Allard, S. — *Russian and the State Treaty: A case study of Soviet policy in Europe*, Pennsylvania State University Press, Philadelphia 1970

Gruber, K. — *Between Liberation and Liberty*, Praeger, New York 1955

Foreign Policy – general

Bielka, E.
Jankowitsch, P.
Thalberg, H.
Portisch, H. (*ed*)
— *Die Ära Kreisky: Schwerpunkte der Oesterreichische Aussenpolitik*, Europaverlag Wien, 1983
25 Jahre Staatsvertrag, Bundesregierung, 1980

European Community

Buiss, F.
Stankowsky, J.
Ohlinger, T.
— *Oesterreich und die EG Binnenmarkt* Signum, Wien 1988
Verfassungsrechtliche Aspekte eines Beitritts Oesterreichs zur EG, Signum, Wien 1988

Mitteleuropa

Busek, E. and Brix, E. — *Projekt Mitteleuropa* Uberreuther, Wien 1986

Toscano, M. — *Alto Adige, Süd Tirol: Italy's frontier with the German World*, University of California Press, Berkley 1976

Neutrality

Emcora, F. — *20 Jahre Neutralität Oesterreichs*, Metzner, Frankfurt-am-Main, 1975

4   The Political Process

Government

Fischer, H.   *Das Politisches System in Oesterreich*
                          4th ed., Europaverlag, Wien 1987
Klose, A.   Machtstrukturen in Oesterreich,
                          Signum, Wien 1987
Knoll, R.   *Oesterreichische Konsensdemokratie in*
                          Theorie und Praxis: Staat,
                          Interessenverbaende, Parteien und die
                          politische Wirklichkeit, Boehlau,
                          Koeln/Graz
Weissensteimer, F.   *Die Oesterreichische Bundeskanzler*
and Weinzierl, H.   Bundesverlag, Wien 1987
Kazler, A.   *Parteien Gesellschaft im Umbruch:*
                          Partizipationsprobleme der Gross-
                          parteien, Bohlau, Wien 1987

Parties

SPÖ

SPÖ   *Perspektiven 90,* SPÖ, Wien 1985
Kleiner, F.   *Denkanstoesse zum uberleben:*
                          Diskussionsbeitrag zu einem neuen SPÖ
                          Programm, Europaverlag, Wien 1976
Kuhz (*ed*)   *Die Aera Kresiky: Stimmen zu einen*
                          Phaenomen, Molden, Wien 1975
Kaufman, F.   *Sozialdemokratie in Oesterreich: Ideen*
                          und Geschichte einer Partei von 1889 zur
                          Gegenwart, Amaltha, Munich 1978
Klein, Loew S.   *Bruno Kreisky: Ein Portraet in Worten*
                          Jungbrunnen, Wien 1983
Hindels (*ed*)   *Roter Anstoess, Der Oesterreichischer*
Pelinka   Weg Jugend und Volk, Wien 1980
Steger, G.   *Der Brueckenschlag: Katolische Kirche*
                          und Sozialdemokratie in Oesterreich,
                          Jugend und Volk, Wien 1982

ÖVP

Vytiska, H.	*Die Logische Nachfolger: Alois Mock, Eine Politische Biographie,* Multiplex Mediaverlag, Wien 1983
Pelinka, A. (*ed*)	*Populismus in Oesterreich,* Junius, Wien 1987
In Fischer op cit;	*'Struktur und Funktionen de politischen Parteien'.*
Koren, et al	*Politik fuer die Zukunft: Festschrift fuer Alois Mock,* Bohlau, Wien/Graz 1984
Reichold, L.	*Geschichte der ÖVP,* Verlag Styria 1975

FPÖ

Pirenger, K.	*Geschichte der Freiheitlichen: Beitrag der Dritten Kraft zur Oesterreichischen Politik* Pietsch, Wien, 1982

GREENS

Pelinka, A.	*Gruen Alternative aspekte in der Ideologie und Programmatik der Parteien,* Verlag fuer Politischen Grundforschung, Wien 1986
Gonner, A. Kitzmueller, E.	*Gruen Ausblicke,* Junius, Wien 1988

General political Crisis

Lenhardt, D.	*Midlifecrisis der Republik,* Uberreuther, Wien 1986

Constitution

Brauneder, W.	*Oesterreichische Verfassungsgeschichte,* Manz, Wien 1987
Querdich, R.	*Parteien und Verfassungsfrage in Oesterreich, Die Entstehung des Verfassungsprovisoriums, 1918–20,* Oldenburg, Munich 1987

Martzka, M. (*ed*)	*Sozialdemokratie und Verfassung,* Europaverlag Wien 1985
Walter, R. and Mayer, H.	*Grundriss des Oesterreichischen Bundes-Verfassungsrechts*
Heller, H.	*Constitutional Law,* Boston Kluner Law and Taxation Publishers
Koja, F.	*Die Verfassungsrecht der Oesterreichischen Bundeslaender,* Springer, Wien 1988

Coalitions

Lamodynsky, O.	*Der Proporzpakt,* Uberreuther, Wien, 1987
Rauchsteiner, M.	*Die Zwei: Grosse Koaltion in Oesterreich* Oesterreichischer Bundesverlag, Wien 1987

Parliament

Schambeck, H. (*ed*)	*Oesterreichs Parlementarismus: Werden und System,* Duncker und Humblot, Berlin 1986
Cerny, W. and Fischer, H.	*Kommentar zur Geschaeftsordnung der Nationalrat und zur Unvereinbarkeitsgesetz* Verlag der Oesterreichischen Staats drueckerei, 1982

5   Austro-Keynesianism

Bundesministerium der Finanzen	*Erfolge, Probleme, Chance der Oesterreichischen Wirtschaft, zur Mitte 1977,* Wien 1977
Matzner, E.	*Wohlfahrtstaat un Wirtschaftskrise, Oesterreichischen Sozialisten suchen einen Ausweg,* Rohwalt, Wien 1978
Bund, M.	*Der Oesterreichischer Weg in der Wirtschaftspolitik,* Wien 1978

Hoell, O.	*Austria's Technological dependence: Basic Dimensions and Current Trends,* Laxenberg Papers, (1980) No. 2
Hussain, M.	*Oesterreichische Aussenwirtschaft in Wandel* Campus, New York, 1978
Steifel, D.	*Gross Krise in einem Kleinen Land: Oesterreichische Finanz und Wirtschafts- politik 1929–38,* Bohlau, Wien 1988
Pelinka, A.	*Modelfall Oesterreich: Moglichkeiten und Grenzen,* Braunmueller, Wien 1981
Hankel, W.	*Prosperity amidst Crisis: Austria's Economic Policy and the Energy Crunch* Westview Press, Bolder 1981
Seidel, H. and Kramer, H.	*Die Oesterreichische Wirtschaft in den Achtziger Jahre,* G Fischer, Stutgart 1980
Brueckmueller, E.	*Sozialgeschichte Oesterreichs,* Herold, Wien 1985
OECD	*Integrated Social Policy, A Review of the Austrian Experience,* OECD 1981

6 Social Partnership

Fischer, H.	*Das Politisches System in Oesterreich,* 4th Edition, Europaverlag, Wien 1987. (Matzner 'Sozialpartnerschaft')
Lachs, J.	*Wirtschaftspartnerschaft in Oesterreich,* OGB-Verlag, Wien 1976
Wimmer, E.	*Sozialpartnerschaft aux Marxistischer Sicht,* Globus, Wien 1979
Nick, R. and Rehnika, A.	*Buergerkrieg, Sozialpartnerschaft; Das politisches System Oesterreich, I und II Republik: ein Vergleich,* Jugend und Polit Wien 1983
Halle, A.	*Politik im Netzwerk, Parteien, Parlament und Verbaende in Oesterreich,* Wisslit, Konstanz, 1987
Schopfer, R. (*ed*)	*Phaenomen Sozialpartnerschaft,* Bohlau, Koeln/Graz 1980
Gerlich, et al (*ed*)	*Sozialpartnerschaft in der Krise,* Bohlau, Koeln/Graz 1980

8 Democratic Reform

Moser, B.   *Die Verfassunsreform Diskussion in Oesterreich,* Politische Akademie, Research Report 27/85

Koja, F.   *Das Verfassungsrecht der Oesterreichische Bundeslaender,* Signum, Europabibliotek, Wien 1988

Kirsch, G. *et al*   *Beitraege zu Oekonomischen Problemen des Foederalismus,* Duncker and Humblot, Berlin 1987

Schambeck, H.   "Entwicklungstendenzen des Foederalismus" in Koren *et al, Politik fuer der Zukunft,* Bahlau, Wien 1984

Ucakar, K.   *Demokratie und Wahlrecht in Oesterreich: Zur Entwicklung von politischen Partizipation und staatlicher Legitimations politik,* Verlag fuer Gesellschaftskritik, Wien 1985

9 A Summing Up

Pretterebner, H.   *Fall Lukona: Ost-espionage, Korruption, und Mord im Dunstkreis der Regierungsspitze: ein Sittenbild der Zweiten Republik,* Pretterebner, Wien 1987

Bassett, R.   *Waldheim and Austria,* Viking, London/New York

Index